NEAL-SCHUMAN

Internet Policy Handbook for Libraries

MARK SMITH

NEAL-SCHUMAN NETGUIDE SERIES

NEAL-SCHUMAN PUBLISHERS, INC.

NEW YORK   LONDON

Published by Neal-Schuman Publishers, Inc.
100 Varick Street
New York, NY 10013

Printed and bound in the United States of America.

ISBN 1-55570-345-3

Contents

Preface   v
Acknowledgments   ix

1   The Policy Development Process   **1**
When Should Policies Be Written and Adopted?   1
What Should Policies Cover?   2
Who Should Develop and Write Policies?   4
What's the Difference between Policy and Procedure?   5
How Should the Public Be Made Aware of Internet Policies?   6

2   Linking the Internet to the Library's Mission   **9**
How Can a Library's Internet Policy Reflect Its Mission?   10
What Values Should the Policy Articulate?   12

3   Physical Location and Access Considerations   **19**
How Can Logistical Arrangements Help Implement Policy?   19
Who Can Use the Internet?   24
How Do Libraries Implement Scheduled Use Policies?   27
What Special Access Considerations Affect Academic Libraries?   29
What about Children and Young Adults?   31
Are Acknowledgment Forms Helpful?   35

4   Defining Acceptable Use   **39**
What Is Acceptable Use?   39
Can Libraries Restrict Access to Internet Content?   41
Are Interactive Internet Services Acceptable Uses?   42
Should Libraries Provide E-mail Services?   44
Is Telnet an Acceptable Use?   45
Can the Library's Internet Connection Be Used to Conduct
    Commercial Business?   46
What about File, Disk, and Directory Access?   47
How Have Libraries Written Acceptable-Use Policies?   50

5 Prohibited Uses and Their Consequences   **59**
What Uses Have Libraries Prohibited?   60
Should Patrons Have to Sign an Acceptable-Use Statement?   66
What Are the Consequences of Unacceptable Use?   66
How Have Libraries Incorporated Unacceptable Uses into
     Their Policy Statements?   67

6 Filtering Considerations   **75**
What Considerations Should Inform the Filtering Decision?   76
What's the Difference between Filtering and Materials Selection?   79
What Are the Choices?   80
How Does Filtering Software Work?   82
What Alternatives to Filtering Do Libraries Use?   86
How Can Policy Statements Reflect Filtering Choices?   94
How Does Filtering Policy Work in the Real World?   96

7 Guided Use and Library Policy   **101**
Should Policy Impact Guided Use?   102
What Kinds of Guidance Do Libraries Offer?   104

8 Web Publishing Policies   **115**
What Should a Web Publishing Policy Include?   116

9 Next Steps: After the Policy Is Written   **131**

Appendices

A Sample Internet Policies   **133**
Public Library Policies   133
Academic Library Policies   144
School Library Policies   159

B National and State Library Association Policies   **167**
American Library Association Policies   168
State Library Association Policies   185

C Internet Policy Checklist   **193**

D Loudoun County Court Case Memorandum Opinion   **197**

Index   217

Preface

Only recently, librarians and library advocates were debating whether the Internet would make libraries obsolete by the year 2000. In what has turned out to be a remarkable chapter of American library history, not only has this question been decided favorably for libraries, but our profession and our institutions have emerged materially strengthened and have earned newfound respect. Policy makers at the local, state, and national levels—and much of the general public as well—have recognized the vital role libraries can and should play in providing public access to electronically networked information. They have backed up that recognition with unprecedented funding in the form of operating expenditures, state and federal grants, and telecommunications discounts. This massive effort to wire the nation's school, academic, and public libraries has ensured that almost any library that wants to be connected to the Internet can be.

This success is not without its downside, however. Every library that has connected to the Internet has found it to be a medium unlike any other. The Internet brings its own unique, sometimes very troubling, set of challenges. While the proliferation of sexually explicit material on the Internet has been the most widely (and often sensationally) publicized of these problems, it is by no means the only issue associated with introducing Internet access in libraries. Deciding who should have access to the Internet, under what conditions, for what purposes, and with what restrictions carries significant risks for library managers and can be nearly as controversial as the filtering question. Establishing sound access policies will clarify the relationship between patron and staff, define administrative intent, and provide a firm bedrock on which to build library procedures.

The Neal-Schuman Internet Policy Handbook for Libraries is intended to guide library administrators—directors and departmental managers in public, school, and academic libraries—through the many complex decisions inherent in managing public Internet access. The *Handbook* systematically takes you through each possible element of an Internet policy. It identifies the options available to you at each decision point. Because every policy decision implies a road not taken, the *Handbook* explores the potential positive and negative impacts for each option.

Chapters 1 and 2 briefly review general principles of library policy development: the importance of policy reflecting the library's mission, when to write a policy, what should be included in it, and who should be involved in writing it. Chapter 3 discusses basic physical considerations and logistics: workstation placement, security, and privacy screens; it also deals with considerations of procedural access including decisions about sign-in sheets, time limits, password access, and other means to control who uses what machine for how long and under what conditions. Chapters 4 and 5 discuss acceptable and prohibited uses, the heart of the Internet policies, beginning in Chapter 4 with defining the parameters of what is acceptable and following in Chapter 5 with prohibited uses and their associated consequences. Chapter 6 is devoted to the filtering controversy and explores both sides of this difficult question, what libraries are doing about it, and the pros and cons of filters, no filters, and mixtures thereof. Readers wanting a more extensive treatment of the issue of Internet filtering should consult *A Practical Guide to Internet Filters* by Karen Schneider. Chapter 7 deals with questions of how to handle training for Internet use in the library. Finally, Chapter 8 is devoted to policies that govern the creation and placement of Web pages on the library server.

Each chapter includes relevant extracts from some policies and reproduces others in their entirety. Many of these policies are available at library Web sites and the Web addresses (or URLs) are provided for most references. In order to provide a wider range of representative policies, additional policy statements (both from individual libraries as well as those from the American Library Association and state library organizations) are included in the appendices. Appendix C provides a checklist for Internet policy development. Finally, the last appendix reprints the court opinion in *Mainstream Loudoun et al. v. Board of Trustees of the Loudoun County Library*, a civil action over the right of a public library to enact a policy prohibiting library patrons' access to certain content-based categories of Internet publications.

The Neal-Schuman Internet Policy Handbook for Libraries never recommends one policy option over another because policy is, in large part, a local decision that the library makes in response to local circumstances. Rather, the *Handbook* organizes and analyzes the range of policies that libraries are using to manage Internet access. The *Handbook* is designed as a major part of a library manager's information base. Nevertheless, readers must keep in mind that many aspects of Internet policy implementation require legal interpretation, especially those impacting First Amendment rights. In the course of implementing policy there will be times that administrators need both technical and legal advice. Administrators are urged to seek further advice on technical and legal issues when necessary from both internal and external experts as well as from published materials like this *Handbook*.

An unfortunate outcome of the hysteria surrounding controversial material on the Internet has been that many library managers find themselves implementing policies that do not reflect their own personal beliefs or even their best professional judgment. This happens because even the library director is only one of many individuals who influence policy development. In the face of pressure from library boards, city councils, school boards, university administrators, the public, and other staff members, library administrators have to make hard policy choices. In these cases, successful administrators first understand the framework for making Internet policy decisions and then become articulate in explaining the implications of each policy option. *The Neal-Schuman Internet Policy Handbook for Libraries* is intended to serve as a guide towards that understanding and articulation.

Mark Smith
Texas Library Association
November, 1998

Acknowledgments

My heartiest thanks to the many librarians who provided their advice and encouragement while I was writing this book. In particular, thanks to the directors and staffs of the many libraries and other institutions whose policies are cited here and for all librarians who have wrestled with the thorny issues of the Internet. Your efforts have made it easier for those of us who follow.

I am indebted to the many friends and colleagues who have generously contributed their time and expertise to my efforts, especially Christine Peterson at the Texas State Library and Archives Commission and Robert White of the Bergen County Cooperative Library System in New Jersey for their advice on the manuscript. Many thanks, as always, to Anne Ramos, the "librarian's librarian," for her cheerful help in research. I owe special thank to my boss, Patricia Smith, executive director of the Texas Library Association, for urging me to write this book, to my editor, Charles Harmon, for his excellent suggestions, and to Don Wood of the American Library Association for keeping me informed of late breaking policy developments.

Finally, I must thank my wife Catharine and my son Peter for their patience during the many days and nights I've been at work on this book.

1

The Policy Development Process

The first step in the creation of a specific area of library policy is to review the process of creating library policies. The process is important, and you will want to make it work as smoothly as possible.

WHEN SHOULD POLICIES BE WRITTEN AND ADOPTED?

Without a doubt, the best time to write a policy of any kind is before the service is introduced. Unfortunately, this is a luxury that most libraries rarely enjoy. Policies such as those governing collection development, for example, almost always follow the activity in question. With new services like the Internet, however, there is a chance that you can have your policy in place before you introduce the service.

There are several advantages to writing your Internet policy before offering public Internet access. First, you can involve the entire staff in the adoption of this new service; by enlisting their help in creating the policy framework in which they will operate, you can mitigate any uneasiness about its introduction. Second, you can consider exactly how this service fits into your overall library program, the terms under which you will offer it to the public, and how you will integrate and relate it to other library services and activities. Finally, and perhaps most importantly, you can take time developing a policy that reflects the objectives and values of your library.

A policy written after the service has been introduced tends to be driven not only by the organizational values of the library but also by the problems already encountered. Both the staff and the public will already have developed ways of using the service based on how it was introduced. All will have to accept—and then learn—a new set of rules. However, don't let this stop you from developing a new policy or revisiting an inadequate one. A late policy is far preferable to no policy at all, because no policy at all means that the staff is making up the policy ad hoc, and difficult situations can arise anytime. Unequal enforcement of library policy can lead to disgruntled patrons and, eventually, to lawsuits.

WHAT SHOULD POLICIES COVER?

Policies in general—and perhaps Internet policies in particular—can be complex or simple, all-inclusive or selective. Many Internet policies are five or ten pages, some with numbered sections. Others are succinct, such as this one from the Berkeley (CA) Public Library (*www.ci.berkeley.ca.us/bpl/*):

> In response to advances in technology and the changing needs of the community, the Berkeley Public Library endeavors to develop collections, resources, and services that meet the cultural, informational, recreational, and educational needs of Berkeley's diverse, multicultural community.
>
> The Berkeley Public Library does not monitor and has no control over the information accessed through the Internet and cannot be held responsible for its content. As with other library materials, restriction of a child's access to the Internet is the responsibility of the parent/legal guardian.

That's it: a reiteration of the library's mission, a statement that the library will not filter, and a disclaimer about what might be encountered on the Internet.

Perhaps the single hardest decision you will have to make in creating your policy is what to include and what to leave out. This book covers most of the things you could include in your policy, why you would choose to include them, and the consequences that you might encounter by adopting a specific policy. It is not this book's function, however, to tell you what to include or exclude from your policy; that is a purely local decision that will be influenced by a number of factors. The following six questions, however, will help you frame the scope and contents of your policy.

What Type of Library Do You Manage?

This may seem facetiously simple, but the type of library will render many of the policy elements unnecessary. For example, many school librarians will not be overly concerned with questions of purpose, since the K–12 library's overall purpose is highly focused on curriculum support. Similarly, academic librarians will usually not have to consider how best to protect children using their Internet workstations since, under most circumstances, there will seldom be children in the library. These same academic librarians, however, will need to look at guidelines on the content of Web pages that are created and maintained by students, faculty, and staff on the library's server. This concern arises somewhat less frequently in the public library or school environment.

To What Extent Is Your Library's Policy Predetermined?

Some aspects of your library's Internet policy may already be covered in the policy statement of your parent institution. For example, a citywide, data-processing policy may disallow patrons from using their own software on library computers. In this case, there is no practical need for the library to reiterate this policy. Or if the configuration of your computers is such that a telnet prompt is not available, you don't really need to address whether telnet use is allowed.

What Is Your Library's Mission?

This is especially critical for public libraries that have been through a formal or informal role-setting process. Internet policies in a library heavily geared toward business reference and job searching will incorporate somewhat different elements from a library that stresses children and youth. (The impact of a library mission on Internet policy development is treated in depth in Chapter 2.)

What Is the Character of Your Community?

Is your community politically conservative or liberal? Is there a concentration of young families or a large percentage of older retirees? Are you located in a rural area or in the suburbs? The nature of your community will determine the content of your Internet policy, just as it will drive all policy decisions of the library.

What Are the Motivating Concerns of Your Library Board, Superintendent, or College Administrators?

Are they cautious or adventurous? Do they tolerate risk? Are they committed to First Amendment rights? Are they forceful advocates of the library? Will they support you in a challenge? All these are questions that only you can answer. The level of trust between you and the board as well as their advocacy stance, political influence, and their tolerance of risk will determine the depth, breadth, and coverage of your policy.

What Other Policies Are Already in Place?

Policies already adopted by the library will influence what is included in your Internet policy. Your collection-development policy, freedom-to-read policies, and fee policies are all parts of the framework of your library and will determine what goes into your Internet policy.

WHO SHOULD DEVELOP AND WRITE POLICIES?

In some communities, school districts, and on some campuses, the entire community has participated in the development of quality policies that are sensible and enforceable. But this is the exception to the rule. Library policy should in general be written by library administrators and the board that oversees the library's operation. The library administration comprises paid staff who, in fact, were hired (one would hope) precisely because they understand what is technically possible, politically advisable, and professionally ethical. The library board—a vital partner in policy development—was appointed to oversee the work of the library staff and to represent the greater community in the work of the library. These groups, in collaboration with one another, should develop the policy based on community wishes and technical specifications.

Does this mean that the public should be left out of the process? Absolutely not. Library policy in its most effective and useful form should be developed in consultation with the community. There are a number of ways to ensure citizen participation in policy development: town hall meetings, draft publications on the library's Web page, print formats, and the use of citizen advisory groups. All of these are effective, and some form of citizen review is vital, but in the end the entity that should write the policy is the library staff in direct consultation with the library board.

To complicate things, however, there is another entity in the mix: the funding authority. This is the board or agency that governs operations of the library: the city council, school board, university board of directors, county commissioners. If you want your policy to have the support of your institution, these decision makers have to be on board from the beginning. Getting formal mayoral and council approval for your policy up front will not guarantee their support should it be challenged, but it may avoid having to make an embarrassing reversal when a complaint or controversy becomes public. This is especially important with such potentially sensitive matters as the Internet filtering policy.

In some cases, there may not be an official channel through which to secure approval of your policy; for example, in some cities, the city council does not formally approve the policies of city departments. Even in such a situation, however, it is advisable to inform your governing administration of your policy's contents. Among the city and county officials that should be informed are the city manager, mayor, council, and the city or county attorney. This last participant is particularly important because of the potential for legal challenges to your Internet policy. If you are going to want the city or county attorney to defend your policy, you are strongly advised to get them on board in the developmental stages.

The same cautions apply to school and academic libraries, even though such libraries cannot adopt policies without the approval of their parent institutions.

So the model for policy planning and adoption should be one that involves library administrators, governing authorities, and input from the community. Such a model looks like the one in Figure 1–1. Policy development is a circular process that is most effective when open to continuous scrutiny and revision. The early experience of libraries with Internet policy suggests that, because of the nature of technological evolution and community reaction, these policies must be constantly revisited and modified. We will discuss specific instances of this situation in this book, especially in regard to what protocols (e.g., HTTP or telnet) will be enabled and what to do about filtering.

WHAT'S THE DIFFERENCE BETWEEN POLICY AND PROCEDURE?

Policies and procedures statements are the twin pillars on which organizational management rests. But how do policies differ from and relate to procedures? This can be a confusing point. Policies are statements of parameters of library service that define how a library will deliver its resources to the community. Procedures are the instructions that convey those policies into practice. Policies are nearly always created for distribution to the public; procedures are nearly always for staff use only.

Library administrators and managers should always strive to keep policies from devolving into procedures. And when writing policies, they should always keep in mind how a policy will be translated into procedure. Policymakers should continually question if the rules they are creating can be enforced and how; if they are unenforceable or require too much interpretation by staff, they are not effective. Front-line staff must be able to apply policies fairly and without ambiguity; they should find their work easier, not harder, because of the policies. Policies that inadvertently create situations that lead to ambiguous interpretation put staff in conflict with patrons and tend not to be enforced at all or, at best, enforced unequally from one situation to the next. This is a recipe for disaster.

The best policies are the ones that establish a sound basis for devel-

Figure 1–1.   Policy Planning and Adoption Model

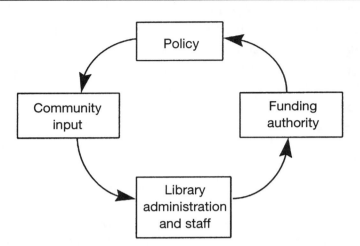

oping procedures that provide practical and helpful guidance for staff. This is not to say that staff should have no prerogative in enforcing policy, but rather that staff prerogatives should be delineated within parameters with which both staff and administration are comfortable. Also, different staffs in different environments will have differing tolerance for the amount of judgment that they will be called upon to exercise.

As this book moves through specific policies, it considers the procedural implications of particular policies and identifies those that leave open a wide range of interpretation. In all cases, however, you should think about how a given policy will be implemented in your library setting.

HOW SHOULD THE PUBLIC BE MADE AWARE OF INTERNET POLICIES?

One of the classic questions regarding library policy is how to inform the public of the policy and how to post the policy so that it is widely available. Fortunately, librarians no longer debate *whether* to post policies, and it seems now to be understood that a policy is not of much use unless it is widely available. The question that remains, then, is how to post the policy so that the public knows about it.

Libraries can inform the public using all the customary mechanisms: bulletin boards in the library, copies distributed upon request or to newly registered patrons, policy books kept at the front desk, even on the backs of library cards. But remember that the Internet offers another medium: if your library has its own Web page, then you know that it is a simple matter to post your policies there for review not only by your own local users but also by anyone, anywhere, with Internet access. This creates a fortuitous situation for library managers: they can view the policies of hundreds of libraries across the United States, learn how other libraries are addressing similar issues, and even borrow language that they like for their own policies.

There are a number of Web sites that collect library Internet policies. The best of these for public library policies—and one used often in researching for this book—is an archive maintained by David Burt of the Lake Oswego (Oregon) Public Library; it is located at *www.ci.oswego.or.us/library/poli.htm*. Burt's site includes not only policies arranged by size of library but also his analysis of various factors related to the policies, such as the percentage of libraries that have included particular elements in their policies.

An excellent online source for academic policies is the EDUCAUSE site at *www.educause.edu/ir/library/master_subjects_1.html*. There are other sites as well, though they are not as thorough. Rice University maintains one on K–12 policies and related documents (*gopher://riceinfo.rice.edu:1170/11/More/Acceptable*), but it is somewhat out of date. Similarly, a site maintained by Stacey Kimmel on the Lehigh University server gathers the World Wide Web policies of dozens of academic libraries around the world at (*www.lehigh.edu/~sek2/wwwpols.html*). It is an excellent site for Web policies, but it contains very few Internet policies. The Ohio State Library maintains a list of public and school libraries in Ohio at *winslo.ohio.gov/libaccep.html*.

It is possible—though somewhat more laborious—to find school, academic, and especially public library Internet use policies by visiting individual sites. These readily available resources can aid your own policy development; indeed, many of the policies referenced in this book can be obtained from the libraries' Web pages. Remember: the end of each chapter lists the URLs for all policies I cited in that chapter if available via the Web.

SUMMARY

Policy is a process, not a destination. The most successful policies are those that are regarded by administrators, staff, and sometimes the public, as organic documents that evolve and change. Internet policy is no different, and the principles that apply to the development of any library policy will guide the development of the Internet policy as well. Library staff and the public should be encouraged to guide the shaping of the policy through this evolution, since they are the ones that have to live most closely with it.

2

Linking the Internet to the Library's Mission

Before you write your Internet policy, you must first answer a basic question: "Why offer the Internet?" In the midst of all the hubbub involved in connecting the library to the Internet, it is often instructive to pause and ponder this.

There are many good reasons to have the Internet in the library, but in terms of policy development, the reason should relate to the library's stated mission. If your library does not have a mission statement, you should consider creating one to resolve a number of issues associated with writing an Internet policy. A mission statement accomplishes many things, including:

- articulating the organizational values of your library
- providing a foundation on which to build library policies and procedures
- ensuring that all parties involved in the administration of the library share basic guiding principles of access and use

In the school and academic library settings, mission statements tend to focus on common elements such as supporting the instructional and curricular goals of the parent institution. In the public library environment, the library's mission can emphasize the role that the library has adopted in its community, which can vary greatly, depending on the demographics and temperament of the community. Since the landmark publication of *Planning and Role Setting for Public Libraries*, public libraries have prioritized their services so that library staff efforts focus on those services that are most important to the community. Role setting means that one library may stress reference and information services, another will decide that children's services are of primary importance, and yet another will emphasize recreational reading. The recent "Re-Vision" process, the first major revision of *Planning and Role Setting*, which produced *Planning for Results: A Public Library Transformation Process* (PLA 1998) has not changed the basic premise of defining the library's purpose in relation to the community it serves. For public libraries, the mission statement is the best place to reference the roles that the library has adopted. So what does all this mean for the Internet policy?

HOW CAN A LIBRARY'S INTERNET POLICY REFLECT ITS MISSION?

It means that for many libraries, the very first item in the Internet policy is the mission statement of the library, a statement of purpose for having the Internet, or a statement that relates the library's Internet service to the mission statement. The "Computer and Internet Usage Policy" of the Spokane (WA) Public Library (*http://splnet.spokpl.lib.wa.us/internet-policy.html*) begins:

> The mission of the Spokane Public Library is to ensure that the people of the City of Spokane have the right and means to free and open access to ideas and information which are fundamental to a democracy. The Library will protect intellectual freedom, promote literacy, encourage lifelong learning, and provide library materials and information services.

They go on record in this first paragraph to restate the shared principles of the library: access, inclusion, intellectual freedom, and a commitment to lifelong learning. The writers of this policy have established the ground rules for the Internet policy that will follow.

Or consider the opening lines of the Queens Borough (NY) Public Library "Internet Policy for Public Use" (*www.queens.lib.ny.us/public.internet.policy.html*):

> The mission of the Queens Borough Public Library is to provide quality services, resources and lifelong learning opportunities through books and a variety of other formats to meet the informational, educational, cultural and recreational needs and interests of its diverse and changing population.

Again, the most common opening lines of Internet policies is a restatement of library mission, which for many means stating up front that the library is about open access to information. By doing so, these libraries have seized the initiative in a perceived debate over the issue of whether to filter or otherwise restrict access to Internet content by persons in the library. The prevalence in so many policies of an up-front commitment to the principles of intellectual freedom indicates the degree to which this issue has dominated Internet policy development. (We will discuss filtering and other access issues in Chapter 6.)

Although intellectual freedom issues are certainly important—and perhaps uppermost in our minds—there are other library missions that find their way into Internet policies. Note, for example, the line in the Queens Borough policy above about the "interests of its diverse and changing population." This commitment to an inclusive vision of library patrons in the opening sentence of the Internet policy signals that the library's sensitivity to diversity will drive the ways in which the Internet is used in the library. What practical difference could this make? Perhaps it defines what is presented on the library's Web page or affects deployment of the physical network, or perhaps it supports bilingual services, training, or other actions. However, as we mentioned in Chapter 1, these issues are not addressed *in* the policy, they are procedural and follow *from* the policy.

How does role setting drive the library's Internet policy? Consider the opening statement of the Fort Smith (AR) "Internet Access Policy" (*www.fspl.lib.ar.us/irpolicy.html*):

> Fort Smith Library's Internet access is intended primarily as an information resource. The Library does not provide electronic mail or access to chat, news, or discussion groups.

So Fort Smith's commitment to information services as opposed to recreational services has resulted in an Internet policy that disallows at least some recreational forms of usage. By contrast, the Danbury (CT) Public Library policy (*www.danbury.org/org/dpl/policy.htm*) encourages Internet use because "it offers unlimited information of every kind, both educational and recreational." This policy adds another dimension, an organizational commitment "to providing its customers with the latest advances in information technology." The Bellingham (WA) Public Library's policy (*www.city-govt.ci.bellingham.wa.us/cobweb/library/internet.htm*) references other roles of the library: "The Bellingham Public Library will protect intellectual freedom, promote literacy, encourage lifelong learning, and provide library materials and information resources."

Again, the most commonly found type of mission statement, especially for public libraries, is the library's commitment to access to information. This is not surprising since that's what a library is all about. But the phenomenal publicity surrounding the issue of Internet filtering has also compelled library administrators to develop strongly worded affirmations of their commitment to First Amendment principles, often informing the reader that the library has adopted the ALA's Library Bill of Rights and other such documents. The opening paragraph of the Ela Area (IL) Public Library policy (*www.ela.alibrary.com/iap.html*) contains the following sentence, which is typical of this approach: "Access to the Internet is compatible with the library's endorsement of the Library Bill of Rights, the Freedom to Read, and the Freedom to View documents."

WHAT VALUES SHOULD THE POLICY ARTICULATE?

The organizational values that affect a library's approach to public service, define the primary clientele, and establish standards of access should be reviewed when writing the Internet policy. This review of organizational values will ensure that the Internet policy is consistent with other policies and will remind your board and other policymakers of the basic tenets that they have already approved. Let's look at a series of examples of very specific areas where you will want to be sure that your Internet policy is consistent with your library's overall mission.

Who Do You Serve?

Some libraries' mission statements clearly pronounce that they exist primarily to provide library service to a discrete group that library policymakers regard as their primary clientele. These libraries will set forth that they will serve residents of the city, for example, but not the county; that they exist to serve faculty and staff of the college, but not residents of the community; or that they provide service to students of their campus only and no others. A library's other policies should follow from this presumption so that, for example, service is provided for free to one group but a fee may be charged to others—if indeed they may use it.

A library's Internet policy should follow this same approach. For example, you might allow cardholders to reserve Internet time but allow noncardholders to use the Internet only when there are no other cardholders using the workstation. Similarly, if you have adopted a policy that makes little or no distinction between the privileges of cardholders and noncardholders, then your Internet policy should give no preference to one group over the other.

Do You Emphasize Certain Types of Service?

As has already been pointed out, libraries adopt service roles that drive a whole set of administrative decisions, from the collection development policy to information access policies. This consistency of approach should apply to the Internet policy also. A library that emphasizes children's and youth services, for example, might plan to place Internet workstations in the children's room, provide special guidance to children and parents in using the Internet, and perhaps offer a different sort of training than would be needed for adult users. Or a school library in a magnet high school or middle school where the curriculum is focused on a special area such as the performing arts or science may want to limit Internet use to that which supports the purpose of the program.

Do You Support Recreational Use or Only Informational/Research Use?

This is an important question to ask yourself in the course of developing your Internet policy, since the answer will define how you decide to offer Internet service. Does your library emphasize services that are informational and educational in nature? If so, you probably see your library's primary mission as providing such core services as reference, information and referral, curriculum support, and homework centers. Collection development in the information/research library is likely to be concentrated in the areas of reference, nonfiction, and perhaps periodicals. Recreational uses such as pleasure reading and audiovisual collections, although not ignored, are probably a lesser priority. If this is your library's approach, then it should do the same with the Internet, gearing its use toward informational purposes. In this case, it would be consistent to allow access only to those resources that have information value—no chat rooms or multi-user interactive games (see Chapter 4).

Another library might consider its primary focus to be a popular collection that supports informal reading, entertainment, and recreational uses. This library would be strong in fiction, biographies, videos, and CDs, and might tend to offer services such as adult programming and instructional classes. Here, it would be consistent to allow patrons to access any materials that are popular in nature—even games, chat rooms, and unrestricted surfing.

Do You Charge Fees?

The library's overall policy toward charging fees for service should be considered when deciding whether to charge for Internet services. For example, many libraries provide a level of basic service for free, but charge for other, more staff- and resource-intensive services. In such a library, a consistent policy might be to provide basic access to the Internet for no fee, but to charge for either longer time at the workstations or for special services such as the provision of e-mail access or downloading files. Bear in mind that if you do not charge a fee for any other library service, charging for Internet access might be inconsistent.

Are There Types of Service That Your Library Does Not Provide?

There may be some types of services your library does not offer. It is standard practice, for example, for libraries to state in their policies that they will not provide product referrals in response to the common patron query of which encyclopedia (or dictionary or atlas) to buy. Typically, libraries will answer such queries with factual information about the range of products available, comparison prices, and other material. In the area of Internet policy, a consistent policy would be not to recommend specific Internet service providers or specific brands of computer hardware or software.

Another example is training. If your library typically provides training for the public, especially in the use of new services, then it would be consistent to offer training for the Internet that is similar in scope and complexity. So if you typically provide only one-to-one, informal patron instruction, it could seem to be inconsistent to offer group classes for Internet training. (This is not a clear-cut issue, however, since, the Internet is sufficiently complex to warrant more training, at least in the months just following the introduction of Internet service.)

What Is the Relationship of the Internet to the Library's Collection Development Policy?

If the collection development policy stresses certain types of materials over others in prioritizing how the print collection will be built, then you might want to set up the Internet policy so that certain parts of the Internet are more accessible for patrons than another. For example, if the library provides links on its own home page to particular sites on the Web, these sites should convey the same type of subject matter that has priority in the library's collection development policy. Similarly, any print guides produced by the library should guide the user to sites that further the priorities of the collection development policy.

But the pitfall here is in viewing the Internet as essentially the same as other resources owned and managed by the library. The nature of the Internet is so markedly different that the old model of library selection cannot apply to it. Because of the vast, sprawling, and uncontrolled nature of the Internet, attempts to replicate the process of selection in terms of Internet content will only lead to frustration for the library (see further discussion of this subject beginning on page 79). Still, to the extent that the library attempts to serve as a guide and gateway to the Internet, those procedures should be consistent with priorities established in other policies, including the collection-development policy.

Is Your Library an Access Provider, an Information Provider, or Both?

If your library has addressed these concerns in other parts of the policy, you may already know the answer to this question. But if it has not, you should review your policies and mission to determine the answer to this question. Chances are, your library is an information provider at some level and that it provides access on some levels as well. But some libraries tend more heavily toward access provision than others. Is some part (such as periodicals or audiovisual materials) or all of the collection closed stack? If so, you do not allow access as freely as if your library were open stack. Does your library allow patrons to conduct their own online searches of commercial databases directly or are those conducted by staff? What about OCLC access—can patrons query the OCLC database directly? Can patrons place their own holds on library materials or submit their own interlibrary loan requests? In many libraries these services are provided only by staff, who serve as information brokers. In other libraries, patrons access these services directly. Some libraries provide extensive reference and research services to patrons, and others simply make those resources available and assume that patrons will be able to help themselves.

The implications of these matters for the Internet policy is that they may determine whether you see it as your library's role to retrieve information via the Internet or to provide access to the Internet itself. If the goal is simply supplying information, then you may choose not to allow patron access to the machine at all. Or, if you do allow patrons to access the Internet on library workstations, you may choose to impose time limits, to limit the types of services available, or to limit access to preselected sites. If your library tends toward providing access to resources, however, you may offer patrons full Internet access via library workstations. You might also go into the Internet provider role, in which citizens can access the Internet from home through the library's connection, establish mailboxes on the library's server, or conduct library business (e.g., renewing books, placing holds, requesting materials) from home. It is important to note, however, that there is a range of choices between the poles of information provider and access provider, and most libraries are on the continuum between the poles. Just keep in mind that your Internet policy should emulate the degree of access to information that you provide in other library services.

Do You Provide Training and Assistance to Patrons?

Many libraries train patrons either in the use of resources or as a form of programming. Typically, academic and school libraries offer a great deal of formal and informal training, and public libraries tend to provide either informal or one-on-one training. Whatever your library's approach, you will want to offer at least as much training in the Internet as for other types of services. This is important, since your patrons have come to expect a certain level of assistance from the library. If they are accustomed to looking to the staff for help in selecting books, in conducting their research, in performing database searches, and in other uses of the library's services and collections, it will be important that the same level of training and staff support be there for the Internet.

Has Your Library Adopted the Library Bill of Rights as Part of Its Policy?

Many libraries have voluntarily adopted policy statements from the American Library Association, most notably the Library Bill of Rights. Such library administrators and boards that adopt these statements have decided that their libraries will conform to the ethics contained in those statements about how the library provides information to the public. So when adopting a library Internet policy, the library must determine whether it is in line with these policies on information access. For many libraries, the entire Internet policy consists of an affirmation that the library supports these principles of open access and therefore that it will not restrict patron access to information. Although such statements do not address the range of elements that form a comprehensive Internet policy, at least they are clear about the Internet policy conforming to other policies adopted by the library.

Are There Special Policy Considerations for School and Academic Libraries

The roles of school and academic libraries are a bit more obvious—support the curriculum, teach information literacy skills—but statements of purpose and mission do appear in school and academic policies, though sometimes in unexpected ways. For example, consider the unusual, tiered statement used by the University of Pennsylvania (*www.upenn.edu/computing/help/doc/passport/policies*):

The priorities for use of University-wide computing resources are:

Highest: Uses that directly support the educational, research and service missions of the University.

Medium: Other uses that indirectly benefit the education, research and service missions of the University, as well as and including reasonable and limited personal communications.

Lowest: Recreation, including game playing.

Forbidden: All activities in violation of the General Standards or prohibited in the Specific Rules interrupting this policy.

Here we have a hierarchical approach to the values that have informed the development of the overall library policy and, in particular, the Internet policy. Like many institutions, recreational uses receive a low priority, but they are not forbidden, as are violations of the acceptable use policy.

The acceptable use policy of NuevaNet, the computer system of the private Nueva School in Hillsborough, California (*gopher://riceinfo.rice.edu: 1170/00/More/Acceptable/nueva*), is somewhat similar in that it identifies multiple missions:

NuevaNet is a service provided by and in consonance with the dual mission of the Nueva School:

Mission I: To improve innovative education for gifted and talented children through access to unique resources and collaborations;

Mission II: To improve learning and teaching through research, teacher training, collaboration, and dissemination of successful educational practices, methods, and materials.

Should your Internet policy open with reference to your mission statement? This, again, depends on the temperament of your board, your administrators, your staff, and your community. It is not absolutely imperative that the mission statement be a part of the Internet policy, but it can't hurt. At the very least, frequent restatement of the library's mission can only serve to remind library administrators, advisory and governing boards, staffs, and the public of the library's defining values. It also serves to remind readers that the persons who wrote the policy kept in mind the library's mission and built the policy upon its premises. Finally, it reminds funding authorities and governing boards that they have already signed off on the guiding principles of the library's overall policy. This last is particularly useful if you have any reason to believe the public's reaction to the policy is likely to cause them to revisit the underlying mission of the library.

3

Physical Location and Access Considerations

Once your library has decided to offer Internet access, you need to initiate a discussion with your staff about how best to offer the service. This process will yield a great deal of valuable insight to use in policy development. This dialogue with staff can also give you a chance to help alleviate their fears about the new service and allow the entire staff to develop a sense of ownership of and excitement about it.

The first set of issues that you and your staff will want to consider are those having to do with physical arrangement. Where will the workstations be? How will monitors be arranged? What provisions will be made to ensure the security of the hardware? Will you offer printing? If so, where will the printer be located? These may seem like simple questions on the surface—and for some libraries they are—but for others, the answers may be very involved.

HOW CAN LOGISTICAL ARRANGEMENTS HELP IMPLEMENT POLICY?

How Does the Library's Mission Determine the Location of Internet Workstations?

If yours is a public library that is geared toward business reference, your logical decision will be to favor location of your Internet service in your business reference center. If, however, you emphasize children's services, you will want to have Internet access in the children's room (and configure access to appeal to children, such as via special Web pages). Mission may be less of a factor for school and university libraries, where the location of the Internet workstations will likely depend more on traffic patterns and security issues.

How Will the Library's Access Policy Impact Workstation Location?

If, like many libraries, access to information is the central, guiding issue in your library's Internet policy, it is likely that the location of the workstations in your library will be determined by your philosophy of access. You will not be concerned with monitoring what your patrons view on the workstations and instead will locate them in high traffic areas and in as many departments as possible (including the children's area). If, however, you are more concerned with problems caused by patrons who view inappropriate materials in the library, you may choose to locate the workstations beside the circulation desk so that staff can monitor what people are accessing on the machines. You may also be guided by the degree to which you allow for quiet, individual research areas for other purposes. Academic and research libraries may situate terminals in study rooms or other quiet areas because this is consistent with the library's mission of providing space in which to do research. Another consideration is whether there are some groups in your library who will not have full Internet privileges. If, for example, you require parental approval for children to use the Internet, you will have to be sure the Internet is in a place where staff can see it and easily monitor who is using it.

Who Gets to Use the Workstation, When and for How Long?

Many libraries require patrons to reserve time to get on the Internet, and some have manual sign-up sheets on which the library staff log patrons in and out (by phone, e-mail, and/or in person). If you and your staff feel that manual sign up is a violation of a user's privacy (though it may be argued that simply knowing that someone has accessed the Internet divulges nothing about the nature of that person's information habits, other than the medium), there are automated means by which you can charge out computers to patrons as though they were books, erasing evidence of use after each patron. In this process, the library creates a catalog record for the workstation. When a patron wants to use it, staff charge the workstation to the patron on their card with a specific due time. Or you can look into "time-out" software, which starts up when a session is initiated and shuts the machine down or at least warns the patron when the session is over or nearly over. This effectively cuts off use after a certain time, but libraries have found that negative public relations result from arbitrarily ending a patron's session, perhaps in the middle of an application or search. Also, you have to determine how the session is initiated, either by patron password or by staff.

If you offer automated means of reserving and timing patron use of machines, you remove from staff the burden of monitoring use, which means that workstations do not have to be situated with monitoring in mind. But if you must manually reserve Internet use, you will probably have to place machines in proximity to staff. Obviously, the main motivation to using any kind of timing or reservation system is to give all users fair and equal access to the service. The best way to ensure this is to provide enough machines to meet demand.

One final caveat: Reservation systems help those patrons who are on a more rigid schedule. In a library with a limited number of workstations, people who can only use the workstations at peak usage times such as around lunch, in the evenings, and on weekends may often not be able to get a machine, but those who are on a more flexible schedule may be able to visit the library at nonpeak hours and get ready access. With reservations, access during peak times would not be hit or miss.

Who Can Access the Printer?

If you intend to offer access to a printer, you will either need to locate the machine near the printer or place the printer behind the desk and direct patrons to pick up their pages at the desk. If you do not want to allow printing from the Internet workstations, their location will be independent of the printer.

Will Patrons Be Allowed to Use the Floppy Drive?

Many libraries do not allow patrons to upload and download materials from floppy drives (this issue is discussed more fully in Chapter 4). If you do, then locate the machines close to the staff areas so staff can keep an eye on things to prevent abuse of the drive and to help with technical problems as they arise.

An automated alternative used by many libraries is locking software, the most popular of which is called Fortres. Fortres can lock down specific capabilities of the machine; for example, it can prevent patrons from writing to the floppy or hard drives, accessing a C-prompt, exiting Windows, or using specific programs. Staff can easily access the software by password to override or modify the settings.

Another option that does not require staff monitoring is to use a mechanical lock on the floppy drive door so that patrons cannot insert disks. However, this option only protects this drive and would not disable patron access to software or to the hard drive.

Protection software or a locking device or cover can help you feel somewhat more secure in locating machines where they cannot easily be monitored by staff and can release staff from the burden of having to play watchdog. A related question is whether the library will allow patrons to use their own software on the computer or to download and run programs from the Internet on the library's workstations (most do not for reasons relating to system security). This issue is discussed more fully in Chapter 4.

How Can Location Facilitate (or Hamper) Patron Assistance?

In many libraries workstations are distributed throughout the library, but there is a very good reason to locate the machines close by the circulation desk, reference desk, or other staff area: patron assistance. Most public service library staff try to be vigilant regarding the needs of their patrons. They keep an eye on users and come to their aid when they seem to be having difficulty. This is particularly important for Internet use; as a new medium, it is unfamiliar to many patrons and even experienced patrons need assistance navigating the jungles of cyberspace. The support that a trained information professional can offer to the user is one of the main benefits of libraries' providing access to the Internet. For all these reasons, many libraries have built into their Internet policies specific language addressing their commitment to patron assistance and training (see Chapter 7). If your library encourages staff to aid patrons who seem confused, you will want to situate your workstations close enough to the staff desks to make this feasible.

Will Privacy Screens Be Installed?

Whether to use privacy screens depends to a large extent on whether you will use filtering software (this matter is discussed fully in Chapter 6). Many libraries are experimenting with privacy screens as an alternative to filtering so that patrons can view what they choose yet not offend others in the library or inadvertently expose children to others' viewing choices. Privacy screens attach to the front of the monitor and permit only the user seated directly in front of the monitor to view the screen. They are particularly useful in libraries that do not have space to isolate computers for private use by patrons, or that for other reasons need to have the screens facing the public area.

But some librarians have found that privacy screens cause specific problems. Users with bifocals have difficulty seeing through the screen. It is also difficult for librarians to assist without getting into an awkward position behind the patron. And should the librarian or patron choose to take off the privacy screen, it can be quite cumbersome to replace, as the Austin Public Library found out while experimenting with privacy screens. Other attempts to protect the privacy of library users have included placing the workstations in cubicles or at desks, or locating them in private rooms. These approaches usually do not allow staff to observe the patron or be aware of a need for assistance.

Another option, and one discussed in Chapter 6, is the use of recessed monitors, or privacy desks, in which the monitor is positioned below the surface of the desk. Privacy desks allow only the person seated at the computer or standing behind the user to see the screen. Although more expensive than privacy screens, they are easier for the user to see and easier for library staff to view when assisting patrons. One problem with recessed monitors, however, is that they are not ergonomically sound. Looking down at a computer screen over a long period of time will cause back and neck aches in some people. For this reason, such desks work much better in areas where patrons will be on them for short information transactions rather than in research areas where they may use them for longer periods.

How Should Monitors Be Oriented?

Some libraries have a clause in their policies to address location of the computers and orientation of the monitors. The acceptable use policy for the Valley Information Alliance in South Texas states that "if the information being accessed is sensitive, or inappropriate for viewing, the patron's viewing area may be positioned to provide the viewer privacy, and so that others might not inadvertently become exposed to material which they may consider inappropriate." Other libraries have adopted policies similar to that of the Taylor (TX) Public Library (*spinoza.pub-lib.ci.taylor.tx.us/taylorpl/ policy.html*): "Designated Internet stations will be located where they can be monitored by staff for assistance and security." This library has situated the computers so that the monitors are visible to staff at the public desks. The hope is that this will restrain patrons from viewing inappropriate sexual materials on the screen that might offend—or, as some have phrased it more strongly, harass—other library patrons. Should patrons access objectionable materials in the library anyway, then staff will be able to see what they are viewing and tell them to stop accessing those sites.

Even though this is the practice of many libraries, it is, nevertheless, problematic. For one thing, this procedure is based on the assumption that staff will continually monitor what patrons are viewing on library workstations. Aside from the burden that this places on staff, it almost certainly assures an uneven (read "unfair") implementation of the policy. Also, suppose a patron does view something the staff considers inappropriate in the library. Now the staff must confront the patron and request that they not view materials that may (or may not) be constitutionally protected speech. What if the patron does not desist? The staff is forced to escalate the confrontation or let it go, in which case the patron continues to view the material—in plain sight of everyone else in the library. In essence, this policy requires that you address whether patrons have a reasonable expectation of privacy in a public space. This is a question to refer to legal counsel.

Are There Other Factors to Consider in Locating the Workstations?

There are some rather mundane physical constraints that may have the final word on where to place the workstations. These include:

- Where are the electrical outlets?
- Where are the network jacks (if applicable)?
- What type of connection will be used (e.g., dial-up, ISDN, T-1)?
- Where is there room for the machines?
- Does the library have existing furniture for the machines or room for new furniture?
- How many machines are there?

One final concern about location: should it be addressed in your policy, or is it a procedural issue? Some libraries do reference it, but most do not, handling it as a procedural matter. But whether it is addressed in the written policy or not, physical location of the workstations is an important issue that will probably impact how your library staff can implement other aspects of your Internet policy.

WHO CAN USE THE INTERNET?

It is now time to consider a series of policy questions that center on how to control procedural or operational access to the Internet.

Who will be allowed to use the Internet? All library visitors? Only cardholders? Will they have to sign up to use the Internet? Will there be a time limit for patrons at workstations? Will minors need to have parental permission to use the Internet? These are just a few of the questions you will be pondering as you formulate your policies regarding access. As with most policies, there are pros and cons to each choice, and you will have to carefully weigh each decision to find the appropriate balance regarding access. Occasionally, you may find your library's mission of unlimited access in conflict with your need to ensure that every patron has some access to online resources.

Academic and school libraries will usually allow only students, faculty, and staff of the institution to use the workstations. Most academic policies will contain sentences—usually in the introduction, like the following of Dartmouth College—that specify that the institution provides "access to information resources, including computer networks and computer equipment, to its students, faculty, and staff (*www.dartmouth.edu/comp/comm/citbook/compcode.html*)." Occasionally, however, especially in the case of community college libraries and combined school/public libraries, the policy will specify access by the community.

Academic library policies, in particular, often have to deal with complexities in the area of access beyond who may use the machines and address more than just Internet access (see the section on academic library access policies, on page 29). In public libraries, however, the issue is a bit more straightforward: access is usually available to all users, and most libraries do not issue passwords for logging onto the system.

Most public libraries have opted to permit all persons in the library to get on the system, regardless of whether they are cardholders. If this is so for your library, you might be tempted simply to leave this matter unaddressed in your policy. This is probably not advisable. Everyone from the board down to the staff will feel much better, and you will be on safer grounds, if your policy specifically states who you will allow to have Internet access—even if it is everyone who walks in the door. You may, however, wish to limit use to only those persons who have a current, valid borrower's card with your library. This tends to be a public library issue, although academic libraries with high levels of walk-in traffic from the general public may find they have to address this matter.

The following five questions may help in deciding how to handle this issue.

1. *How many workstations do you offer?*

    If you have only a few, you may want to limit access only to cardholders.
2. *How many noncardholders use your library?*

    If you have relatively few nonresidents coming in, you may have little need to impose a limit. But if your walk-in numbers are high, how will you monitor cardholder access? Do you have other reasons for requiring sign in? (We will discuss sign-in policies later in this chapter.)

3. *Do you have staff to monitor who uses the Internet?*

Staff availability as well as their tolerance to enforce limits will be a factor in your access decision. Every policy decision should assess the level of work that will be required of staff and whether you have enough staff to monitor patrons.

4. *What is your library's policy toward in-house use of other materials?*

Does your library permit access to other materials on a walk-in basis, or are these services only for cardholders? Do you have a compelling reason for setting a different policy for how patrons access the Internet as opposed to traditional, print-based services?

5. *Are there state laws or rules that pertain?*

Some states have laws governing access to public information, which includes any information in a public institution.

Once you have answered these questions, you may find it to your benefit to limit access to cardholders, but then you must decide how.

The Farmers Branch (TX) Manske Library Internet Use Policy (*www.ci.farmers-branch.tx.us/library/pol_int.htm*) stipulates, "You will need a Farmers Branch Manske Library card," and directs users to sign in and out at the reference desk. In this library, patrons must show their current library cards to use the Internet workstations. It is not enough to simply be *eligible* for a card, although you may opt to set eligibility as your requirement.

Another option is to prefer cardholders to noncardholders without categorically excluding anyone. The Bellingham (WA) Public Library (*www.city-govt.ci.bellingham.wa.us/cobweb/library/internet.htm*) gives preference to users with a card, but allows use by noncardholders. Their policy reads, "A current Bellingham Public Library card in good standing will be required in order to reserve time on the computer in advance. Computers may be used without a Library card, on a walk-in basis, if not previously reserved." This policy allows staff a way to avoid the embarrassing situation of having to turn away noncardholders when there are machines that are not being used.

If you are going to allow only cardholders to use the workstations, however, be sure to consider how staff will bounce noncardholders. You will need clearly stated guidelines (procedures) on what to do if someone wants to use the Internet but doesn't have a card. Staff will appreciate guidance, especially when a patron is reluctant to relinquish a machine.

HOW DO LIBRARIES IMPLEMENT SCHEDULED USE POLICIES?

Your policy on whether to allow noncardholders to use Internet workstations in the library will, in part, determine your policy of whether to require patrons to schedule their use of an Internet workstation. If your policy
is to allow only cardholders to use the Internet, you will need a mechanism to check for cardholder status. You could do as the Lawrence (KS)
Public Library (*www.ci.lawrence.ks.us/iag.html*), and direct that "you'll need
a current Lawrence Public Library card. We'll hold your library card while
you use the Internet Access computer." This policy goes on to state that
time limits are not imposed and that use is on a first-come, first-served basis with no reservations. Or you may choose to control cardholder access
by using a reservation system operated either by automated or nonautomated
means. (See the discussion on page 20 on controlling patron time on workstations.)

It is indeed becoming common practice to require users to sign up for
time on an Internet workstation. In this way, staff can more easily monitor
who uses the machine as well as impose time limits, which policymakers
in libraries with high demand and too few machines may find necessary. It
is very difficult to set time limits without the use of a sign-in sheet since
staff would otherwise have to monitor the time a patron has been on and
play traffic cop to move people off and on machines. The Bellingham policy
is remarkable on this point, because it very carefully and extensively outlines the parameters of the sign-in access (see Figure 3–1).

With such a detailed policy, this library should have no problem with
staff not being clear on how to implement the policy. But you need not
feel you must have such a thorough policy regarding sign-in sheets, reservations, and time limits. Just be sure to consider the following questions
when writing this section of your policy:

- Will your staff apply all rules evenly and equitably, especially those
  that require monitoring of the facilities?
- Are there any terms or circumstances that will require staff to ne-
  gotiate with patrons? (For example, will the mayor and council be
  held to the same time limits as all other citizens?)
- Do you have good reasons for the limits you are imposing? Every
  limit is a barrier to use; even though there may be very good reasons for establishing limits, library managers should carefully consider what problem they are attempting to avoid in instituting them.
- How will you handle walk ins when no one is waiting? The
  Bellingham policy addresses this issue by allowing access if there
  is no prior reservation or the party with a reservation has not yet
  arrived.

Figure 3–1	SAMPLE POLICY ON TIME LIMITS

When reserving library computers:

a.   All Internet users should sign-in at the Reference Desk.

b.   You may reserve the Internet computer up to 2 hours a week, minimum of 30 minutes per sign-up; and you may reserve a time slot up to 7 days in advance. (Example: Monday to Monday; Tuesday to Tuesday; etc.)

c.   Reserving time on the Internet stations may be made in 30 min., 60 min., 90 min., or 120 min. consecutive blocks of time, up to the 2 hours maximum. Only one block of time per day may be reserved in advance.

d.   All "walk-in use" counts toward the 2 hours weekly maximum. Once you have used an Internet station for the 2 hours maximum, any other pre-reserved time you have that week will be canceled.

e.   Latecomers forfeit the unused portion of their reserved time. Really latecomers (more than 15 minutes) lose their entire reserved time.

f.   Due to heavy usage, all time that is canceled less than one hour previous to the reserved time shall be counted towards the 2 hours weekly maximum. Also, a "no show" for reserved time shall count towards that person's 2 hours weekly maximum.

g.   If you have reached the 2 hours maximum use per week, but there is an Internet station available, you may sign-in to use available time. However, you will be bumped if someone else comes along who has not used or exceeded the 2 hours weekly limit.

h.   Problems that may arise if two people who both have exceeded the 2 hours weekly maximum will be resolved at the discretion of the librarian on duty.

Source: Bellingham (WA) Public Library (*www.city-govt.ci.bellingham.wa.us/cobweb/library/ internet.htm*)

- Are there enough staff to enforce the limits?
- Is confidentiality an issue? In some situations librarians are concerned that requiring a sign in violates patron confidentiality. Check to see if this is so in your state, and if necessary, investigate other means (such as patrons' initials) for signing in users.

WHAT SPECIAL ACCESS CONSIDERATIONS AFFECT ACADEMIC LIBRARIES?

The nature of campus computer networks in higher education creates a somewhat different situation in academic libraries. Public library patron access to the Internet is typically limited to Web access via a browser, but colleges and universities will often issue user passwords to students and faculty that allow them to reach a much more extensive range of computing services. Electronic mail, file access, access to commercial databases, and access to licensed commercial software of campus LANs (local area networks) and WANs (wide area networks) are but a few of the plethora of services available through academic sites. Because these often involve direct access to campus mainframes and networks, and because these arrangements are often governed by the legal constraints of the commercial license an institution has signed with a database or software vendor, it is essential to have in place strict policies for computer access. Sometimes these policies will be drafted by the library, but more often the library policy will derive from and be consistent with computer access policies adopted by the institution as a whole.

These policies are usually very strictly stated and the consequences very carefully defined. Take for example, the policy of the University of Texas at Austin, which is titled "Looking for Trouble?" It asks the reader, "Tired of using the Internet? Want to lose your computer account? Get expelled from UT? Go directly to jail?" The body of this policy carefully outlines the procedural access parameters that govern access to the University of Texas network computing services (*www.utexas.edu/cc/policies/trouble.html*):

1. You are the only person who can use a computer resource (such as your IF number) that the University has provided specifically for your use.
2. Do not give your password to anyone else, even people you trust, like your boyfriend, girlfriend, brother, sister, or friend who has offered to help you fix a problem. If you suspect that someone may have discovered your password, change it immediately.

Prohibitions on attempts to breach security, or "hacking," are common in academic computing policies. The University of Texas policy states:

> Never try to circumvent login procedures on any computer system or otherwise gain access where you are not allowed. This is not acceptable under any circumstances and can result in serious consequences, including disciplinary action by the Office of the Dean of Students or the Office of the Executive Vice President or Provost.

This should take care of all but the most brazen and determined hackers.

The "Dartmouth College Computer and Network Policy" (*www.dartmouth.edu/comp/comm/citbook/compcode.html*) outlines the criteria the institution follows to qualify a student or faculty member for access to the system:

> The names of members of the Dartmouth community are entered into the Dartmouth Name Directory (DND). An entry in the Dartmouth Name Directory (DND), an electronic database administered by Computing Services, grants access to network services that originate at Dartmouth College and that require user authentication, including BlitzMail and access-restricted information resources available through the Dartmouth College Information System. Increasingly, access to the Dartmouth network and Dartmouth network services will be determined by whether one has a DND entry and the attributes associated with that entry. Some members of the Dartmouth community are also granted user names and accounts on various computing systems in order to complete work for Dartmouth College. Within this section, a DND entry, user name, or account will be referred to as an "account."

The access policy of Cortland College outlines the terms of access to which a user agrees (*snycorva.cortland.edu/acs/policy.html*):

> Use of Cortland College's large computer systems requires that a username be issued by the College, granting access to a particular system. Usernames are issued to individuals. The use of the username is the responsibility of the person in whose name it is issued. The following will be considered theft of services, and subject to penalties described in Section 3, below.
> (1) Acquiring a username in another person's name;
> (2) Using a username without the explicit permission of the owner and of the Computer Center;

(3) Allowing one's username to be used by another person without explicit permission of the Computer Center.

One question that may arise is whether the library must adopt these policies if they are already part of the university's policy system. It is not necessary to do so, especially if there are no other policies that specifically govern access in the library, but if the library is going to adopt a separate policy, then it is best to reflect the campuswide policy. Since the library is the principal site of student network access, academic library managers will want to review whether the campuswide policy is sufficient for the library and whether it is advisable to adopt an acceptable use policy for the library. If so, reiterate that the rules and policies of the institution apply to these other services as well, because it may well fall to library staff to intervene in the event that a student's actions are found to be unacceptable by the terms of the policy.

WHAT ABOUT CHILDREN AND ADULTS?

Another area of procedural access that must be addressed is that of children's use of the Internet. Will children be allowed to use the Internet? Will they be allowed to use any machine in the library, or only those in designated areas? Must they have a parental consent prior to being allowed to use the Internet?

Obviously, these questions will not greatly trouble academic libraries, and school libraries may require some parental permission, but public libraries will find this issue to be a great challenge. (Keep in mind, though, that academic libraries often serve students who are under 18 and thus still minors, and that school libraries often serve the entire community during the summer). The main concern, of course, is the presence of pornography and other adult materials on the Internet, which we will discuss more fully in Chapter 6. For libraries that decide not to filter, a common solution is to require parental consent for Internet use by minors.

The Port Isabel (TX) Public Library, for example, requires that "children under the age of eighteen (18) should have parental permission to use the Internet." This library's parental release form is reproduced in Figure 3–2.

Other libraries that neither filter nor require parental release might require or suggest that parents accompany children using the Internet in the library. An example of a suggested monitoring can be found in the language of the Grande Prairie (IL) Public Library "Internet Use Policy (*www.grandeprairie.org/netuse.html*)," which reads, "Parents and legal guardians who are concerned about their children's use of the Internet

Figure 3–2	SAMPLE PARENTAL PERMISSION FORM

PORT ISABEL PUBLIC LIBRARY

AGREEMENT

I, _____ am the parent/gardian of
(Print name)

_____ a child under the age of
(Print name)

eighteen (18).

I have read and understand the Internet Access Guidelines and the Policies concerning its use. I understand that this access is designed for educational purposes.

I recognize that restricting access to controversial materials is impossible for the Port Isabel Public Library and I will not hold the Library or its personnel responsible for materials accessed on the network.

I accept full responsibility for supervision if and when my child's use of the Internet Access computer is not educational in setting.

I hereby give permission for my child to use the Port Isabel Public Library Internet Access computer.

_____   _____
Parent/Guardian Signature   Date

_____   _____
Address   Telephone Number

should provide guidance to their own children and should monitor their use of this resource." By contrast, the Evanston (IL) Public Library policy (*www.evanston.lib.il.us/library/internet-access-policy.html*) states a bit more strongly that "parents are expected to monitor and supervise their children's use of the Internet." The Internet policy of the Public Library of Charlotte and Mecklenburg County in Charlotte, North Carolina (*www.plcmc.lib.nc.us/find/policy/internet.htm*), states, "Children 12 years and under must be accompanied by a parent, guardian or authorized teachers."

It is common for schools to require parents or guardians to sign release forms to allow their children to use the Internet in the school. Two examples are given in Figures 3–3 and 3–4 (*www.benton.org/Library/KickStart/kick.communityresources.html*).

Figure 3–3	SAMPLE STUDENT/PARENT CONSENT FORM

STUDENT SIGNATURE AND PARENTAL CONSENT FORM
[LOS ANGELES UNIFIED SCHOOL DISTRICT]

LAUSDnet (Internet) Account

(Note: If a student is too young to read the Acceptable Use Policy, please provide assistance. The purpose of the Acceptable Use Policy is to provide information, not to exclude anyone.)

Student last name _____

Student first name _____

School name _____

Teacher name _____

Date student completed Internet Test _____

I have read the Acceptable Use Policy. I have completed the Student Internet Test. If I follow the rules I may keep my account on LAUSDnet. If I do not follow the rules in the Acceptable Use Policy, I understand that my network account will be taken away from me. I understand that there will be no second chances.

Student Signature _____

Date _____

PARENTAL CONSENT

I have read the LAUSDnet Acceptable Use Policy and the LAUSDnet Student Internet Test. I understand that the Internet is a worldwide group of hundreds of thousands of computer networks. I know that the Los Angeles Unified School District does not control the content of these Internet networks. When using the Internet, I realize that students may read material that I might consider controversial or offensive. The Los Angeles Unified School District has my permission to give an Internet account to my child. I understand that my child may keep this address as long as procedures described in the Acceptable Use Policy are followed.

Parent or guardian signature _____

Date of signature _____

Source: Los Angeles Unified School District.

Figure 3–4	SAMPLE NETWORK USE CONSENT FORM

PARENTAL CONSENT

I have read in full the Norwood Network Acceptable Use Policy (including the User Responsibilities listed on the reverse) and agree to support and uphold the Policy for my personal use and use of my child(ren). I understand that any violation of the Policy may result in loss of my privileges to use the Norwood Net. I also understand that if I knowingly allow others to violate these rules, I may lose my personal access. My signature shows this understanding.

Please sign the appropriate space(s):

Norwood Faculty/Staff: _____

Date _____

Norwood Parent: _____

Source: Norwood Independent School District.

For libraries that are concerned with the American Library Association's position on parental release, it should be noted that ALA statements on access to information find that minors should have free access to all resources in the library. There certainly is no obligation that a library conform to the ALA position unless, of course, the library has stated that it adopts such positions as library policy (ALA intellectual freedom statements, policies, and other documents may be found on the ALA Office of Intellectual Freedom Web page at *www.ala.org/oif.html*).

ARE ACKNOWLEDGMENT FORMS HELPFUL?

Many libraries require patrons to sign a user agreement form in which they acknowledge that they have read the policies concerning Internet use in the library and agree to those policies. Figure 3–5 contains the text of one such form.

Figure 3–5	SAMPLE REGISTRATION AND USER AGREEMENT

REGISTRATION AND USER AGREEMENT

1. I have read the policies concerning the use of the Bloomingdale Public Library's Internet Computers and agree to abide by the policies.

2. I agree to pay any repair or replacement costs of equipment or software damaged by myself or by minors for whom I am responsible.

3. I understand that the library is not responsible for any damage to personal disks due to system malfunction, or any other reason.

4. I understand that copyright laws restrict duplication of copyrighted software, and I will follow all copyright laws.

5. I understand that if I fail to abide by the Internet Computer policies, I will lose eligibility for use of the Library's Internet Computers.

6. If I am a non-resident, I understand that my Internet Card entitles me to use of the Internet access only.

Signature _____

Date _____

For Patrons Under the Age of 18:

As the parent or guardian of _____ I give permission for my minor to use the Internet Computers at the Bloomingdale Public Library, with the understanding that I am responsible for monitoring their appropriate use of the Internet Computers and that I am responsible for any damage that may occur.

Parent's Signature_____

Date _____

Source: Bloomingdale (IN) Public Library

Note that this library also requires parents of minors to sign, making this both a parental release and an acknowledgment of the rules and the parent's responsibility.

Is it necessary that patrons sign such a form? This depends on the library's level of comfort with patron access. In many libraries—especially smaller libraries—staff can oversee Internet usage and intervene in case of misuse. However, it can be prudent to verify that patrons understand and have acknowledged the policies of the library whether they are Internet policies, circulation policies (which are often printed on the back side of library cards and signed by patrons), or meeting-room policies.

Whatever the nature of the Internet policy that is ultimately adopted, it is very important that the library examine closely all questions having to do with procedural access. These procedures become the core of the relationship between the staff and the public regarding the use of Internet in the library. It is of utmost importance that the library feel comfortable with these policies before initiating access, and that they be reviewed periodically once Internet access has been introduced.

4

Defining Acceptable Use

The term "acceptable use" has become nearly synonymous with Internet policy. Librarians now use the term "acceptable-use policy" so frequently that it has earned its own shortcut abbreviation, the AUP. To refer to the library's Internet policy as its "acceptable-use policy" is not accurate, however, since the Internet policy may include other elements other than a statement of what is permitted in the library. These other aspects of the Internet policy have nothing whatever to do with acceptable use, though admittedly they may be influenced by the library's attitude toward it.

But if the acceptable-use statement is not always the totality of the Internet policy, it is typically its heart. In most policies, the largest part consists of determining what patrons can and cannot do on the Internet. Some libraries combine acceptable and unacceptable uses in the same section, but others break it out into distinct treatments. This book treats acceptable and prohibited uses as distinct topics so that the differences are highlighted. This chapter looks at possible elements to consider in developing your acceptable-use statement, next at the list of practices that you may want to specifically label as restricted or prohibited.

WHAT IS ACCEPTABLE USE?

There is a vast range of choices about what constitutes acceptable use, and to a great extent, the library's mission will shape what is permitted. In some cases, the type of library may also define what is acceptable, as will the policies of the parent institution (in the case of school and academic libraries).

There are, however, certain points that tend to recur in acceptable-use statements, and these tend to be very similar across library types. This chapter explores the dilemmas you will want to pose to your staff, library board, citizens' group, and other groups involved with creating your policies. The responses will sometimes be simple, other times more complex, but when you have resolved them, you will have defined the majority of the issues comprising the acceptable-use policy.

Before we go into specifics, however, please note that some policies contain overarching statements of the acceptable use of the Internet in the library. These are not so much acceptable-use statements as values statements for all parties to the Internet connection—the user *and* the institution. For example, the Canyon (TX) Public Library's statement begins:

> All users of electronic information resources such as the Internet are expected to use these resources in a responsible manner, consistent with the educational and informational purposes for which they are provided.

Statements like this one are very useful in providing a backdrop for and often serve to introduce a list of the elements of acceptable use, as does the Canyon Public Library's policy.

Some libraries specify in their policies that the use of the Internet must be consistent with specific purposes—either those that form the stated mission and supporting roles of the library, or those specific to a particular function within the library such as the children's program, the science and technology collection, or the business reference center. For example, a special-collection library on a university campus might state that patrons may only use the Internet workstations to access resources that are related to the subject of that collection. In this case, a patron in an engineering library would be expected to refrain from using the Internet workstation to surf the Web for recreational purposes. In a school library, students might have to limit their searches to materials needed to complete assignments.

You may find that you have very cogent reasons for limiting access based on narrowly stated purposes. You may have a limited number of workstations and a high level of demand, a very narrowly defined mission for the library, or a need to demonstrate that the Internet is being used for serious, informational research. But as with other limitations placed on library services, it is important that those creating the policy understand and articulate these reasons. It is even advisable to publish this reason in the policy since, without fail, the public will question the need for the restriction.

You should take into consideration whether the library has adopted any overarching statements regarding free access to information. If so, a limitation on what a person can access on the Internet may conflict with the library's stated policy of unrestricted access. It is important to keep in mind the distinction between restricting acceptable use by purpose or type of use and restricting the class of material accessed. It is not a contradiction for a library to adopt a policy that states that patrons must use the Internet in ways consistent with the purposes of the library, yet state that the library is not responsible for the content of the Internet and will not attempt to regulate access based on the content of the material. The question of acceptable use based on content of materials is addressed next.

CAN LIBRARIES RESTRICT ACCESS TO INTERNET CONTENT?

There are materials that may be considered inappropriate for access in the library. Sexually explicit materials may come to mind first, but there are other types of materials that a library may find inappropriate, such as ones that promote violence, racism, sexism, or values considered to be in conflict with those of the dominant community.

The most commonly prohibited material, however, is sexually explicit in nature. Some policies regard accessing sexually explicit materials in view of other patrons as a form of harassment and inform the public that staff will intervene. For example, the policy of the West Warwick (RI) Public Library (*www.ultranet.com/~wwpublib/libpol.htm*) states that patrons "should be aware that there are some information resources which are inappropriate to a library setting. Because the library is a public place, the library staff has the authority to end an online session when inappropriate material is displayed on the screen." See also the box on Loudoun County, page 90.

This dilemma should be considered very carefully. The First Amendment of the U.S. Constitution protects the rights of citizens from the intrusion of government in what they see, say, hear, view, and read. Furthermore, the U.S. Supreme Court in its 1997 landmark ruling overturning the Communications Decency Act, ruled that the Internet is a forum for the exchange of ideas and, as such, should be accorded protection under the U.S. Constitution. What does this mean for your Internet acceptable-use policy? It means that if your library is a publicly funded entity, any restrictions placed on what people view or read on the Internet in your library could be construed as government interference in a citizen's right to constitutionally protected speech. Note, however, that we specify *publicly funded* libraries. There may be a little more leeway within private institutions, but this is something to check with an attorney.

There are notable exceptions, however, such as speech that is prohibited by either state or federal statute. For example, many states have harmful-to-minors statutes prohibiting the display of harmful materials to a child. These statutes typically have very carefully worded statements of what is considered harmful. Another exception could be speech in public schools. Because teachers and school librarians operate *in loco parentis*—that is, they have the obligations of parents in the absence of parents—they must ensure the well-being of the children and make decisions in their best interest. This gives teachers and librarians in schools more latitude than, say, public library staff, to restrict children's Internet access by content.

Public libraries and publicly funded college and university libraries, however, must be very cautious in adopting Internet acceptable-use policies that make access of certain materials unacceptable by nature of their content. Chapter 6 covers this issue more fully in its discussion of filtering Internet access.

ARE INTERACTIVE INTERNET SERVICES ACCEPTABLE USES?

Sometimes library managers approach Internet services purely as an information resource that is just an extension of the print collection or a complex version of an electronic database. But our patrons consider the Internet as not just a one-way information resource but also a dynamic, two-way medium for stimulating and entertaining interaction. Indeed, the prime motivation for some patrons to get on the Internet is to use services such as chat rooms, e-mail, interactive games, or online shopping and are reasonably dismayed when library policies make these interactive uses off limits. The decision to deem these activities unacceptable may be based on sound reasoning, but seem often to arise from misinformation about the nature of the service or the technology. Let's begin our review of the limits of acceptable use by reviewing these interactive uses of the Internet.

Can Users Enter Chat Rooms?

Chat rooms have become one of the most popular attractions on the World Wide Web. Though they have a stigma of being sexually oriented, in fact there are thousands of chat rooms for all purposes ranging from women's health issues to politics to music, or just meeting other Internet users to "talk." Chat rooms have, in fact, become a legitimate source of information for many people.

Chat rooms are like bulletin boards that operate in real time. Users have software that allows them to post messages on the Internet that are quickly read and responded to by other users who are online in the chat room. This technology creates a kind of delayed-response conversation.

Okay, you say, these chat rooms may be a strangely disconnected way to interact with fellow human beings, but they don't sound all that harmful. So why do some libraries exclude chat rooms from the range of use allowed in the library?

For a variety of reasons. The primary one is because they are equated with sexually explicit speech. There are many chat rooms where users act out imaginary but graphic sexual encounters with other persons in the "room." The speech on these sites is unpredictable at best and frankly uninhibited. So, though there are many nonsexual sites, many people tend to think of chat rooms as being synonymous with sex and choose to play it safe by declaring chat rooms off limits for the library computer. It should be noted, however, that there are many legitimate chat rooms in which users converse about a wide variety of mutual interests that have nothing to do with sex.

Some libraries restrict chat room access out of a concern that there are predatory adults lurking on the Internet who would harm children and young people. Unfortunately, there have been terrifying cases of adults who manage to lure children and teenagers to meet them in person after initial encounters on chat rooms. And there are those on the Internet who misrepresent themselves as being women when they are men, older when they claim to be younger, and so forth. It may not occur to younger children to question someone who seems to be a peer and suggests they meet. Stories of harm coming to people—young and old—who have met over the Internet have received a lot of media coverage, though it could be argued that, all things considered, children might be relatively safer in a chat room in the library than in some other, less protected environment. Nevertheless, many libraries have played it safe by making chat rooms a nonacceptable use of the Internet on library workstations.

Another concern, perhaps the most legitimate, is that chat rooms will cause patrons to hog workstations so that other patrons cannot use them. Many Web users find chat rooms addictive and end up spending hours glued to the screen. Libraries that may otherwise choose not to limit access may prefer instead to disallow the use of workstations for chat rooms, to limit their access to nonpeak times, or to require that patrons use them for "legitimate" information needs. Before you decide what to do about chat rooms, you would do well to spend a few minutes in some chat rooms to familiarize yourself with the technical process of accessing the rooms and observing the type of interaction that occurs there.

Can Users Play Interactive Games?

Many of the same issues regarding chat rooms also arise in the discussion of interactive games, which are games played simultaneously by multiple players who might be literally anywhere in the world. The movements of a given player are (or may be) known to all the other players. Interactive online games are extremely popular, especially among high-school and college students.

These games tend to be violent and sometimes involve controversial, occult themes, such as devil worship or sorcery. The controversies over the content of the games is part of the reason that some libraries consider them problematic enough to declare them an unacceptable use of library Internet resources. This approach might be appropriate in a school library, but public libraries might run into freedom of speech issues if they limit access to such games. This would be a case of restricting access because it is based on content rather than use. But there are other reasons to deem use of interactive games inappropriate. Like chat rooms, interactive games can become quite addictive and tie up library Internet stations. Some people are concerned these games make fertile hunting grounds, as some games allow users to "meet" and online game players tend to be youths. The nature of the games, however, makes it hard to overtly lure someone off the game since the point is to play the game and not to engage in conversation.

SHOULD LIBRARIES PROVIDE E-MAIL SERVICES?

There are three aspects to consider with e-mail. First, does the library offer e-mail accounts to patrons? Second, does the library allow e-mail to be sent from the library's Web browser? Third, will patrons be allowed to establish free, Web-based, e-mail services in the library?

Does the Library Offer E-Mail Accounts for Patrons?

This is not really an issue of acceptable use—either the library offers it or not. On the other hand, the question should be considered with the discussion of acceptable use since your policymakers must decide whether those who use your library should expect to have an e-mail box on the library server. A survey of Internet policies reveals that very few public libraries actually offer e-mail accounts to patrons despite the widespread expectation among the public that the library will do so and the apparent belief among library staffs that they will be expected to provide them. Despite being a value-added service, especially in those areas that have no other local Internet service provider, offering e-mail consumes a significant investment of staff and library resources. The parent institutions of academic libraries, however, often have the policy of establishing e-mail boxes, and elementary and secondary schools often assign the library the task of managing e-mail accounts for students on the school or district server.

Can Users Send E-mail from the Web Browser?

Most standard browser software, such as Netscape and Microsoft Explorer, allows users to send e-mail messages from within the browser. You can choose whether to configure your browser to allow mail, but in many cases it is a relatively simple operation for a user to configure the browser and to send e-mail. One advantage is that patrons can send information on Web pages to their own e-mail accounts without downloading and printing, a cleaner solution for everyone involved—or at least for those with accounts.

But sending mail through the browser is problematic, essentially because there is no way to receive a response. Also, patrons can send e-mail virtually anonymously (mail is tagged with the library's domain name and the e-mail address placed in the mail set-up file). There have been many instances of patrons sending junk or unsolicited e-mail content from the public workstation. Should this happen, you will find it very difficult to track down the person who sent the mail.

Can Users Access Web-based E-mail in the Library?

The Web now abounds with free e-mail accounts, such as those from Yahoo Mail and HotMail, and users can set up free e-mail accounts with those companies. There are few reasons why a library would want to limit the ability of a user to do so. First, these services are established on the provider's server, not the library's. Second, there is no security issue at all; the patron is simply visiting another Web site.

IS TELNET AN ACCEPTABLE USE?

Once upon a time, before the World Wide Web, telnet was one of the commands that allowed a user to surf the Internet. Services that did not allow users access via telnet were of only limited use. This issue is less important today than it was a few years ago because the advent of the World Wide Web has meant that virtually every resource is accessible via a Web browser. But there is still the need, although diminished, for allowing patrons telnet access, since some sites are only available via telnet. Users who are authorized by their network administrator to access a remote system many times must enter that system via telnet to perform any functions on the remote server; for some systems, this could mean remote access to an electronic mailbox. The most significant reason to allow telnet access, however, is to reach library catalogs, many of which are still only available via telnet.

Offering telnet access is not as much of an issue as it once was, primarily because telnet is just another client software application installed on the workstation (like the Web browser) that poses little threat to system security. There are some situations, however, in which telnet access may continue to represent a security risk, especially where a patron is offered access to a Unix prompt. If you are ever unsure about what level of access you are offering your patrons, seek the advice of someone with the technical expertise to analyze any security risks in your system.

Nearly all public and school libraries and most academic libraries have stopped offering telnet access. The same goes for FTP (File Transfer Protocol) capability, which allows patrons to ship files directly from one server to another. These tools are indispensable for system operators, programmers, and others, but they are of only limited use for the retrieval of information by most library patrons.

There is software available that can be installed on library computers to prevent patrons from accessing many of the activities that we have described in the last several pages. This software, called protocol blocking, functions similarly to filtering software, but it restricts patron access by function, not content. However, protocol blockers do not work as well for chat rooms since these sites are Internet based; libraries that block chat rooms usually must do so by blocking the IP address.

CAN THE LIBRARY'S INTERNET CONNECTION BE USED TO CONDUCT COMMERCIAL BUSINESS?

Another consideration in the development of the acceptable-use policy is whether to allow patrons to use the library's Internet access and workstations to conduct business over the Internet. This might seem at first a simple question, but it can become somewhat tricky. If you choose, as many library managers have, to deem this type of activity unacceptable, you should be clear about what is meant by commercial business. Certainly, using the university's server to launch a Web page that sells a product would be a clear violation, as would using a public library's computer to order and pay for goods and services online (many libraries specifically single out this practice as unacceptable out of fear of being financially obligated for the purchases). What about patrons who use the Internet workstations to send out resumes? Not the same, you say? Maybe not, but what if that person is a self-employed consultant? It is certainly a reasonable policy to prohibit commercial uses of the Internet in the library; however, be sure you and your staff understand exactly what is meant by commercial activity and under what circumstances staff should intervene.

WHAT ABOUT FILE, DISK, AND DIRECTORY ACCESS?

A related concern is whether patrons will be able to access the hard or network drives for the purposes of opening, modifying, and saving files. If your policy prohibits the downloading of software, you will most likely not want to allow patrons access to the hard drive. Conversely, if downloading software in your library is permitted, then you may want to give users access to the hard disk unless the download is allowed only to floppies. Just keep in mind that giving patrons access to the hard drive invites trouble. Obviously the main concern is security: a user might be able to open, delete, move, and copy files; copy software; and perhaps even change system configurations. Libraries can protect access to the hard drive by password, but a determined user with moderate computer skills may be able to get around that. Such an action by a patron would be considered an attempt to breach system security.

Chapter 3 discussed security software such as Fortres, which allows library staff to lock down certain features of the workstation, including hard-drive and floppy-drive access. Depending on your policy, you may want to investigate such offerings.

Are Certain Files Off Limits?

Just as you may wish specifically to disallow access to the hard drive, you may also prohibit patrons from accessing the library's internal network. This is a particular concern for Internet workstations, because often they must be connected to the library's LAN to get outside access, making it possible, for example, for a user to access files on a shared drive or, upon discovering a password, to get into the internal files of the library. In this scenario, it could be possible for a patron sitting at an Internet workstation in the reading room to be reading memos taken from your directories.

There are technical barriers that can be put in place to help prevent this, but the wise policy will address network access explicitly so that attempts to circumvent the restriction will be considered a violation of the library's acceptable-use policy.

Is Uploading or Downloading Permitted?

Some policies do not allow patrons to load their own software on Internet computers or, for that matter, to use those computers for any purposes other than accessing the Internet. Library managers who write these policies are attempting to avoid harming the machine by keeping out software that could conflict with other software on the machine (a particular problem for Apple computers), carry viruses, or gobble up disk space. However, many Web sites have multimedia features that require software be downloaded from that Web site to the computer before seeing, hearing, or reading a particular file. For example, patrons visiting the site *www.bobdylan.com*—a site devoted to the music of singer songwriter Bob Dylan—will find that there are many clips of Dylan's music to be heard, but only if they download and install a specific software application (RealAudio—a standard software for audio capability that arguably should have been installed on the machine before making it available to patrons) onto the local hard drive. The software is normally harmless and takes up little space; however, it does stay on the machine after the session unless it is specifically removed. So if the library has a policy that prohibits downloading software, sites such as this—which are the rule rather than the exception—will be meaningless to patrons. And these are the very sites that people most want to visit because they are the most stimulating and interesting.

Applications such as RealAudio, called "plug-ins," are needed to view and hear the multimedia aspects of the Internet and can become common across the Internet in a relatively short time. The library should have a plan for staying current with plug-ins, systematically loading these resources onto machines, and handling situations where the use of Web-site resources requires downloading of a type of software not currently loaded on the workstation.

One way to deal with this last point is to require patrons to request that library staff actually download the software from the Internet. Staff can download the file into the appropriate directory and keep track of what plug-ins are available on the machine by periodically reviewing the files, updating obsolete programs, and deleting those that are no longer needed. Of course, this requires some technical capability on the part of a staff member and places an additional burden on staff (which should always be considered carefully).

Can Patrons Use Their Own Diskettes?

One of the essential questions regarding system security is whether you will let patrons use their own disks at your computers. Most libraries do not allow it because of concerns over viruses, which run rampant on the Internet. Some are massively damaging; many are simply irritating; but all will cause problems. When patrons bring disks from home and use them on the library's computers, the risk increases that a virus could inadvertently be transmitted to the library's computer or network. For this reason, many libraries specifically disallow the use of personal disks. The Lawrence (KS) Public Library policy (*www.ci.lawrence.ks.us/iag.html*) states:

> You will need to ask a reference librarian if you wish to save files. Diskettes are available from reference librarians for a minimal charge. You may not use your own diskettes. (This is to minimize the potential for the introduction of a computer virus into the Internet Access computer, which could then be spread to subsequent users of the computer.)

This policy also contains a disclaimer that no patron is absolutely safe from the risk of computer virus when using a library computer.

If you opt to let patrons use their own diskettes, it is a good idea to require that they submit their disks to virus scanning first. This can be done by staff, but it will be time-consuming and, should staff find and not be able to clear a virus, the patron will not be able to use the disk. A fact of life, however, is that no virus-scanning software is foolproof.

An alternative is to sell disks in the library. A diskettes is relatively inexpensive, usually no more than a dollar and often much less. This way, the library can sell factory fresh, preformatted disks that have a very low risk of virus. The Cedar Falls (IA) Public Library (*www.ci.oswego.or.us/library/cedar.htm*), for example, directs users: "You will need to ask a reference librarian if you wish to save files. Diskettes are available for a minimal charge."

Can Patrons Use Nonlibrary Software.

Another area of concern is whether to allow patrons to use their own software. Most libraries do not, and many libraries expressly address this in their Internet policy precisely because it is a big risk even though it's not directly related to Internet access. When the library offers computer access, there may be some legitimate reasons for a patron to bring along software, but when it comes to the Internet, most policies—like this one from Bloomingdale, Illinois (*www.xnet.com/~bdale/inetpol.htm*)—state that "Internet computers are to be used for Internet access only. Patrons may not use personal software."

Do You Allow Downloading?

Downloading materials from the Internet is, in some ways, what Internet access is all about in terms of offering your patrons access to this new medium of information. But allowing downloads implies some risk. As always, there is the threat of viruses to the library's Internet workstation, especially if the download is to the computer's hard drive. In addition, many files on the Internet are quite large. Downloading them may tie up the computer for a long time, especially if the library's connection is slow. Copyright is another issue: some libraries discourage downloads to guard against patrons obtaining unauthorized copies of copyrighted material.

The strategy adopted by many libraries is thus to sell preformatted disks or check disks for viruses, to forbid downloads to the hard drive, to limit the size of downloads, and to remind patrons of the copyright law. For example, the Peachtree (GA) City Library (*www.geocities.com/Athens/9755/rules.htm*) states that "printing and downloading of material from the World Wide Web or Telnet is encouraged as long as it does not violate the general ideas of copyright and plagiarism. Downloading material to a floppy disk is free." In this way, the library's risks are minimized and patrons can enjoy the full benefits of taking home with them information obtained via the Internet.

HOW HAVE LIBRARIES WRITTEN ACCEPTABLE-USE POLICIES?

Now that you have reviewed each of these issues and decided your course, you need to write the policy. The following approaches to writing policies are the most often used, though there are other models as well:

Three Different Approaches to Policy Formulation

1. Include in the policy two detailed and specific lists, one of practices that are allowed and another of those not allowed in your library.
2. Address only what is *not* allowed and allow the library user to infer that what is not expressly disallowed is allowed.
3. State in broad, general terms the purpose of the Internet service in the library, then go into more specific detail about what is not allowed.

Which of these three is the best approach? There is no "right" answer. It depends on the preference of the governing authority of your institution, the adaptability of your staff, and the organizational climate of your institution. A broad policy allows latitude in interpretation and enforcement; a specific policy provides a clear basis for the development of procedures for implementation.

Figures 4–1, 4–2, 4–3, and 4–4 offer up examples of different approaches. Figure 4–1 gives the entire text of Denver's Internet policy, the online version of which is followed by two buttons that ask the user to choose either "Agree" or "Don't Agree" before continuing. The Denver policy illustrates a broad statement of purpose followed by a specific list of practices not allowed. Note that chat rooms, e-mail, and non-Internet uses of workstations are not allowed. By inference, we can conclude that other uses such as downloading files and the use of machines for commercial purposes would be considered permissible. The Nassau Community College policy in Figure 4–2 anticipates some of the unacceptable practices discussed in Chapter 5. It provides an example of a policy that is very broad and brief in describing acceptable use, but very specific in describing unacceptable use. And the "Internet Statement" in Figure 4–3 mixes a few specific citations of acceptable and unacceptable uses. Note that the statement explicitly states that downloading information to a floppy is permissible, that library-authorized games are permissible, but chat rooms, downloading software, and unauthorized games are not allowed.

Finally, let's look at the rather lengthy appropriate-use statement for Brown University in Figure 4–4, which is very specific and mixes both allowable and unallowable use in a single list. This policy—which, like many universities, is of the parent institution rather than the library—is remarkable not only for its length and thoroughness but also because, with only a couple of exceptions, all statements are affirmative rather than negative. Brown has also identified some appropriate or inappropriate uses that are not covered in this book, such as political activity and civility.

As you may have noted in reading the sample policies above, there is no well-defined line between acceptable- and unacceptable-use statements. This chapter has explored some of the questions that will lead you to a decision about what you will consider acceptable use. Chapter 5 presents, in a bit greater detail, some of those practices that are considered unacceptable in many libraries, more examples of how policies describe restricted use, and the range of consequences available when a patron violates the library policy.

Figure 4–1   BROAD ACCEPTABLE-USE POLICY FOR A PUBLIC LIBRARY

THE INTERNET AT THE DENVER PUBLIC LIBRARY

The Denver Public Library cannot control the information available over the Internet and is not responsible for its content. The Internet contains a wide variety of material and opinions from various points of view. Not all sources provide information that is accurate, complete or current, and some may be offensive.

Persons using any of the computers in the Library shall not use the Internet for any form of electronic communication including conversation groups ("chat rooms") or electronic mail (e-mail) services. The computers shall not be used for word processing or other office functions including the design and maintenance of Web pages.

Source: Denver Public Library (*www.denver.lib.co.us/ipolicy.html*).

Figure 4–2   BROAD ACCEPTABLE-USE POLICY FOR A COLLEGE

ACCEPTABLE USE POLICY FOR COMPUTER FACILITIES AT NASSAU COMMUNITY COLLEGE

Nassau Community College provides computing resources to support the academic research and instructional activities of the institution. The resources are intended for the sole use of College faculty, staff, students and other authorized users. Computing resources include host computer systems, personal computers and workstations, communications networks, software, and files.

Nassau Community College reserves the right to monitor its computing resources to protect the integrity of its computing systems, workstations, and lab facilities.

Accounts issued to the individuals are intended for the sole use of that individual, and are non-transferable.

The owner is responsible for all usage on their assigned account.

The following types of activities are examples of behavior that are unethical and unacceptable, and in some cases may violate state or federal law:

- altering system software or hardware configurations;

- accessing another individual's account, private files, or e-mail without permission of the owner;

- misrepresenting one's identity in electronic communication;

- violating copyright and/or software agreements (See also Using Software, A Guide to the Ethical and Legal Use of Software for Members of the Academic Community);

- violating rules or codes set by services subscribed to by the college;

- using Computing resources to threaten or harass others;

- using the College systems for commercial or profit-making purposes without written authorization from the college administration;

- disobeying lab and system policies, procedures, and protocol (e.g., time limits on workstation usage).

Policies and regulations of the college, and state and federal law, are applicable to computing resources. Alleged violations will be processed to college policies and the processes outlined in the Student Handbook, and Personnel Policies and Procedures.

Source: Nassau (NY) Community College (*www.sunynassau.edu/policies/labpol.htm*).

Figure 4–3   SPECIFIC ACCEPTABLE-USE POLICY FOR A PUBLIC LIBRARY

AACPL INTERNET STATEMENT

The Anne Arundel County Public Library provides access to the Internet to assist Anne Arundel County residents of all ages in receiving accurate answers to their questions and easy access to resources for personal enjoyment and learning.

The Internet is an unregulated medium. Not all sources on the Internet provide information that is current, accurate, or complete. The Anne Arundel County Public Library is unable to control or monitor the content of the materials on the Internet which changes quickly and without warning.

Parents: Some of the material on the Internet may be objectionable. You may see things on the Internet that you do not wish your children to view. Please provide guidance to your children in their use of the Internet. The Library has material ("Child Safety on the Information Superhighway") that can help you work with your children to safely cruise the information highway.

Patrons can use the public information stations to access information from the catalog and the Internet provided they do not corrupt, damage or otherwise compromise the library equipment or software.

There is a one hour time limit for the use of the computers when other patrons are waiting. This may be more strictly enforced at busy times than at slower times. Due to the heavy use of the computers access to chat lines is not permitted. Playing games on the computers is prohibited except for library authorized games.

Downloading information to a floppy disc is permissible. Discs may be purchased from library staff.

Software may not be loaded or downloaded from the Internet onto the library's computers.

Staff are not trained to assist patrons in the use of e-mail.

Source: Anne Arundel County (MD) Public Library (*web.aacpl.lib.md.us/disclaim.htm*).

Figure 4–4	SPECIFIC ACCEPTABLE-USE POLICY FOR A COLLEGE

GUIDELINES FOR APPROPRIATE USER BEHAVIOR

The following list, while not exhaustive, provides some specific guidelines for responsible and ethical behavior:

1. Use only the computers, computer accounts and computer files for which you have authorization. Do not use another individual's ID or account, or attempt to capture or guess other users' passwords. Users are individually responsible for all use of resources assigned to them; therefore, sharing of accounts is strongly discouraged.

2. Obey established guidelines for any computers or networks used both inside and outside the University. For example, individuals using Brown's public computing clusters must adhere to the policies established for those clusters; individuals accessing off-campus computers via external networks must abide by the policies established by the owners of those computers as well as policies governing use of those networks. (See Appendix B for a summary of CERFnet guidelines.)

3. Do not attempt to access restricted portions of the operating system, security software, or accounting software unless authorized by the appropriate University administrator. Breaking into computers is explicitly a violation of Internet rules of conduct, no matter how weak the protection is on those computers.

4. Abide by all state and federal laws. (Appendix C provides an extract of some relevant Rhode Island and federal laws.)

5. Respect the privacy and personal rights of others. Do not access or copy another user's electronic mail, data, programs, or other files without permission. Guidelines in the Tenets of Community Behavior and Academic Code regarding plagiarism or collusion on assignments apply to course work completed with computers just as they do to other types of course work.

    Brown endorses the following statement on software and intellectual rights distributed by EDUCOM, the non-profit consortium of colleges and universities committed to the use and management of information technology in higher education, and ADAPSO, the computer software and services industry association:

    "Respect for intellectual labor and creativity is vital to academic discourse and enterprise. This principle applies to work of all authors and publishers in all media. It encompasses respect for the right to acknowledgement, right to privacy and right to determine the form, manner and terms of publication and distribution.

    Because electronic information is volatile and easily reproduced, respect for the work and personal expression of others is especially critical in computer environments. Viola-

Figure 4–4	**(Continued)**

tions of authorial integrity, including plagiarism, invasion of privacy, unauthorized access and trade secret and copyright violations, may be grounds for sanctions against members of the academic community."

6.   Abide by all applicable copyright laws and licenses. Both university policies and the law expressly forbid the copying of software that has not been placed in the public domain or distributed as "freeware" or "shareware."

7.   Use appropriate standards of civility when using computing systems to communicate with other individuals. When sending personal messages to other users, always identify yourself as the sender. Using Brown's computing resources to harass other individuals deliberately is explicitly prohibited.

8.   Be sensitive to the needs of others, and use only your fair share of computing resources. For example, users of shared resources, such as the central computer or the public clusters, should use these facilities for only the most essential tasks during periods of peak demand. Broadcasting non-critical messages to large numbers of individuals and sending chain letters are examples of activities that cause network congestion and interfere with the work of others, and thus are not allowed. (See Appendix B for a summary of CERFnet guidelines.)

9.   Treat computing resources and electronic information as a valuable university resource. Protect your data and the systems you use. For example, back up your files regularly. Set an appropriate password and change it regularly. Make sure you understand the access privileges you have set for your files. Do not destroy or damage any computing equipment, networks or software. The willful introduction of computer viruses into the Brown University computing environment or into other computing environments via Brown's network violates University standards and regulations.

10. Use Brown's computing facilities and services for university related work. Activities that would jeopardize the University's tax exempt status are prohibited.
     PERSONAL FINANCIAL GAIN: Use of University computing resources for personal financial gain requires prior approval. Contact the Vice President for Computing and Information Services for detailed information.
     POLITICAL ACTIVITY: Refer to the "Guidelines for Political Activities" in the Brown University Student Handbook for information on acceptable and unacceptable uses of university resources for political activities. (A copy of the relevant section is included in Appendix D.)

Figure 4–4	**(Continued)**

11. Stay informed about the computing environment. The computing environment is continually evolving, as new products are introduced and others become obsolete. Services change as the number and needs of users change. Brown publishes information in a variety of ways, including logon messages, general news items that users are prompted to read, news items associated with particular compilers or software packages, on-line documents about software, policy and procedures, newsletters, and in some cases, letters mailed to individuals. Users are responsible for staying informed about changes in the computing environment and are expected to adapt to changes in the University computing environment.

Source: Brown University (*www.brown.edu/webmaster/TM009.html*).

5

Prohibited Uses and Their Consequences

Chapter 4 discussed the process of defining what is included in a library's acceptable-use statement. A number of sample statements of acceptable use, however, also presented what the library considered unacceptable use. You may wonder, isn't prohibited use simply the reverse of acceptable use? Isn't anything that is not part of the acceptable-use policy automatically considered prohibited use? The answer is: Sometimes, but not always. Many libraries specifically identify actions that will not be tolerated in the library and issue a clear statement of the penalties for violating those rules. As seen in the last chapter, many libraries combine these elements in a common document (often called simply the "acceptable-use policy"), but others distinguish between them and state them as separate parts of the Internet policy.

It comes down to a question of degree of severity between the limits of acceptable use and behavior that is considered unacceptable and could result in a loss of privileges. For example, an acceptable-use statement might require patrons to sign up to use the Internet; but it would probably be acceptable to use the workstation without a reservation in most libraries, assuming no one was waiting who had a reservation. In contrast, an unacceptable-use statement might forbid intentional attempts to breach system security for any purpose, with violation resulting in a loss of use privileges and possible criminal charges. In an academic setting, the offender might also be expelled from the institution. Policy statements of unacceptable use are often a reiteration not only of a violation of library policy but also of some higher rule—either civil or criminal law or the policies of the parent institution.

WHAT USES HAVE LIBRARIES PROHIBITED?

This chapter looks at the elements most often specifically prohibited in library policies, reasons you might want to include them in your unacceptable-use statement, a discussion of the range of consequences of unacceptable use, and examples of policy statements of unacceptable use. Particulars covered are:

- copyright violations
- misrepresentation
- unlawful speech, hate speech, and harassment
- illegal activities
- viewing, displaying, or transmitting sexually explicit materials
- sexual harassment
- commercial activity
- attempts to violate system security and user privacy

Copyright Violations

Libraries have an obligation to protect the rights of owners of copyrighted materials that are in the libraries. The temptation is great, opportunity abounds, and the mechanism of enforcement is weak, so there is an ongoing danger that library patrons will violate copyright law. The most common example of this practice is the unauthorized photocopy of extensive portions of copyrighted works held in the library. For this reason, libraries post warnings on photocopy machines informing patrons that it is a violation of federal law to make unauthorized duplicates of copyrighted materials.

Libraries may begin to place such warning labels on their Internet workstations and printers as well, because standard Internet browsing software makes it very easy to violate federal copyright law. At the time of writing, however, those laws are undergoing revision that could impose further restrictions on the use of copyrighted materials available electronically. It is currently a simple matter to download an image or other copyright-protected material from the Internet and reproduce, save, or distribute that image—almost any case of which would be a violation of the rights of the copyright holder and could subject the violator to prosecution under copyright laws. But would the library be liable as well? This is not clear, and new laws being considered might greatly restrict the range of fair use allowed of online materials.

In the interim, most libraries want to demonstrate that they have done whatever is reasonably within their power to prevent library patrons from violating copyright laws when using library resources. One way is for the library to adopt in its Internet policy a statement that patrons may not violate copyright laws and that there is a penalty for violators of that policy. Indeed, copyright violation is one of the most common items in unacceptable-use statements. It is especially important for libraries that allow students, faculty, and others to mount Web pages on their servers to consider specifically stating that use of copyrighted materials without express permission on such a Web site is unacceptable.

Misrepresentation

A cartoon from the early 1990s showed a dog sitting at a computer speaking to another dog. The caption read, "On the Internet, no one knows you're a dog." Many have remarked on this democratizing nature of the Internet. Presumably, users on, say, listservs or newsgroups will not be able to recognize your race, age, socioeconomic status, or even sometimes your gender, so that you will be judged on the merits of your comments rather than on some superficial characteristic.

But this potential anonymity carries a darker side that some users take advantage of for less noble reasons. Many reports have circulated that some persons misrepresent themselves on the Internet with the intention of harming someone else, either through fraud, a con game, or seduction. According to these reports, these people send e-mails that seem to come from someone else, or describe themselves as being someone they are not, for example hiding their age or gender. More technically sophisticated and malevolent violators may try to use a false identity to violate the security of your system or others.

Some libraries have adopted policies that prohibit the use of library Internet workstations to misrepresent oneself. Whether your library does so in its unacceptable-use policy will depend in part on whether your library provides e-mail accounts to patrons, allows patrons to e-mail documents and mail from library terminals, permits users to post to news groups and listservs, or lets them enter chat rooms. If not, there will be very little opportunity for a patron to use a library connection to send a misrepresenting message.

Unlawful Speech, Hate Speech, and Harassment

Similar to misrepresentation is whether your unacceptable-use policy will define speech that is not acceptable on Internet computers. This is a sensitive topic, since librarians are rightfully careful not to restrict patron speech that is constitutionally protected, which is virtually all speech. However, there are types of speech that are not protected by the First Amendment of the U.S. Constitution. For example, it is illegal to threaten the life of the president of the United States (though it is not illegal to advocate the violent overthrow of the government in general). It is also illegal in many states to send "harmful" materials to a minor via the Internet.

If your library allows patrons to send e-mail from the library Internet workstations, to have e-mail accounts on the library server, or to maintain Web pages on the library server, you may want to consider stating that the use of library resources to post or distribute speech that violates federal and state law is not allowed.

Other Illegal Activities

It should go without saying that no illegal activities will be allowed using library resources. Nevertheless, illegal activities are frequently identified in a library's unacceptable-use policy. It might seem a bit obvious to do so, but referencing illegal activities gives the library the chance to state that it does not condone and, in fact, actively prohibits such use.

Examples of illegal activities in which library users might engage (other than copyright violation, threats, and other such conduct already mentioned) include using e-mail for any of the following purposes: purchasing or selling drugs or other controlled substances, operating prostitution services, conducting gambling operations, trying to violate the security of a computer system, downloading or offering for download pirated software, or commiting vandalism against another system.

Viewing, Displaying, or Transmitting Sexually Explicit Materials

Much has been written and said about the decisions libraries have had to make regarding patron access to sexually explicit materials and pornography via the library's Internet workstations (see Chapter 6 on the use of blocking and filtering software). Even if a library decides not to filter and states that it will not limit access by class of materials, that library may still wish to impose some restrictions on the use of sexually explicit materials in the library and reference that restriction in the unacceptable-use statement.

This may seem contradictory, and in some cases there may be an inconsistency between the library's access policy and its unacceptable-use policy, but a library may have legitimate concerns regarding sexual materials that intersect a policy of open access. Most significantly, not all speech is constitutionally protected: many states have laws that restrict the exposure of minors (usually defined as persons aged 18 and younger) to certain types of obscene material. Usually these laws characterize the materials as "harmful" to minors and provide relatively specific definitions of the nature of that material. The Texas statute is representative of such statutes, especially in the way it very carefully and narrowly defines "harmful" materials:

> "Harmful material" means material whose dominant theme taken as a whole:
> (A) appeals to the prurient interest of a minor in sex, nudity, or excretion;
> (B) is patently offensive to prevailing standards in the adult community as a whole with what is suitable for minors; and
> (C) is utterly without redeeming social value for minors.

These statutes differ slightly from state to state, but they usually specify the type of material restricted and the nature of the restriction. Also, federal statute—upheld by judicial review—finds that materials depicting persons under the age of 18 engaged in sexual activity is not constitutionally protected. Furthermore, there have been several attempts to create a federal-level prohibition very similar to the restrictions described above, which currently only exist in some states.

Your unacceptable-use policy could reference such materials that are in violation of state and federal statutes with a statement such as the following: "Library resources may not be used in such a way that may be considered a violation of state statutes restricting the sale, exhibition, and distribution of materials harmful to a minor."

The only problem with this "tap on the shoulder" approach is that it leaves everything up to the discretion and interpretation of the staff member who happens to notice such inappropriate viewing. In some extreme cases, this will be a relatively easy call, but in others, a library employee might consider something "harmful" that in fact may fall under constitutionally protected speech. After all, we are talking about materials that have been the subject of fluctuating judicial opinion for decades. Remember that judges have found some materials to be obscene—such as James Joyce's *Ulysses* and Allen Ginsberg's poem *Howl*—that are now considered masterpieces of modern literature. Does your staff have the expertise to tell the difference? And even if they do, such a provision in your unacceptable-use statement puts staff in the unfortunate role of enforcer to patrons who may be offended and outraged when they are told not to view such materials in public. This element of your policy should receive a good deal of scrutiny and deliberate thinking before implementation.

Another issue surrounds access—specifically, staff access—to sexually explicit materials via library Internet connections and, like all others, it has been controversial. Some employers have written into their policies that staff may not use library resources to view materials that are sexually explicit in nature. Such a situation became the basis of an important early test of the government's limits in restricting access by its own employees. The State of Virginia restricted staff access to sexually explicit materials, which prompted a group of state university professors to file a class-action suit on behalf of all state employees. In a summary judgement in the case of *Urofsky v. Allen*, the U.S. District Court ruled that restricting employee access to materials based on their material represented an unconstitutional interference by government in the right of citizens to free access to constitutionally protected speech. (Let's be clear about one point: This discussion should not be construed to imply that employers do not have the right to limit staff uses of resources to those that are work related; the courts have ruled repeatedly that employers can limit the actions of employees regarding their use of networked resources.) The court found that *Urofsky v. Allen* involved a content-based restriction and, therefore, was unconstitutional.

There is another issue regarding sexually explicit materials: the allegation by some that viewing such materials in a library setting constitutes a form of sexual harassment and, therefore, should be considered unacceptable use. This thus falls into the larger discussion of the entire issue of sexual harassment.

Sexual Harassment

Does viewing sexually explicit materials in the library constitute sexual harassment? Some legal opinion says it creates an atmosphere of harassment, others claim there must be a more deliberate and prolonged action on the part of the offending party.

Regardless of the controversy, the issue of sexual harassment can be treated as independent from whether to allow patrons to view sexually explicit materials. Simply state that library Internet resources may not be used to sexually harass others, and you describe a range of conduct that is considered unacceptable use.

Commercial Activity

Although there is no law against using the Internet for commercial activity, there may be institutional prohibitions against such use. Of particular concern to academic and school libraries, it may also pertain to public libraries as well. Many—if not most—colleges and universities specifically prohibit the use of student and faculty Web pages to sell goods and services over the Internet or even to link to for-profit sites. A public library's policy on this may be affected by the terms of its contract with the Internet service provider (ISP); in some cases, favorable rates for service are dependent on the library not doing business over the Internet. Be sure and check the terms of the contract with your ISP when considering this aspect of your policy.

A related item to think about incorporating in an unacceptable-use policy is the purchase of goods and services over the Net while using library computers. The rationale for considering such a practice unacceptable is that the library may be liable for payment for items ordered online.

Attempts to Violate System Security and the Privacy of Users

After copyright violations, this is probably the most common topic in unacceptable-use statements. System administrators are justifiably concerned that giving the public access to Internet services in the library can make the library's own computer system vulnerable and also lower the library's defenses against those who would harm other systems. To limit this exposure, system administrators take technical steps—such as creating proxy servers and firewalls—to prevent malicious users from using public-access catalogs and other public files to get into operating systems and data files containing patron transaction information, student records, and other confidential materials. It is true that determined hackers armed with the right kind of technical expertise or, perhaps, an illicitly obtained password, can do considerable damage to a system, ranging from vandalizing files to illegally obtaining patron records and other internal information. In these cases, the library's unacceptable-use statement has no impact. It remains a wise strategy, however, to include these items in the policy so that all library users understand that the library takes seriously its responsibility to protect system resources both locally and elsewhere. It may even persuade some users not to take an action that would even appear to be an attempt to violate system security.

Many states have laws protecting the confidentiality of patron records, but even if they don't, library staff have a professional, and perhaps ethical, obligation to protect the privacy of library users. Libraries need to take the same precautions to protect the safety of patron records as the integrity of the system. Stating that this is unacceptable use will not prevent anyone determined to violate security, but it may provide an additional deterrent and will allow staff to move quickly to curtail the privileges of anyone found using library resources in this way.

SHOULD PATRONS HAVE TO SIGN AN ACCEPTABLE-USE STATEMENT?

Should your libray require that patrons sign a form acknowledging that they have read the acceptable-use statement and agree to its terms? Many libraries do. In effect, it turns the library policy into something like a memorandum of understanding between the library and the user, though the degree to which the document is binding is uncertain. But whatever the legal implications, library staff—especially those at the front desk who must confront angry patrons over the enforcement of rules—will find their job somewhat easier when they can show patrons that they have been presented with the rules and have agreed to abide by them.

Libraries have different ways of obtaining the signature. Many state this and other policies on the application form for a library card. Others present a separate form with the terms and the patron signs it. Staff keep it on file for future reference, although this means they have to check that the form has been completed before allowing a patron to use the Internet workstation. A third option—one that works especially well in libraries that require a sign up to use the Internet—is to obtain the signature on a form (which can be a card) that the patron fills out when requesting time on the workstation.

Whatever method you use, instruct your staff to actually point out to patrons that they are signing an acceptable-use agreement and should be familiar with its terms. This provides an added level of assurance that the patron has read and understands the policy.

WHAT ARE THE CONSEQUENCES OF UNACCEPTABLE USE?

Stating the consequences of unacceptable use in the policy can serve both as a deterrent and as a clear basis for staff actions. Different libraries will have different levels of consequence depending on their populations. School and academic libraries can withhold grades or even expel students who violate a policy or use system resources in connection with the commission of a crime. This penalty might be too harsh, however, if the violation is the conduct of commercial business over the Internet or the display of inappropriate materials. Public libraries have more limited consequences at their disposal—usually loss of computer privileges and, in some cases, library privileges, although they may decide that some offenses merit a zero-tolerance approach that suspends a patron's privileges without any warning. Other, lesser offenses may involve issuing one or two warnings prior to suspension, which should be stated in the policy along with the consequences. Regardless of the consequences, there should be a clearly stated effect of noncompliance in the policy that gives staff a guideline for immediate action. And, if the offense happens to also be a violation of federal or state law, you are required by law to report it to the authorities.

HOW HAVE LIBRARIES INCORPORATED UNACCEPTABLE USES INTO THEIR POLICY STATEMENTS?

The policies in Figures 5–1, 5–2, and 5–3 give examples of different approaches to describing prohibited use in the library policy. The one in Figure 5–1 includes nearly every one of the points discussed in this chapter and a couple of others besides—such as not disregarding time limits while others are waiting and prohibiting access to chat rooms. The Cincinnati and Hamilton County Library has combined all elements of acceptable and unacceptable use under a single heading that tells the public what uses are restricted. Patrons can conclude from this that all other uses are allowed. Also note that this policy carries a statement of the consequences of violations of the rules and a somewhat novel one at that—disconnection of the computer by library staff.

Note the combination of the statement of open access for all persons with the restrictions that users may not view or print sexually explicit materials nor access in the children's area sites unsuitable for minors. Although seemingly contradictory, it is actually saying that there are no restrictions on who may use the workstations but that there is a restriction on what they can access. This is a common practice in library Internet policies, but if the library has a policy that leaves decisions about what patrons may view up to library staff, give the staff guidelines about what constitutes "appropriate" material and what is considered "sexually explicit."

Figure 5–2 shows a good example of a school policy, though the concerns expressed in this policy are very similar to those of any type of library, since unacceptable use tends to encompass the same behavior across library types and sizes. It is clear that failure to comply with these terms will result in the temporary or permanent loss of system privileges. You will note that seven of the twelve restrictions cited relate to misrepresentation, privacy, and system security. Number five, however, adds an interesting—if somewhat difficult to define—violation: the wasteful use of finite resources. And number twelve refers to rules for the type of content that is allowed on Web pages maintained by students on the library's server (see Chapter 8 for more on Web guidelines).

The academic policy in Figure 5–3 is remarkable in its thoroughness at addressing unacceptable use, which is referred to as "specific rules." Elsewhere in the policy are contained the "General Standards for Acceptable

| Figure 5–1 | **PUBLIC LIBRARY UNACCEPTABLE-USE POLICY** |

INTERNET USE POLICY

In keeping with our mission to make accessible the broadest possible range of information in a variety of formats, the Public Library of Cincinnati and Hamilton County provides public access to the Internet.

The Library cannot control and is not responsible for the content or accuracy of information accessed over the Internet. Any restriction of a child's access to the Internet is the responsibility of the parent or legal guardian.

Users who fail to abide by the Internet Use Policy and Internet Use Rules will be instructed to choose another Internet site or terminate the Internet session. Failure to comply with these instructions will result in disconnection of the computer by library staff.

INTERNET USE RULES

Restrictions

Individuals are expected to use the Internet in a responsible manner. Restrictions include the following:

- Users may not view or print sexually explicit materials inappropriate for use in a public setting.

- Users may not attempt in any way to alter, damage, abuse, or sabotage computer equipment or software; alter configurations; or install any software.

- Users are liable for costs arising from malicious damage to Library equipment or software.

- Users may not use any Library terminal for illegal purposes.

- Users may not violate licensing agreements or Copyright Laws.

- Users may not use Library terminals for any activity that is deliberately offensive or creates an intimidating or hostile environment.

- Users may not disregard time limits on the use of a Library terminal while others are waiting.

- Users may not use Library terminals to access chat rooms.

- Users may not use Library terminals for recreational games when others are waiting.

- Users are not permitted to access sites which may be unsuitable for juveniles in the children's area of Library location.

Source: Public Library of Cincinnati and Hamilton County, Ohio (*plch.lib.oh.us/about/policy.html*).

Figure 5–2	SCHOOL UNACCEPTABLE-USE POLICY

INTERNET USE POLICY

USAGE GUIDELINES

The Internet account holder is held responsible for his/her actions and activity within his/her account. Unacceptable uses of the network will result in the suspension or revoking of these privileges. Some examples of such unacceptable use are:

1. Using the network for any illegal activity, including violation of copyright or other contracts;

2. Using the network for financial or commercial gain;

3. Degrading or disrupting equipment, software or system performance;

4. Vandalizing the data of another user;

5. Wastefully using finite resources;

6. Gaining unauthorized access to resources or entities;

7. Invading the privacy of individuals;

8. Using an account owned by another user;

9. Posting personal communications without the original author's consent;

10. Posting anonymous messages;

11. Downloading, storing or printing files or message that are profane, obscene, or that use language that offends or tends to degrade others;

12. Violating the Content Guidelines as outlined below.

Source: Community High School, Ann Arbor, Michigan (*communityhigh.org/about/CHS_policy.html*).

Figure 5–3 COLLEGE UNACCEPTABLE-USE POLICY

SPECIFIC RULES INTERPRETING THE POLICY ON
ACCEPTABLE USE OF ELECTRONIC RESOURCES

The following specific rules apply to all uses of University computing resources. These rules are not an exhaustive list of proscribed behaviors, but are intended to implement and illustrate the General Standards for the Acceptable Use of Computer Resources, other relevant University policies, and applicable laws and regulations. Additional specific rules may be promulgated for the acceptable use of individual computer systems or networks by individual Schools, departments, or system administrators.

CONTENT OF COMMUNICATIONS

- Except as provided by applicable City, State, or Federal laws, regulations or other University policies, the content of electronic communications is not by itself a basis for disciplinary action.
- Unlawful communications, including threats of violence, obscenity, child pornography, and harassing communications (as defined by law), are prohibited.
- The use of University computer resources for private business or commercial activities (except where such activities are otherwise permitted or authorized under applicable University policies), fundraising or advertising on behalf of non-University organizations, or the reselling of University computer resources to non-University individuals or organizations, and the unauthorized use of the University's name, are prohibited. The Vice Provost for Information Systems (or designee) may specify rules and specific forums where limited use of University resources for non-recurring exchange and sale of personal items is permitted.

IDENTIFICATION OF USERS

Anonymous and pseudonymous communications are permitted except when expressly prohibited by the operating guidelines or stated purposes of the electronic services to, from, or through which the communications are sent. However, when investigating alleged violations of the *Guidelines on Open Expression*, the Committee on Open Expression may direct the University's Information Security Officer, or an authorized system administrator, to attempt to identify the originator of anonymous/pseudonymous messages, and may refer such matters to appropriate disciplinary bodies to prevent further distribution of messages from the same source.

The following activities and behaviors are prohibited:

- Misrepresentation (including forgery) of the identity of the sender or source of an electronic communication;
- Acquiring or attempting to acquire passwords of others;
- Using or attempting to use the computer accounts of others;
- Alteration of the content of a message originating from another person or computer with intent to deceive; and
- The unauthorized deletion of another person's news group postings.

Figure 5–3	(Continued)

ACCESS TO COMPUTER RESOURCES

The following activities and behaviors are prohibited:

- The use of restricted-access University computer resources or electronic information without or beyond one's level of authorization;
- The interception or attempted interception of communications by parties not explicitly intended to receive them;
- Making University computing resources available to individuals not affiliated with the University of Pennsylvania without approval of an authorized University official;
- Making available any materials the possession or distribution of which is illegal;
- The unauthorized copying or use of licensed computer software;
- Unauthorized access, possession, or distribution, by electronic or any other means, of electronic information or data that is confidential under the University's policies regarding privacy or the confidentiality of student, administrative, personnel, archival, or other records, or as defined by the cognizant Data Steward;
- Intentionally compromising the privacy or security of electronic information; and
- Intentionally infringing upon the intellectual property rights of others in computer programs or electronic information (including plagiarism and unauthorized use or reproduction).

OPERATIONAL INTEGRITY

The following activities and behaviors are prohibited:

- Interference with or disruption of the computer or network accounts, services, or equipment of others, including, but not limited to, the propagation of computer "worms" and "viruses", the sending of electronic chain mail, and the inappropriate sending of "broadcast" messages to large numbers of individuals or hosts;
- Failure to comply with requests from appropriate University officials to discontinue activities that threaten the operation or integrity of computers, systems or networks, or otherwise violate this policy;
- Revealing passwords or otherwise permitting the use by others (by intent or negligence) of personal accounts for computer and network access;
- Altering or attempting to alter files or systems without authorization;
- Unauthorized scanning of networks for security vulnerabilities;
- Attempting to alter any University computing or networking components (including, but not limited to, bridges, routers, and hubs) without authorization or beyond one's level of authorization;
- Unauthorized wiring, including attempts to create unauthorized network connections, or any unauthorized extension or re-transmission of any computer or network services;
- Intentionally damaging or destroying the integrity of electronic information;
- Intentionally disrupting the use of electronic networks or information systems;
- Intentionally wasting human or electronic resources; and
- Negligence leading to the damage of University electronic information, computing/networking equipment and resources.

Source: University of Pennsylvania (*www.upenn.edu/computing/help/doc/passport/policies.html*).

Use," which state the guiding principles users are expected to follow in using the university's resources. Thus this policy has a very clear distinction between acceptable and unacceptable use. Most of the elements of unacceptable use that we have discussed in this chapter are reflected in this policy, with the exception of viewing inappropriate materials. Academic library policies tend not to be overly concerned with the exposure of patrons to materials they may find offensive or that may be considered harmful to children for two reasons: first, there are few children using academic libraries, and second, there is very little material that cannot be considered to have legitimate research value. Note however, that the Penn policy prohibits only speech that is a violation of state and federal laws, and that it stresses system security. Generally speaking, schools and academic libraries have a greater concern for system security when those institutions permit students and faculty to maintain their own Web pages on the school or university center server.

The University of Pennsylvania also has a statement of the consequences of noncompliance:

> *Enforcement and Penalties for Violation:* Any person who violates any provision of this policy, of the *Specific Rules* interpreting this policy, of other relevant University policies, or of applicable City, State, or Federal laws or regulations may face sanctions up to and including termination or expulsion. Depending on the nature and severity of the offense, violations can be subject to disciplinary action through the Student Disciplinary System or disciplinary procedures applicable to faculty and staff.
>
> It may at times be necessary for authorized systems administrators to suspend someone's access to University computing resources immediately for violations of this policy, pending interim resolution of the situation (for example by securing a possibly compromised account and/or making the owner of an account aware in person that an activity constitutes a violation). In the case of egregious and continuing violations suspension of access may be extended until final resolution by the appropriate disciplinary body.
>
> System owners, administrators or managers may be required to investigate violations of this policy and to ensure compliance.

Lest the policies of the University of Pennsylvania seem overly detailed and meticulous, keep in mind that they provide clear guidance to staff and administrators on how to enforce rules of Internet use and what the range of options is in the event that these rules are violated. The policy also provides a detailed list of all the applicable laws governing computer use, citing eleven sets of statutes including the federal copyright law, the federal and Pennsylvania child pornography laws, antidefamation laws, and the Pennsylvania computer crime law. (For further reference, the entire text of the University of Pennsylvania's policy on the acceptable use of electronic resources is reproduced in Appendix A of this book.)

The policies excerpted above represent comprehensive treatments of prohibited use. Although a thorough policy may be preferable when it comes to interpretation and enforcement, it is possible to reference unacceptable use more briefly by simply listing those elements that are prohibited without giving great detail or much explanation. As for violations of federal and state laws, many libraries find it sufficient simply to state that it is not acceptable to use library computing resources to violate state and federal laws.

6

Filtering Considerations

The question of whether to filter access to the Internet in libraries has created an intensely heated policy debate about library service. The debate has extended far beyond an internal discussion among library managers to become the subject of federal and state legislation, lawsuits and judicial review, and what seems to be limitless commentary and debate in the general press and library media. The motivating element in the discussion, of course, is the unease among community leaders, parents, and others about the proliferation of sexually explicit materials on the Internet. The presence of such content has caused some members of the community to suggest that the library should protect children from exposure to these materials, contending that they are inappropriate in the library setting. Many librarians, intellectual freedom advocates, and First Amendment experts, however, question whether the use of filtering software in the library is appropriate, effective, or even legal.

This chapter will not tell you whether to filter. This is a decision that should be made locally, but one that is too often made without adequate information and is motivated by emotional arguments. This chapter will provide you with information that you and others in your community should consider before making this decision: relevant documents that pertain to this issue, including state and federal law, related court decisions, policy documents of the American Library Association and other organizations; how the software works and what software products are available; the competing arguments on both sides of the issue; and the potential consequences of either position. You will read the case histories of a couple of libraries involved in setting this policy, and the consequences of their policies. The chapter closes with a review of alternatives to filtering.

Filtering is an issue larger and more complex than any other covered in this book. For this reason, you would do well to explore this issue. There are several documents cited in this chapter to point you to further reading on various aspects of the topic, but the most thorough treatment of filtering is *A Practical Guide to Internet Filters* by Karen Schneider (Neal-Schuman, 1997).

WHAT CONSIDERATIONS SHOULD INFORM THE FILTERING DECISION?

The first thing to acknowledge is that there *is* sexually explicit material on the Internet. To argue otherwise—as some have done in defense of open access—could lead funding authorities, library boards, and the public, to charge that the library manager has misled them into believing that the prevalence of sexually explicit materials on the Internet is overstated and that such materials are hard to find. While the percentage of all Internet sites that contain sexually explicit materials is very low (as low as one-half of one percent), that still means there are thousands of sites on the Internet that trade in sexually explicit materials. Some provide free access to images and text, but most sell subscriptions that require a membership fee. Many place disclaimers on the introductory screen warning of the adult nature of the materials; many do not allow users to see much without providing a user password; but most provide some free samples and many of these show nudity and persons engaged in sexual activities. More responsibly maintained sites show nothing until visitors have verified that they are at least 18 years old (of course, anyone can click that they are 18), but others present sexual materials when the site first loads. Still others maintain sites that are named to mislead visitors into thinking they are visiting an entirely different—and less sensitive—site. The most notorious of these is whitehouse.com, which draws visitors who might believe they are visiting the official White House site (which, by the way, is whitehouse.gov) and then "treats" them to several images that are not appropriate for children by any measure of community decency.

The well-known presence of these materials—intensified by reports in the news media about persons who prey on young people—has caused many parents, community leaders, and decision makers to pressure libraries into restricting access to these materials with filtering software. To many, this seems like a logical solution to the problem. Most libraries would not purchase sexually explicit magazines for the library shelves, so why not similarly limit what people can see on the Internet?

The American Library Association, civil libertarians, and First Amendment specialists counter that there are several problems with filtering software: first, libraries have an ethical responsibility to open avenues to information, not close them. Second, filtering software cannot distinguish between constitutionally protected speech and that which is not protected. Third, the software is not infallible, meaning that it will often filter materials that are in no way objectionable and sometimes leave some offensive sites unfiltered.

There are several relevant documents that you should become familiar with before you decide whether to filter.

Library Bill of Rights, Access to Electronic Information, Services, and Networks, and Statement on Library Use of Filtering Software

In 1948, the American Library Association adopted a policy statement titled the Library Bill of Rights that "affirms that all libraries are forums for information and ideas" and that basic principles should guide their services, including that "materials should not be excluded because of . . . their creation." Many libraries in the United States have adopted this policy as their own and thereby have committed their libraries to uphold this policy of unfettered access to information (the Library Bill of Rights and the other ALA documents cited here are reproduced in their entirety in Appendix B). In 1996, ALA adopted a report titled "Access to Electronic Information, Services, and Networks: An Interpretation of the Library Bill of Rights" (*www.ala.org/alaorg/oif/oif_q&a.html*). This document clarified and updated the Library Bill of Rights for the digital age and concludes that "users should not be restricted or denied access for expressing or receiving constitutionally protected speech," and that "the rights of users who are minors shall in no way be abridged." The American Library Association adopted a further clarification on the association's position on filtering in its "Statement on Library Use of Filtering Software" (*www.ala.org/alaorg/oif/filt_stm.html*). This document states that "The American Library Association affirms that the use of filtering software by libraries to block access to constitutionally protected speech violates the Library Bill of Rights." These documents are important to consider as you decide your policy on filtered versus open access, especially if your library has adopted the ALA's Library Bill of Rights.

Reno v. American Civil Liberties Union

In 1996, the U.S. Congress passed the Telecommunications Act that deregulated the telephone companies. An amendment to that legislation, the Communications Decency Act (CDA), made it a crime to transmit obscenity and child pornography via computer communications. The very day that President Clinton signed this bill into law, the American Civil Liberties Union and a host of coplaintiffs filed suit to stop implementation of the CDA. In June 1997, the Supreme Court ruled in *Reno v. American Civil Liberties Union*, unanimously upholding a lower-court decision that found that speech over the Internet should be accorded full protection under the First Amendment, and that "the interest in encouraging freedom of expression in a democratic society outweighs any theoretical but unproven benefit of censorship." The entire text of the Supreme Court Decision in *Reno v. American Civil Liberties Union* can be found on the Web (*www.aclu.org/court/renovacludec.html*) and proves very informative reading for anyone considering an Internet policy because it establishes judicial precedence regarding efforts of the government to limit free speech on the Internet. In other words, because *Reno v. American Civil Liberties Union* affirms First Amendment rights in cyberspace, the decision strengthens the hand of a patron who would sue a filtering library on the basis of an infringement of First Amendment rights. A judge has, in fact, ruled in such a case in Loudoun County, Virginia (see page 90 and Appendix D). Interestingly, another suit in Livermore, California, has been brought by the parent of a child who viewed sexually explicit materials in the library, alleging that the library was negligent by not having filtering software in place.

Filtering Facts: David Burt's Case for Filtering

One of the most tireless crusaders for filtering in libraries is David Burt, an employee of the Lake Oswego (Oregon) Public Library. In addition to operating an archive of Internet policies (that have been of great use in the production of this book), Burt also publishes an online digest of information called *Filtering Facts* (*www.filteringfacts.org*). The site provides an exhaustive case for filtering Internet access in libraries and is heavily weighted toward material that answers antifiltering discussions in the library media.

The Anti-Obscenity Statutes of Your State

Be sure as you consider filtering that you are very familiar with the anti-obscenity statutes that exist in your state. Most states have such statutes, and U.S. statutes apply as well—especially in the area of child pornography, where the courts have upheld the government's contention that it has a compelling interest in limiting free speech. Be sure to share copies of the anti-obscenity statute with members of your library board, the city council, the school board, the library staff, and anyone else who has an immediate interest in the library's policies. It is important that everyone understand what the statute says and how it pertains to the library's activities in the area of library Internet services. Be sure to consider what the statute specifically outlaws, the methods of communications that are affected, and whether the statute allows a defense to prosecution for governmental use or in the case of parental consent. You may find it helpful or necessary to consult an attorney who can advise you on the implications for these statutes in terms of library Internet services.

WHAT'S THE DIFFERENCE BETWEEN FILTERING AND MATERIALS SELECTION?

Remember the discussion in Chapter 2 about how important it is to make sure your Internet policy is consistent with your other policies? You might now be thinking, "We select materials for the library based on what is appropriate for our needs and our clientele, so why shouldn't we use filtering software to 'select' what is appropriate to our community and by age group? Isn't this simply making our Internet policy consistent with our collection development policy?"

This argument is often made in favor of filtering, and although it is true that both processes result in limiting the range of materials that the patron can access in the library, there are significant differences between selecting materials and using filtering software to limit access. Selection is a positive decision based on stated criteria of evaluation (the collection development policy) that is carried out by professional librarians who consider each title individually and make purchasing decisions that are informed by a knowledge of the collection, its strengths and weaknesses, and the needs of certain clients. By contrast, filtering usually (though not always) represents decisions, made by anonymous persons outside the library staff and the community, that have a coincidental or accidental relationship to the library's collection development policy. Furthermore, in the case of keyword filters, decisions are not based upon an evaluation of individual sites but on all sites containing a specific word. The analogy to print media would be to tell our book vendor that we do not want any book shipped to the library that contains a word from a preselected list, regardless of the overall content of the book. Installing filtering software is passive, selection is positive and action oriented. Selection is about deciding what goes into the library, filtering is the process of deciding what stays out of the library. Unlike the careful, thoughtful process of evaluation that is conducted in selecting materials, filtering software cannot compare, consider, or evaluate; all it can do is say yes or no to sites based on a set of criteria of which the library manager may or may not be aware. This is not to say that you should not filter, only that filtering and selection are not analogous.

WHAT ARE THE CHOICES?

Once you have acquainted yourself with the literature, the library's policymakers must decide: To filter or not to filter. There are three decisions your library can make regarding filtering access. They are not to filter, to filter all machines, or to filter some machines. Let's briefly discuss each option.

Choosing Not to Filter

Your library might choose this option for any of a variety of reasons, such as:

- You, your board, your city council, and at least a vocal contingent— if not a majority—of the community you serve believe that access to information should be unrestricted.
- Your library has adopted the ALA's Library Bill of Rights and the Freedom to Read Statement as a part of its overall library policy, and your policies promote open access to all materials by all ages.
- You are more concerned that you may be sued for a violation of First Amendment rights than that you may be prosecuted for criminal violations under state or federal obscenity statutes.
- You are concerned that filtering software might create a liability situation because parents believe that the presence of the filtering software is an implied contract to protect children using the Internet.
- You do not believe that the library should operate *in loco parentis.*

Many libraries have begun their Internet services with a policy of open access and have been able to maintain that position, but others have faced demands from outraged citizens and have had to introduce filtering software. The end of this chapter contains case studies of three libraries that initially decided not to filter and the aftermath of that policy. If you decide not to filter, become familiar with your state's anti-obscenity statutes so that you can be sure that you and your staff are operating within the range of allowable use. Also, it is recommended that you develop a set of policies, procedures, and practices that will minimize children's risk of inadvertent exposure to sexually explicit or otherwise inappropriate materials (see the end of this chapter and Chapter 7). These policies will be very helpful procedurally and demonstrate the library's commitment to protecting children.

It is imperative to seek concurrence on your decision not to filter from your mayor and council, school board, county commissioners, or other governing board. You must be sure they will back you up should your policy come under attack.

Deciding to Filter

You will probably choose this option if one or more of these situations apply to your library:

- You are required to install filtering software by the city, county, or other funding authority.
- Your policy does not address—or de-emphasizes—its role in providing unrestricted access to the Internet (for example, your library has not adopted the ALA Library Bill of Rights).
- You or your library board believes the library has a responsibility to protect children in the library that outweighs the right of citizens to access materials that may be constitutionally protected.
- You believe that the risk of criminal prosecution under anti-obscenity statutes is more significant than the risk of civil action on First Amendment grounds.

Before filtering, consult your city or county attorneys to ensure that they concur that you should filter and that they are comfortable with the level of risk of a challenge on First Amendment grounds.

Filtering Selected Workstations

This compromise position represents libraries' attempts to balance the needs of clients who want free access to information on the Internet with the concerns of parents and others that children be protected in the library. Most public libraries following this strategy filter access on computers located in the children's area but leave those in adult areas unrestricted. Of course, this does not mean that kids will not be able to use the machines in the adult areas nor that they will be protected from seeing sexual materials if walking by a computer. Again, be cautious of the level of safety the policy seems to promise to parents lest the library be held accountable should a child happen to view inappropriate materials on a nonfiltered, or even a filtered, workstation.

Sometimes funding authorities require this level of filtering before the Internet service is activated. Other times, libraries come to this configuration as a compromise in response to demands of the community to filter sexually explicit materials in the library. Whatever the cause, selective filtering represents to many library administrators the most intelligent compromise to this dilemma.

HOW DOES FILTERING SOFTWARE WORK?

Not all filtering software is the same. There are numerous brands on the market, and each works a bit differently. Some products are keyword blockers, some are site blockers, and others use a combination of the two. Keyword blockers restrict access to any Web pages that contain one of a set of predetermined keywords. Site blockers restrict access to certain URLs from a predetermined list and must be regularly updated with new releases.

Who decides which keywords and URLs are blocked? That depends on the software. Some software packages, like Net Nanny, allow users to view and edit the lists. Others, like Cyber Patrol, allow the user to turn on and off large categories of blocked sites easily, but require a higher level of technical expertise to unblock individual sites. How important is it to be able to fine tune the list of blocked words and sites? Very important, because the default lists are overly cautious and are almost certainly inconsistent with your town's community values. The preset lists for the products contain words—for example, "breast"—that cause many legitimate sites to be filtered. There will be many times when you will want to view and edit the lists of blocked sites and words, so complete and hassle-free access to these lists is an important point as you comparison shop.

Another consideration is whether the filtering software allows overrides to turn off the filtering software and at what level. You may want to override the software when you find that a site has been blocked that an adult patron wishes to visit, or for other situations in which you need full access on a machine that you would otherwise block. Most filtering software allow override with the use of a password, though some permit override at the network level as well as the individual computer level.

What features should you look for in purchasing filtering software? Karen Schneider recommends the following concise list of features in her May 1997 article in *American Libraries* (which, in turn, was adapted from materials posted to the PUBLIB listserv by Jerry Kuntz of the Ramapo Catskill Library System in New York):

1. Enabling or disabling blocking based on individual keywords and sites.
2. Access to the filter product's list of blocked Internet sites and keywords.
3. Ability to add and remove sites and keywords from the site list.
4. Ability to block based on developing rating schemes, such as PICS.
5. Ability to block according to "time, place, manner."
6. Variable access command.
7. Methods for alerting patrons these products are in use.

8. Feedback mechanisms for requesting that sites be added or dropped.
9. Ability to request or view site and keyword lists. (Schneider 1997)

The last three are software requirements that would be desirable from the patron's point of view.

Filtering software, however, is fallible, and if you have decided to filter access in your library, it is important to understand those limitations and act accordingly. First, the software is stupid. It cannot do more than what it is told to do by those who program and configure it. Most notably, this means that it cannot distinguish between speech that is illegal (e.g., child pornography) and all other speech that, when it takes place in a public forum, is protected by the Constitution (though one filtering product on the market, X-Stop, claims to filter only illegal speech, a claim many filter reviewers have found questionable). This also means that it cannot absolutely guarantee that no objectionable site will not get by. A keyword blocker, for example, will pass a site through that does not have any keywords that trigger a block even if the photographs are sexually graphic. Similarly, a site blocker will fail to block a site that has not yet been programmed into its list of blocked sites. And you always have to be on guard that having the software will lull some users into assuming that it will keep children from seeing sexually explicit materials on the Internet, creating a potential liability for the library.

Another potential problem with filtering software is that some brands may block according to criteria other than sexually explicit materials—whether you want them to or not. In some cases, the software may block according to whether a site contains hate speech, promotes intolerance, or other ideological issues. In a recent case, the American Family Association (AFA), a conservative religious organization, was placed on a list of sites blocked by Cyber Patrol because of the AFA's opposition to homosexuality. This site was blocked under the category of "intolerance," one of several categories of filter criteria used by Cyber Patrol: ironically, the AFA has been adamantly profiltering. Thus, librarians should note that the criteria for blocking sites is not always predictable nor is it always based on standards that might prevail in your community.

PICS (Platform for Internet Content Selection) represents a somewhat different approach to content-based access restrictions. Somewhat similar to the famous V-chip for television programs, PICS uses information embedded in the Web pages to rate the site based on various criteria, including appropriateness to different age groups. Software working with or in the browser evaluates the site based on the type of rating it has received and the browsing setting. Promoters of PICS believe that it represents a more sophisticated approach than site or keyword filtering, but at this time

FILTERING SOFTWARE PACKAGES

The following list was compiled by Christine Peterson, manager of consulting and continuing education, Library Development Division, Texas State Library.

Bess
N2H2
900 4th Avenue
Suite 3400
Seattle, WA 98164
(800) 971-2622 (206) 336-1501
(206) 336-1556 (fax)
bess@bess.net
http://www.bess.net/

Cyber Patrol
The Learning Company, Inc.
One Athenaeum Street
Cambridge, MA 02477
(617) 761-3000
cust_serv@learningco.com
http://www.cyberpatrol.com/

CyberSitter
Solid Oak Software, Inc.
P. O. Box 6826
Santa Barbara, CA 93160
(800) 388-2761 (805) 967-1614 (fax)
info@solidoak.com
http://www.solidoak.com/cysitter.htm

Cyber Snoop
Pearl Software, Inc.
64 East Uwchlan Avenue, Suite 230
Exton, PA 19341
(800) PEARL96 (800) 732-7596
sales@pearlsw.com
http://www.pearlsw.com/

Elron Internet Manager
Elron Software Inc., Network Management
     Division

(800) 767-6683
(617) 914-5001 (fax)
http://www.elronsw.com/
http://imdemo.elronsw.com/ (demonstration)

I-Guard
Unified Research Laboratories, Inc.
303 Butler Farm Road, Suite 106
Hampton, VA 23666-1568
(757) 865-0810 (757) 865-4528 (fax)
http://www.urlabs.com/public/products/
     product.html

The Library Channel
vImpact, Inc.
7870 Olentangy River Road
Columbus, OH 43235
(888) LIB-GUID (614) 224-7383
(614) 224-6861 (fax)
TLC@vimpact.net
http://www.vimpact.net/tlc/

Net Nanny
Net Nanny Software International Inc.
10900 NE 8th, Suite 900
Bellevue, WA 98004
(604) 662-8522 (604) 662-8525 (fax)
netnanny@netnanny.com
http://www.netnanny.com/

Net Shepherd
Net Shepherd Inc.
800 6th Avenue SW Suite 900
Calgary, Alberta T2P 3G3
(403) 205-6677 (403) 232-6552 (fax)
info@netshepherd.com
http://www.netshepherd.com/

FILTERING SOFTWARE PACKAGES—(CONTINUED)

SmartFilter
Secure Computing
One Almaden Boulevard, Suite 400
San Jose, CA 95113
(888) 683-3030
(651) 628-2718 (fax)
service@securecomputing.com
http://www.webster.com/

Surf Watch
SurfWatch Software, Inc.
175 South San Antonio Road, First Floor
Los Altos, CA 94022
(650) 948-9500 (650) 948-9577 (fax)
info@surfwatch.com
*http://www.spyglass.com/products/
    surfwatch/*

WebSENSE
Net Partners Internet Solutions, Inc.
9210 Sky Park Court
San Diego, Ca 92123

(800) 723-1166 (619) 495-1950
sales@netpartners.com
http://www.netpartners.com/

WizGuard
WizGuard Company
89 Del Sur Street
Vallejo, California 94591-8274
(800) 928-2688
(707) 554-6827 (707) 554-1369 (fax)
info@wizguard.com
http://www.wizguard.com/

X-STOP
Log-On Data Corporation
828 West Taft Avenue
Orange, CA 92865-4232
(888) STOP-XXX (714) 282-6111
(714) 282-6116 (fax)
info@ldc.com
http://www.xstop.com/

Last revision date: 15 September 1998

the system is not yet in wide enough use to allow a full evaluation. As yet unresolved questions include the criteria for rating sites and the consistency of rating between sites. At present, most PICS ratings are done by the authors of the Web pages, raising further questions about the reliability of the system.

If you are planning to purchase filtering software for your library, it is vital that you become an educated consumer by reading as much as you can about the various software packages. Although there is not room here to review the many product evaluations that have been conducted, there is a list of recommended titles at the end of this chapter. [Also, the sidebar on pages 84–85 lists the contact information—including Web sites—for 14 brands of blocking software.] Try to "test drive" the various software in conference exhibit halls, other libraries, and demo versions from the companies. Schneider organized TIFAP (The Internet Filter Assessment Project) to test Internet filters, using volunteers to pose 100 questions with nine filtering products. TIFAP formed conclusions about the use of Internet filters in a library environment in general, and evaluated individual products. TIFAP provides excellent guidelines for your own comparison shopping of the products and your selection of a filter. Be sure to read the results of TIFAP, conducted by Karen Schneider and reported in *A Practical Guide to Internet Filters*. (David Burt takes a somewhat detailed objection to those findings in *Filtering Facts*.)

WHAT ALTERNATIVES TO FILTERING DO LIBRARIES USE?

If your policy will be not to filter access, you will probably still want to minimize the risk that children will be exposed to potentially objectionable material in the library. You also may want to take measures to try to protect patrons and staff from being sexually harassed while in the library. These protections are important for two reasons: they allow the library staff to take a proactive role in guiding patrons to recommended resources (an action that is truly analogous to the materials selection process), and they provide a positive defense—in the event a controversial incident arises—that the library is concerned about the well-being of persons using the library, that the library is a good citizen, and that the library has not ignored the risks associated with the Internet.

Arrangement of Workstations

As an alternative to filtering, many libraries have arranged workstations so that the monitors are visible to the staff at various work areas in the library (such as the reference station, the circulation desk, and the librarian's desk in the children's area—see Chapter 3). The theory is that if the library staff can see what people are viewing, there will be more library control over what is accessed to help head off incidents. Assertive library staff can instruct offending patrons that what they are viewing is objectionable to other patrons, and they can steer children onto more useful and appropriate sites. Using this approach might make some members of the library board, city council, and school and college administrators more comfortable about the decision not to use filtering, but it raises another set of problems.

This approach places a level of discretion on the library staff that is at best uncomfortable and at worst burdensome and unfair to both staff and patron. It will almost invariably lead to content-based restrictions on constitutionally protected speech. Are the staff comfortable in approaching a patron who is, in fact, so brazen that he or she will view such materials in the library? And what guidelines will staff use in intervening? Will they do so only if there is a complaint from another patron? Only if there are children present? Will the policy state very clearly and unequivocally what material is inappropriate, or will staff make that call based on individual preference and tolerance?

Keep in mind that one of the reasons libraries do not like to use filtering software is because the software cannot distinguish constitutionally protected speech from that which is not. Can you or your staff tell the difference? True, you know when you are viewing something that you think is inappropriate, but can you be certain that it is not constitutionally protected speech? And even if you can, can your staff? This is a crucial issue because, when you approach patrons who are viewing sites that contain nudity or sexual material and ask them to stop because their actions are disruptive, you may have unwittingly exercised government interference in the right of a citizen to freely access those materials.

Privacy Screens and Recessed Monitors

Many libraries have experimented with the use of privacy screens, devices that fit over the computer monitor and allow only the person seated at the computer to view what is on the screen. Privacy screens do ensure that those passing by the computer cannot see what is on the screen, but they can be hard to see through, and make it difficult for staff to assist patrons, since the staff member's view of the screen is obscured.

Another solution is to place the monitor below the level of the desk. Special desks are sold by library supply companies and furniture companies that recess the monitor into the desk, with glass covering the desktop over the monitor. Only patrons sitting at the computer and those standing directly behind them—such as an assisting staff member—can see the screen. Both privacy screens and recessed monitors are discussed more fully in Chapter 3.

Guided-Use Policies

Many libraries—those that filter as well as those that do not—have found guided-use policies and procedures very helpful. Guided use includes a variety of activities ranging from one-on-one instruction, to group instruction in formal and informal settings, to the use of literature, guides, and preselected sites on library Web pages. All of these practices are detailed in Chapter 7, but it is appropriate to briefly discuss here the use of literature, guides, and preselected sites alternatives to filtering.

There are essentially two types of printed materials that can be helpful in safeguarding children accessing the Internet in the library. The first type is guides that inform parents about the Internet, specifically stating that it is an unrestricted medium in which there are many sites containing material inappropriate for children for various reasons. One such guide is a document entitled *Child Safety on the Information Highway* (*www.4j.lane.edu/safety*), published by the National Center for Missing and Exploited Children (NCMEC), which contains guidelines for parents in supervising their children's use of the Internet. A number of libraries, such as the Las Vegas Public Library, have placed this publication in its entirety in their Internet policies. Others have set up links to such guides from their Web pages. Another good guide is the "Safety Net for the Internet" page on the New York Public Library site (*www.nypl.org/branch/safety.html*). This excellent resource leads to a variety of guides for parents about the risks of the Internet, how to minimize the dangers, and links to other helpful sites.

The second type of print material is guides to Internet sites for kids. The most famous of these is the "700+ Great Sites for Kids (*www.ala.org/parentspage/greatsites/*)" compiled by the Children and Technology Committee of the Association for Library Service to Children (ALSC), a division of the American Library Association. The ALA also has available other resources that parents, teachers, and librarians can use to steer children and teenagers toward materials that are appropriate and rewarding to their age groups (*www.ala.org*). Many libraries have linked these sources to home pages designed specifically for kids and used them as the default screen display in youth services areas of the library. Other libraries set up these and other guide materials in print formats nearby the Internet workstations.

Figure 6–1   SAMPLE POLICY ON CHILDREN'S USE OF THE INTERNET

CHILDREN'S USE OF THE INTERNET

Parents, guardians, and caregivers are responsible for their children's use of all library materials, including the Internet. Library staff cannot monitor the Internet resources that children may select. Any restriction of the child's access to the Internet remains the sole responsibility of the parent, guardian, or caregiver. Parents and children should read *Child Safety on the Information Highway*, produced jointly by the National Center for Missing and Exploited Children and the Interactive Services Association.

Library staff will be glad to assist you and your child in finding information on the Internet.

POINTERS FOR PARENTS

- Visit the Library often with your child
- Spend time online visiting Internet sites with your child
- Keep yourself informed of current trends related to the Internet
- Encourage your child to ask Library staff for help in finding information on the Internet

(*www.lvccld.lib.nv.us/policy.shtml*)

Source: Las Vegas-Clark County Library District

Parental Permission

One of the most common alternatives to filtering in libraries is requiring express prior written consent from parents before anyone under 18 is allowed to use an Internet workstation. To keep track of who has permission, libraries either keep the paperwork on file and check it each time the minor wants to use the Internet, or they mark the person's library card to indicate a parent or guardian has given permission. Either way, it is a good idea to require children to sign in when using the Internet. However, this method is in opposition to the American Library Association's position on free access regardless of age, which is of consequence only if the library has adopted as its own policy the ALA's Library Bill of Rights and the Freedom to Read Statement.

FOCUS: LOUDOUN COUNTY

In a decision that will have profound implications for public library Internet filtering policies, Judge Leonie M. Brinkema of the U.S. District Court for the Eastern District of Virginia ruled on November 23, 1998 in the case of *Mainstream Loudoun et al. v. Board of Trustees of the Loudoun County Library*. Judge Brinkema found that the library's use of filtering software "offends the guarantee of free speech," and blocked local government officials in Loudoun County, Virginia, from restricting online access.

The case is highly significant because it is the first time any court has ruled on the issue of First Amendment rights as they pertain to Internet usage in public libraries. The judge found that mandatory blocking constitutes "prior restraint," a form of censorship that is rarely upheld by the court; that libraries must consider the First Amendment when making content-based decisions; and that any library procedure that limits adult access under the guise of protecting minors is unconstitutional. Judge Brinkema noted that other libraries in Virginia have used less restrictive means—such as privacy screens and the use of optional filtering on machines used by children—to restrict the display to minors of sexually-explicit materials on the Internet.

The entire text of Judge Brinkema's decision in this case is included in Appendix D of this book.

Figure 6–2   SAMPLE POLICY FOR ACCESS TO ELECTRONIC INFORMATION

ACCESS TO ELECTRONIC INFORMATION

The WCFL Board of Trustees created this policy with the goal of helping the public make the best use of this new world of electronic information, not with the goal of restricting access. The trustees and staff of the Wicomico County Free Library are committed to offering access to the Internet, in text and graphical format, and as funding allows, computers will be installed to provide the access. These computers are available for use by customers of all ages. During the discussion of this policy, the library trustees reaffirmed the basic principle of public library service: library trustees and staff do not have the right to decide what library resources are selected or accessed by you or by your children. Only you have the right to define what material or information you feel is consistent with your personal and family values and boundaries. Only you can apply these values for yourself and your children as you use your library.

Given the unique nature of the Internet, however, the trustees and staff feel it is the library's responsibility to provide the following services which should enhance the entire community's access to this electronic information resource:

- There are terminals in the library which provide text access only to the Internet and computers which provide graphical access.

- The library staff created and maintains a home page on the WWW (World Wide Web), http://*www.co.wicomico.md.us/library.html*, which includes a variety of destinations (links) and search tools selected by the staff. These links have been selected by library staff as a service to help you navigate the WWW. The staff will periodically monitor these selections. Please be aware, however, that these sites can change rapidly and unpredictably without the staff's knowledge.

- Filtering software was purchased and installed on three WELL (Wicomico's Electronic Learning Library) computers in the children's area. The filtering software package was chosen based on reviews in the September 1996 issue of *Internet World*. The library will not edit the blocks provided by the software package.

- Privacy screens were purchased and installed on the computers which provide graphical access to the Internet.

- Copies of a brochure entitled *Child Safety on the Information Highway* were purchased and are being distributed, free of charge.

- The library staff have selected and purchased several excellent books which provide instruction and assistance to the Internet user.

- The library staff will provide individual instruction as well as periodic workshops and programs on effective use of the Internet.

Source: Wicomico (MD) County Free Library (*www.co.wicomico.md.us/library/access.html*).

What School Libraries Are Doing about Filtering

School Library Journal reported in its April 1997 issue that 77 percent of libraries responding to an *SLJ* survey reported that they did not use blocking software. Nineteen percent reported that they did use blocking software, and the remaining four percent did not respond. This statistic may seem surprising since school librarians might be the most likely type of librarian to use blocking software since they operate more clearly *in loco parentis*.

In deciding this issue for your library, investigate what policies already exist at the district or campus level and decide if they do in fact adequately address these questions of open access. It's also a good idea to explore with your principal and superintendent the level of support you can expect in implementing policies that govern library Internet use.

HOW CAN POLICY STATEMENTS REFLECT FILTERING CHOICES?

The policy in Figure 6–1 is typical of those for nonfiltering libraries. It affirms the library's intention to offer open access, affirms that parents should supervise their children's use of the Internet, and references the *Child Safety* document.

The Berkeley (CA) Public Library's "Internet Use Policy" (*www.ci.berkeley.ca.us/bpl/files/usepolicy/html*, see also Chapter 1) is even more succinct. It is representative of library policies that are very short and that essentially disclaim regarding the library's role in monitoring Internet usage. Its second—and final—paragraph affirms that the library will not restrict children's access:

> The Berkeley Public Library does not monitor and has no control over the information accessed through the Internet and cannot be held responsible for its content. As with other library materials, restriction of a child's access to the Internet is the responsibility of the parent/legal guardian.

In contrast to the brevity of the Berkeley Public Library policy, the Wicomico (MD) County Free Library takes what could best be described as a belt-and-suspenders approach to ensuring the safety of children. They declare that not only do they install filters, but also that they use privacy screens and guide use through all three methods we have mentioned above: literature and child safety guides, staff guidance, and preset links to age-appropriate materials. The Wicomico policy is unusual in several regards,

---

Figure 6–3   SAMPLE POLICY ON FILTERING CHILDREN'S WORKSTATIONS: I

INTERNET ACCESS AT THE BOSTON PUBLIC LIBRARY

The Internet is a global electronic network. Resources available on the Internet supplement and complement the collections of the Boston Public Library. All Internet resources accessible through the Library are provided equally to all library users. The Boston Public Library does not monitor and has no control over the information accessed through the Internet, and cannot be held responsible for its content. The Internet and its available resources may contain material of a controversial nature. The Boston Public Library neither censors access to materials nor protects users from information they may find offensive. Library users access the Internet at their own discretion and are responsible for any access points they reach.

The Boston Public Library provides computers with filtering software to limit children's exposure to some websites. The software blocks some specific sites that could be offensive to some users. Filtering software may not block all material users might find offensive. Parents may wish to supervise their children's Internet sessions. Parents may give their children approval to use unfiltered computers.

Source: Boston (MA) Public Library (*www.bpl.org/WWW/Internet_pol.html*).

the most pronounced being that it conveys not just the policy itself but also the process by which the policy was developed. Interestingly, this library declares that staff will not edit the factory settings for blocking software (Figure 6–2).

The decision in Boston to filter public-library access (see Figure 6–3) reverberated throughout the library literature and sparked an intense debate about the problems and merits of filtering. Some commentators might discern some irony in the policy containing the standard disclaimer about the Internet containing potentially offensive materials and declaring that the library "neither censors access to materials nor protects users from information they may find offensive," then goes on to state that the library will offer filtered access (though apparently not at all workstations). Wisely, the policy cautions that in spite of the filters, there remains a risk of exposure to offensive materials and that parental supervision is suggested.

A similar—though more strongly worded—approach is used by the Houston Public Library (see Figure 6–4). This policy filters access only on specifically designated "Children's Workstations," provides a caution that filtering is not an absolute safeguard to safety, strongly recommends parental supervision, and suggests the same online safety guides we've seen in other policies. Although this policy of filtering selected workstations may not conform to the American Library Association's policy of unrestricted access for all patrons regardless of age, it represents a middle-ground strategy that many libraries have found sensible and defensible, and that provides protected use for children on some machines while not reducing all access in the library to levels suitable for young children.

The next section contains several brief, real-world situations that demonstrate how library directors are coping with the decision of whether to filter, and with the pressure to filter from various groups including citizens, city councils, and even staff.

Figure 6–4   SAMPLE POLICY ON FILTERING CHILDREN'S WORKSTATIONS: II

SUPERVISING CHILDREN'S USE

It is the library's policy that parents or legal guardians must assume responsibility for deciding what library resources are appropriate for their children. There will be some resources which parents may feel are inappropriate for their children. Parents should let their children know if there are materials which they do not want them to use. Parents should supervise their child's Internet sessions. Some library computers are designated as Children's Workstations. These workstations use filtering software to access the Internet. No filtering software can control access to all materials that an individual may deem inappropriate. Parents should instruct children in the Rules for Online Safety recommended by the National Center for Missing and Exploited Children. These rules are repeated for children who access the Library's Kids' Page.

Source: Houston (TX) Public Library Internet (*sparc.hpl.lib.tx.us/hpl/policy.html*).

HOW DOES FILTERING POLICY WORK IN THE REAL WORLD?

Chapter 1 discussed how policy is not an event, but a constantly evolving process in which participants continually evaluate where they are, deciding if that is where they should be. The following five examples describe the situation in several libraries during the period 1996–1998. The names of the libraries are not given, but similarities to libraries you know may not be purely coincidental.

Case 1: Filtering from the Outset

This county system in an urban area serves about 2 million persons. Technologically proficient and progressive, this library was an early adopter of the Internet, and the director persuaded the county officials to fund Internet access. In planning meetings, the county administrator communicated to the library director that he favored filtered access. The director discussed the matter with the library managers, none of whom held strong convictions that access should be unfiltered; all had heard horror stories from other libraries that had suffered protracted and damaging political battles with their funding authorities and their communities over this issue. The library administration concluded that the best alternative was to filter access at all workstations from the outset.

Case 2: The Filtering Controversy

This municipal library serves a population of about half a million persons in a city generally thought of as more liberal than most. The library inaugurated Internet access with unfiltered machines. Library policies proclaimed the public's right to know, and the staff provided parental guides to child safety on the information highway and preset Web page sites with age-appropriate materials. Everything went along pretty well—for a while. Then, two incidents caused library administrators to re-evaluate their policy. In the first one, library staff intercepted a patron printing materials that were clearly child pornography from the Internet. In the second case, a branch employee witnessed an adult patron instructing a group of children on how to access sexually explicit materials on the Internet. Library staff expressed their feelings that they were sexually harassed by such activities. Other staff grew concerned that they could be liable to prosecution under the state's obscenity statute. City officials directed the library to install filtering software on all machines, but after it was installed, members of the community began to complain that they could not access sites, and civil liberties groups pressured the library to remove the filters. After negotiations with the groups involved, library staff agreed to unblock all but the most offensive sites and to consider unblocking any site upon patron request. Staff spent many hours fine-tuning the software and unblocking sites, but the civil liberties groups continue to talk of a possible lawsuit against the library for interference with First Amendment rights. The library board has recently recommended to the city council that a few workstations offer unfiltered access.

Case 3: A Library Board Divided

This small, rural community's library received a state grant to install two Internet workstations. Almost immediately, a member of the library board raised questions about the availability of sexually explicit materials on the Internet. With the help of regional, state, and national library groups, the director built a case for open access and was supported by a majority of the library board, including the board chair. The profiltering board members took the issue to the city council, which recommended a compromise: filter one machine, leave the other unfiltered, and schedule a public hearing on the matter. Several dozen residents packed the hearing to voice their concern over the danger of harmful materials on the Internet. After much debate, the city council voted by a one-vote margin to continue the Internet in the library and to have one machine filtered and one not.

Case 4: Going to the Legislature

In a large, county system with established Internet access, members of a national profamily group with ties to the Christian Coalition demanded that the library filter Internet access to protect children in the county from exposure to sexually explicit materials. The response of the library staff and board advocated the American Library Association's position that open access should be guaranteed for all users regardless of age. The profiltering group waged an all-out campaign against the library in general and the director in particular, calling him a pornographer and asking voters to vote no in an approaching referendum on raising the library's tax levy. More significantly, the group, unsatisfied with the response they received from the library board, took their fight to the statehouse, where they found a legislator to introduce a bill to mandate filtering in all libraries. Heavy lobbying by the state's librarians defeated the bill. Eventually, a compromise was reached that requires every library in the state to have an acceptable-use policy.

Case 5: Unfiltered Access

The director of a rural community library serving a town of 13,000 in a conservative area drafted a policy that called for open access to the Internet in the library. She took the policy to the city administrator, who approved the policy with the requirement that she strengthen the section protecting the privacy of users. The policy went into effect, but concerns about Internet content prompted library staff to begin requiring parental approval for children to use the Internet. Staff announced the arrival of the Internet in the library and made the library's policy public. The director braced herself for controversy and demands to install filtering software. None came. The public flocked to use the Internet, and to date no incident involving a child accidentally viewing sexually explicit materials has arisen.

The library did experience two incidents, however, that caused the library director to be concerned about the policy. The first was that in checking the history files, she found that a child pornography site had been accessed. She responded by deleting the history file and installing privacy screens on the computers. The second incident involved a patron who viewed sexually explicit materials in the presence of the library director. The director grew uneasy about the patron's behavior and requested that city police conduct occasional walkthroughs of the library in uniform. No words were ever spoken to the patron by police or staff, and the police never even walked close to the patron, but eventually the patron stopped coming to the library.

REFERENCES

American Civil Liberties Union. "Censorship in a Box: Why Blocking Software Is Wrong for Public Libraries." *www.aclu.org/issues/cyber/box.html.*

"Blocking Software Not Yet Widespread." *School Library Journal* 43 (April 1997): 16.

Burt, David. "In Defense of Filtering." *American Libraries* 28 (August 1997): 46–48.

Champelli, Lisa. "Respond to Inaccurate Perceptions of Porn on the Net." *The Internet Advocate. www.monroe.lib.in.us/~lchampel/natadv1.html.*

Child Safety on the Information Highway. *www.4j.lane.edu/safety/*

Johnson, Doug. "Internet Filters: Censorship By Any Other Name?" *Emergency Librarian* 25 (May–June 1998).

Langland, Laurie. "Public Libraries, Intellectual Freedom, and the Internet: To Filter or Not to Filter." *PNLA Quarterly* 4 (Summer 1998): 14–18.

Minow, Mary. "Filters and the Public Library: A Legal and Policy Analysis." *First Monday* 2 (12). Also available at: *www.firstmonday.dk/issues/issue2_12/minow/.*

Schneider, Karen G. *A Practical Guide to Internet Filters*. New York: Neal-Schuman, 1998.

———. "Figuring Out Filters: A Quick Guide to Help Demystify Them." *School Library Journal* 44 (February 1998): 36–38.

———. "Selecting Internet Filtering Software: Buyer Beware." *American Libraries* (May 1997): 84.

7

Guided Use and
Library Policy

These days, libraries are using a variety of techniques to steer children, young adults, and even adults to sites with content that is consistent with the library's mission, roles, and other policies. Such techniques include developing library Web pages that contain helpful links, offering one-on-one instruction and assistance, and supplying print materials that guide patrons to helpful sites and that counsel parents about how to supervise their children's Internet experience.

These alternatives to filtering comprise only one part of the impetus for libraries to provide guided use and why they reference guided use in their policies. This chapter explores guided use, starting with three seminal questions:

- Why offer such assistance?
- What level of assistance is right for your library?
- Should your policy be specific about what level of guided use you will offer?

Next are other options for guided use and the implications of each:

- printed guides
- library Web pages
- staff intermediaries
- one-on-one assistance
- informal group instruction
- formal group instruction

SHOULD POLICY IMPACT GUIDED USE?

Why Offer Guidance?

To some, this may sound like a leading question. The library exists as a service entity and is geared to servicing the public. To put a new service in the library and not support it with training would represent a poor service ethic indeed. It is a given that, to the extent possible, most libraries will want to help their patrons use this or any other service of the library; and that librarians, having a strong service orientation, will naturally tend to want to proffer as much guidance to patrons as resources will allow. But this is more than a rhetorical question. Different libraries have different types of user populations, some of whom absolutely must have training and assistance, others who can do just fine without it. You must pose the question of why offer assistance to clarify the following issues:

- your motivation for offering training
- the level of expertise of the public you serve
- the degree of priority you will assign to helping patrons use the Internet
- how to ensure that staff provide consistent information about the Internet

There are many reasons to assist: as an alternative to filtering, to stimulate use of the resource, to help patrons get the most out of the service, to give a value-added service to the community that they could not get from home access—to name only a few. How you answer this question determines how you answer the next.

What Level of Guidance Is Appropriate?

Most of this chapter explores the levels of assistance you can offer your patrons. But only you can determine which is right for your library. Your answer will depend on your particular factors:

- patron level of expertise and overall need for assistance
- number of staff available to help patrons
- level of staff expertise
- number of workstations
- type of library
- library's policy on filtering

Because they are staff intensive, training and assistance are costly, but they are potentially some of the most valuable services the library can offer and will distinguish library Internet service from that offered elsewhere and through ISPs (Internet Service Providers). But for training and guidance to be effective, they must be suitable to the library's service population. Would the same type and level of training offered in an academic library be equally appropriate to a rural public library? Would a library Web page alone be adequate training for a group of fourth graders who have had little or no experience with the Internet? Would a guide to Internet sources in a public library be effective in a school library? Is it necessary to require every patron of a public library to attend formal classes in Internet regardless of their individual proficiency? The answers to these questions suggest that one-size-fits-all solutions to training will not work. Even within your library, you may well decide that all levels do not have the same needs.

Should Your Policy Be Specific about What Level of Guided Use You Will Offer?

To think about this question is to contemplate how your staff will interact with the public about the Internet. It also focuses your thinking on whether your policy is the right place to reference what you will do about guided use. An Internet policy varies from library to library, some consisting only of a broad overview statement of philosophy of access, others describing only acceptable and unacceptable use. Others give users a full description of how the library will use the Internet to serve its clientele, including information that is closer to staff procedure than policy. And many libraries use the policy to establish a disclaimer for what the library will not do and what it cannot be held accountable for. The extent to which you describe your practices pertaining to guided use in your Internet policy will depend on which approach best describes your policy document. If your policy is similar to the Berkeley policy (*www.ci.berkeley.ca.us/bpl/files/usepolicy/html*)—the short-and-sweet type of access statement—then it will probably not be appropriate to detail your intentions regarding training in the policy. If, however, your policy tends toward detail, you may want to use the policy as the vehicle that tells the public what level of training and assistance they can expect.

The disclaimer aspect becomes important as you explore the issue of the limits on your staff and your service. Because your library has limited resources and because staff are already stretched thin, you may not be able to offer the training and assistance that the public will sometimes demand. If your community is the kind that expects a high level of interaction, or if your staff is nervous that training people to use this new service will cause them to have to abandon their other duties, then you might need to use your policy to be very explicit about how much training you will do. This means essentially using your policy as a disclaimer about the limits of training that you have the resources to offer. Such a disclaimer is a common element of Internet policies.

WHAT KINDS OF GUIDANCE DO LIBRARIES OFFER?

Printed Guides

This is the most basic and least staff-intensive form of guided use. Printed guides cover any literature that informs the public about how to access the Internet and sites that they can visit. These can include the following types of materials:

- *Parental guides* for parents and/or teachers who supervise children's use of the Internet. *Child Safety on the Information Highway* (*www. 4j.lane.edu/safety*) is one example of this type of material, as is *The Librarian's Guide to Cyberspace for Parents and Kids*, published by the American Library Association. Up to fifty copies of the brochure can be ordered from ALA for free and the ALA will also provide the camera-ready artwork at no charge. The Baltimore County Public Library Web site offers a page called "Parent's Corner" that leads to similar sites and links to resource pages for parents (*www.bcpl.lib.md.us/kidspage/parents.html*).
- *Lists of child-appropriate sites on the Internet* include book-length guides such as *The Internet Kids Yellow Pages* by Jean Armor Polly (Osborne/McGraw Hill, 1996) and the *Librarians Guide to Cyberspace* from the ALA, which contains a list of "50+ Great Sites on the Internet."
- *Resource guides*, intended for students and adults seeking information on specific topics on the Internet.
- *Instructional guides* to help patrons of all ages figure out how to use the Internet effectively, including search tips and instructions on how to use software such as browsers, e-mail programs, and ftp.

Library Web Pages

Any information that you can print can also be put online on a Web page for patrons to access either in the library or from their home or office. The

New York Public Library operates "A Safety Net for the Internet" (*www.nypl.org/branch/safety.html*), an excellent example of a library Web page that contains tips for parents on supervising their children's use of the Internet (see Figure 7–1). In addition, many of the guides to safe use of the Internet mentioned above can be found online and linked from your library's home page. If you wish to guide your younger users to child-appropriate sites, you can link to the ALA's "700+ Great Sites for Kids" (*www.ala.org/parentspage/greatsites/amazing.html*), which has guides to a variety of subjects. An example of a small community library that has built a home page to guide users to a huge range of information resources on the Internet is the Unger Memorial Library in Plainview, Texas (*www.texasonline.net/schools/unger/*). The San Diego Public Library's Web site contains a page with a similar list of preselected Internet sites (*www.sannet.gov/public-library/searching-the-net/subject.html*), as well as a page with links to numerous search engines on the Internet and guidance on what each does and how to use them (see Figure 7–2).

Web pages such as these make use of the medium of the Internet not only to provide an enhancement to Internet access but also to tailor information resources to those items in which the community tends to be most interested. They also take some of the pressure off staff to be the default line of contact for patrons wanting help finding information on the Internet. When Web pages are child specific, they also help the library be a partner in guiding children to the right resources without necessarily having to filter access.

Staff Intermediaries

Staff can instruct patrons in a number of ways. Most of the other examples of guided use in this chapter assume that the library allows patrons direct access to the Internet, but in some libraries, staff conduct Internet searches for patrons. This procedure was once the norm, and perhaps is necessary in those libraries with only one Internet workstation. But it is also much more staff intensive than direct access and most libraries are likely to convert to direct access unless a conscious decision is made to preserve mediated access, in which case the library's Internet policy will certainly want to address why.

One-on-one Assistance

Of the types of guidance offered by staff to patrons using the Internet, one-on-one assistance is undoubtedly the most common in the course of a normal day. In fact, it is probably true in most libraries that, whatever training

Figure 7–1	SAMPLE SAFETY GUIDE FOR PARENTS

A SAFETY NET FOR THE INTERNET

A PARENT'S GUIDE

Who's Afraid Of The Internet?...What Parents Should Know
How To Minimize The Risks
Guidelines For Parents
Further Information and Other Sites To Visit

WHO'S AFRAID OF THE INTERNET?

What Parents Should Know

"Surfing," the "net," "gopher," and the "Web" have nothing to do with water, small animals, or spiders. It is the new language of cyberspace. Your children are learning about it in school or from their friends, while references to the Information Highway and the Internet on television may be leaving you feeling lost in space.

A few tips will ease your fears and allow you and your child to take advantage of this new technology.

The Internet is a global network of information networks accessible with a computer. Entertainment, education, and information are all at your fingertips. You can visit the world's great libraries, take a college course, play a game, check weather forecasts and sports scores. Virtually anything you want to know can be found somewhere on the Internet.

This exciting sensation is world-wide and is not regulated by anyone, which opens the door to some risks. Not all information that appears may be accurate. Also, just as people in person can be rude, obnoxious, and exploitative, the anonymity of the computer allows them to be even more so, if they choose.

Does this mean you shouldn't let your child use the Internet? Of course not, it simply means that you should be on the alert and aware of some of the risks.

How To Minimize The Risks

The best way to assure that your children are having a positive online experience is to stay in touch with what they are doing.

- First, have your child show you how to access the Internet.
- Spend time with them when they are online.
- Explore the wide range of information that is available and discuss with them which topics you consider off-limits.
- Keep the lines of communication open so that you can talk to your children, and they will recognize your interest in what they are doing is genuine.
- Monitor the amount of time your child spends with the computer. Excessive use of online

---

Figure 7–1   **(Continued)**

---

services, especially late at night, may signal a potential problem. The same parenting skills that apply to the "real world" also apply while online.

- Set your rules for the use of the Internet

Guidelines For Parents

Parents who are concerned about their children's use of electronic resources should provide guidance to their own children. It is important that you as a parent assume responsibility for your child's online computer use, at home, at school, or in the library. Part of your family rules may be:

- Never give out identifying information such as home address, school name, or telephone number.
- Decide whether you want personal information such as age, marital status, or financial information revealed.
- Never allow your child to arrange a face-to-face meeting with someone via the computer without your approval.
- Never respond to messages that are suggestive, obscene, threatening, or make you or your child uncomfortable.
- If you or your child become aware of the transmission of child pornography, report it to the National Center for Missing and Exploited Children at 1-800-843-5678.
- Remember that people online may not be who they say they are.
- Remember everything you read may not be true.
- Remember that personal computers and online services should not be used as electronic babysitters.

Make computer use a family activity. Get to know your child's online friends as well as their other friends.

VISIT

The New York Public Library Home Page
http://www.nypl.org

Featuring these two special web sites for children and teens:

Teen Link
http://www.nypl.org/branch/teen/teenlink.html

Explore hotlines, booklists, links to college and financial aid information, sports, homework help on teen home pages.

On - Lion: For Kids
http://www.nypl.org/branch/kids/onlion.html

Provides answers to questions about homework, holidays, history, people and places. Plus, great books for children of all ages to read and enjoy.

Figure 7–1   **(Continued)**

For further information see:
NYPL's Policy on Public Use of the Internet
http://www.nypl.org/admin/pro/pubuse.html

Talking to your child, setting rules together, keeping aware of computer services offered, will make using the Internet exciting for you and your child. The opportunities to expand one's horizons are great. These are challenging times in which we live. Make the most of them by sharing the online experience with your child.

The branches of The New York Public Library offer a variety of resources both print and electronic, for all ages. Ask your librarian to help you to find more information on parenting skills, family activities, and the Internet.

Source: New York Public Library (*www.nypl.org/branch/safety.html*).

Figure 7–2	SAMPLE WEB PAGE LINKS

SAN DIEGO PUBLIC LIBRARY SEARCHING THE NET

INFORMATION BY SUBJECT

Internet sites listed here are selected by the staff of the Central Library sections of the San Diego Public Library for their usefulness in answering questions typically received by the Library. Listings change as new resources become available. Selection criteria include quality and quantity of information, ease of use, accessibility and stability. This is not intended to be a comprehensive directory of all Internet sites on every subject. For more in-depth subject listings developed by others, click on Exploring the Internet.

- Art, Music and Recreation Section
  Includes entertainment and sports

- Children's Room
  Includes K-12 information and teen sites

- History Section
  Other topics are flags, geography, maps and atlases and travel

- Literature and Languages Section
  Also includes books/library science and religion

- Reference
  Includes sites for quick referral in all subjects

- Science Section
  Also includes computer science, patent information, health and technology

- Social Sciences Section
  Includes business and stocks, employment, government and law, charities, real estate, scholarships and statistics

- Special Collections
  Includes San Diego, California and general news sources

Updated June 15, 1998

Source: San Diego Public Library (*www.sannet.gov/public-library/searching-the-net/subject.html*).

and guidance the library decides to offer, one-on-one assistance will be a routine occurrence. Reference librarians, children's librarians, and, in smaller libraries, circulation-desk staff, will find themselves answering many questions about how to search the Internet and to troubleshoot problems with software and hardware. In fact, many libraries have included in their Internet policies a caveat that staff assistance will be provided on a staff-available basis.

The nature of one-on-one assistance differs from library to library. For libraries where direct assistance is the main guidance mode, it may be described in the policy and encouraged in the staff procedures manual. In other libraries, one-on-one may get less emphasis than formally training patrons in a group setting. Naturally, the content of one-on-one training will vary depending on the library, with some offering scripted and formal presentations and others leaving it up to the librarian on duty to offer the greatest level of service possible for the amount of time and money available.

The most common guided-use statements in library Internet policies concern one-on-one assistance. Following are examples from two policies on staff assistance, the first from the Monroe County (NY) Library System (*204.97.3.3/mclspolicies.html*):

> Many Monroe County Library System staff members have already undergone Internet orientation, and more intensive training will follow. However, "surfing the Net" is a new experience for us all, and in many cases we will be learning to use this resource along with our patrons. We will be happy to offer assistance in accessing the Internet, although we cannot provide in-depth training or guarantee that the Internet-trained staff will always be available during library hours. Please use the comment cards available in your local public library to let us know what you think about this service or to ask any questions. Self-guided Internet access materials are also available at local libraries.

As with many policies, this statement stresses the limits of training and assistance that staff can give. The statement is very gracefully crafted, as it tells the user why in-depth training is not yet possible, promises an expansion of service as time goes on, and offers patrons a way to communicate their reaction to the policy. The wording of the Dallas Public Library's (*205.165.160.15/policy.htm*) "Internet Acceptable Use Policy" is similar:

> The Library has prepared a World Wide Web home page to assist users in their Internet searches and staff have identified and recommended specific starting points on the Library's home page.

> While users are encouraged to access the Internet, the information needed may be more easily available through the Library's more traditional resources. Library staff will assist users in locating these materials.
>
> While Library staff are happy to assist users in accessing the Internet, each user is nevertheless responsible for his or her own search. Staff cannot provide in-depth personal training in the use of the Internet or of personal computers.

Interesting points in this policy are its references to the interaction between the Internet and traditional sources and how it reiterates the limits of assistance staff can provide.

Informal Group Instruction

The library may offer instruction on how to use the Internet to groups of patrons at a time. One approach is to offer short, relatively informal sessions with the patrons gathered either around the terminal in the service area or in a meeting room. Unlike one-on-one instruction, this training gets scheduled at the prerogative of the library, not as the need arises from the patron. Many libraries set up group training when the Internet is first introduced in the library, and many require patrons to attend a training session before they are allowed to use the Internet. The policy of the Spokane Public Library (*splnet.spokpl.lib.wa.us/internet-policy.html*), for example, contains a clause that "the Library reserves the right to require all prospective users to attend an orientation session as a condition for access to the Library Internet stations."

Informal group instruction is usually shorter than formal and covers topics that intended to orient the library patron to the Internet and library policy and procedure than to provide systematic, in-depth training in Internet searching, protocols, and use.

Formal Group Instruction

The highest level of training that the library can offer is formal group instruction, which has some or all of the following characteristics:

- Sessions are scheduled to occur at times that are advertised to the public.
- Attendance is limited and registration is required.
- Some or all of the training takes place in a classroom or lab setting.

- Sessions are taught by a trainer and use a curriculum, handouts, exercises, and other techniques of a classroom environment.
- Training is sufficient in length to provide students with at least a basic understanding of Internet resources, protocols, and search strategies, as well as library policies and procedures.

As with informal training, the library may require that patrons attend a formal session of this type before they are allowed to use the Internet, but it is more likely that such a requirement will be for informal rather than formal training. Formal training is much more common in school and academic library environments, which are geared toward teaching situations, but training programs are turning up in public libraries as an additional information service to the community and as a way to take some load off of reference, circulation, and children's room staff.

The Internet policy may or may not reference formal training activities. The Rio Grande Valley (NM) Library System policy (*www.cabq.gov/rgvls/internet.html*) states that "Internet training will be made available on a scheduled basis" and directs patrons to inquire at the circulation desk. The policy of the Medina County District Library in Ohio (*www.medina.lib.oh.us/guidelines2.html*) describes a guided-use program that includes a Web page with preselected sites, one-on-one instruction, and classes: "Library staff will assist individuals in the use of the Library's Home Page and offer basic instruction in the use of selected Internet sites linked to the Home Page. Classes on the use of electronic resources are regularly scheduled at each community library."

The policy of the Juneau (AK) Public Library (*www.juneau.lib.ak.us/library/libsvcs.htm*) states how to find out about its classes in Internet searching and Web page design, and even goes on to offer specialized instruction: "Special classes to meet the needs of particular groups can be scheduled at other times."

One final example, from the Florida Atlantic University (*www.fau.edu/wise/wisetrain.htm*), is typical of the emphasis on training found in many academic universities. And like most school and academic Internet policy documents, this one was apparently written by administration, not library staff. Nevertheless, the policy is very specific about formal group instruction and reads as follows:

Training on how to use the World Wide Web system at FAU and classes for users who wish to become WISE Team developers are being handled by IRM's Academic/Institutional Support Services, End User Services Group. This training is presently available for faculty and staff. Students who will be creating HomePages for their social, athletics, honor society organizations on campus may also attend some of these classes. The current training schedule can be printed out locally for you to select which courses you would be interested in taking.

The policy goes on to describe in some detail how to register for training, classes offered, and course descriptions for each class.

Regardless of what type of guidance is offered to patrons, all these techniques have a common goal: to make the use of the Internet as rewarding as possible for the library patron. They are a value-added service provided by the library to help patrons more quickly locate those materials on the Internet that serve their specific needs.

REFERENCES

American Library Association. *The Librarian's Guide to Cyberspace for Parents and Kids*. Chicago: American Library Association, 1998. (call 1-800-545-2433, press 7 for free copies).

National Center for Missing and Exploited Children. *Child Safety on the Information Highway*. Available at many sites including: *www.4j.lane.edu/safety/*

Polly, Jean Armor. *The Internet Kids Yellow Pages*. New York: Osborne/McGraw Hill, 1996.

8

Web Publishing Policies

Most of the policies discussed in this book so far have been based on the assumption that use of the Internet by library users is unidirectional, that they are only receivers of Internet content. But this is not always true. There is an increasing tendency by libraries to allow users to be information publishers as well as consumers by permitting individuals or groups to create Web pages that they can mount on the library server. Academic and school libraries routinely offer this service to students, because it teaches computer literacy skills. And public libraries are starting to offer this service, for example, the San Antonio Public Library, where a dynamic program called "Youth Wired" encourages teenagers to create their own Web pages.

But this type of use creates a twofold liability for the library. First, it allows users direct access to files on the library's server. There is, as discussed in Chapter 4, some risk involved with allowing users access to the server—for instance, a student could damage other files on the system. This risk can be mitigated significantly, however, by incorporating adequate safeguards such as allowing users access only to their files.

The second, more significant issue, is the content of the Web page. What if a student running a Web page on your server downloads copyrighted material and publishes it online without asking permission? Can your library be held responsible for the violation? What about publishing sexually explicit materials or using the Web page to publish speech that is constitutionally protected but that is offensive and generates complaints?

It is imperative for libraries that allow and encourage students and patrons to mount their own Web pages on library servers to consider all the implications and to provide policy guidelines. In many universities, this will be a function of another department with a name like Information Resources or Computer Services Department. For school libraries, there may also exist standards for Web publishing that have been developed by another department in the district. If there are pre-existing standards, it will be the responsibility of the library to inform students of the standards and to ensure that any project the library participates in conforms to the standards. If there are not standards already, you take the lead on writing the policy, especially if the idea of allowing patrons to publish Web pages originated in the library.

This chapter looks at the various elements that might be addressed in a Web policy and provides some examples of Web policies (see also Appendix A). There is also an excellent archive of academic Web policies that has been collated by the education association Educause (available at *www.cause.org/information-resources/ir-library/subjects/policies-www.html*).

WHAT SHOULD A WEB PUBLISHING POLICY INCLUDE?

There is a dilemma that awaits the administrator, committee, or other group charged with the task of developing a Web policy: balancing the institutional standards with personal expression. This dilemma derives from two institutional values that are sometimes in conflict. Institutions that let students and staff create Web pages do so because they want people to develop new skills of computer literacy and use this new medium to express personal and departmental personalities, goals, and interests. At the same time, the institution has its corporate image and legal responsibilities to consider and does not want its Web page to sponsor, link to, or appear to support a subsidiary page that does not maintain the standards of the institution. This conflict creates the need for a policy statement that Michael Stoner has succinctly characterized in his must-read paper, "Web Policies That Work" (*www.rutledge.com/stoner/polhome.html*):

> You want to ensure that your institution's official Web pages are well-designed, accurate, and in compliance with state and federal laws. But you must also avoid stifling the creativity of those who want to experiment with this exciting medium. To accomplish both goals . . . many campuses are developing policies about who may post and what may be posted on Web servers. With a combination of cooperation and common sense, you too can make the Web a little less wild.

Determining Who May Operate a Web Page

The first and most basic question is: Who may post or modify a Web page on your server? A second, related question is: Will the terms of the Web policy differ from group to group or apply equally to all? You may offer the privilege of creating and mounting a Web page on your server to some or all groups in your institution: students, faculty, staff, or patrons. Within these groups, you may differentiate between official pages to further the work of the school, college, or library—departmental pages, or pages for colleges or divisions within the university—and purely personal pages for individuals. Many institutions offer all of these groups the option of mounting Web pages on their servers, but with differing terms. For example, individual, personal pages for students, faculty, and staff may not necessarily have to meet all the same standards for consistency of design and content as departmental pages. For example, it is logical to require that all departmental pages display the name and perhaps the seal of the university near the top of every page, but the same requirement for personal student pages would be a bit silly. It is also not unusual for faculty or staff to have different privileges from students in terms of the type of material they can link their pages to, the size or complexity of pages, or system resources devoted to the pages.

Requirements versus Recommendations

In writing your policy, consider whether specific elements will be requirements or recommended guidelines. Some standards are sufficiently important that they must be required, such as not to engage in any illegal activities. You may also have hard-and-fast design elements such as the level of HTML used, or the display of a contact name on every page. Other standards, however, especially those involving aesthetics or design principles, may only be recommended in your policy. By the way, recommended policies may prove to be a very good way to resolve disagreements among parties writing the policy about certain standards. But if you do opt to make an element of your policy required, you need to decide what the penalty for noncompliance will be, which is discussed later in this chapter.

Technical and Quality Standards

Defining quality standards for Web pages mounted on the library or institution's server is the next and perhaps most complex area of investigation in designing the policy. Unlike the clear-cut standards of legal use that follow in the next section of this chapter, quality standards vary between institutions and convey the institutional and organizational values of the school, college, or library. Here is where institutional standards of decorum and conduct may come into conflict with personal expression.

To make this issue a bit easier to handle, policymakers should begin by addressing technical standards and hold aesthetic standards until later. Technical standards serve the dual function of providing guidance to Web page designers and ensuring accessibility for users. Common elements found in technical specifications are:

- *HTML (hypertext mark-up language) standards*, specifying which version of HTML designers should use in creating their pages.
- *Handicapped accessibility*, requiring that designers take into account the needs of persons who are blind or visually impaired. (For an in-depth discussion of this topic and to test a specific page for handicap accessibility, visit the "Bobby" site at *www.cast.org/bobby/*).
- *Text, graphics, and forms*, determining what you will allow in terms of design elements. In addition to the graphics that have been on the Web since its inception, other features such as sound and animation are becoming commonplace. Another popular element, found on perhaps a majority of pages, are frames, which split the screen into multiple panels, each of which can be navigated separately. All these features are fun and can enhance the value and interest of the Web page, but not all users can see them. They depend upon users having not only browsing software, but often specific versions of specific software as well. Your policy may require or recommend that pages meet a "lowest common denominator" standard for design either by providing mostly text with minimal graphics or by allowing the user the option to move between single and multiple frames.
- *Size of graphics*, which affects the speed of loading a page. Because huge graphics files including animation and sound will cause a page to take a long time to load, some Web guidelines require or recommend that graphic files be kept below a certain size, usually expressed in number of kilobytes of storage space.
- *Contact person*, who is responsible for maintaining the page, and a way to contact that person. Pages can use the convenient "mailto" function in HTML to allow users to send e-mail directly to the contact person. Some policies suggest or require that an alias such as "Webmaster" or "Webwizard" be used instead of the real name of the contact person.
- *Disclaimer statements*, which some institutions require every page mounted on the server to display. Most often these serve to dis-

tance the page from the institution and—for what it's worth—to attempt to establish a defense to prosecution or legal action for the institution. These say something to the effect of "Opinions expressed on this page are solely those of its authors and do not reflect the opinions of Big State University," or perhaps, "This page was designed and maintained by the X group. The Public Library is not responsible for the content of this page. Complaints and suggestions about this page should be directed to . . . " The question of whether such a statement can provide any legal protection is debatable and should be referred to your legal counsel for further discussion.

- *Title information,* which every page on the World Wide Web displays at the very top of the browser window. You may wish for pages mounted on your server to have a consistent display in that block. Perhaps you would like them to reference the name of the institution—or perhaps you would prefer that they not do so. Keep in mind that some Internet search engines look at this line of the HTML code in searching for a particular subject or keyword.

- *Copyright statements,* which you will probably want to recommend, if not require, on each page. These state that the pages are copyrighted in the name of either the university, school, library, or unit or individual responsible for their creation. You may further wish to state that permission is required to cite or link to the pages.

- *Length and complexity* limitations on the size of pages. You may choose—or be forced by server limitations—to impose certain limits, usually in terms of kilobytes of storage space required for the page rather than number of subpages. But, you may also wish to limit the complexity of the pages so that there can be no more than, say, four levels on any site.

- *Links to orient the user,* usually at the bottom of the page. Many schools and universities require that all individual pages have references back to the home page of the parent institution. Such links are especially important for departmental pages. You may also want to require that some pages link back to previous pages, because even though the standard "back" and "forward" functions of most browsers allow the user to move between previously selected pages, a user arriving at a page from a link on another page or from a search engine may not be able to tell at which site they have arrived.

- *Templates,* which help Web designers create pages that automatically conform to technical standards. These templates would already be formatted with the core elements that you require or recommend in your library, school, or university. For an example of Web page templates, see the Florida Atlantic University site at *www.fau.edu/wise/publish.html.*

Aesthetic Standards

Once technical requirements are sent out, you need to move on to the thorny area of aesthetic standards. You will probably not get far down this path before you realize that tastes differ and that you may not even be able to establish consensus among the policy developers about what to include. Even if you do, there will be some designers who wish to deviate from the standard. But as a starting point, here are some of the elements of aesthetic standards found in Web policies.

- *Backgrounds, colors, headers, and the like.* You or your institution may require all pages to have a similar "look," especially departmental pages. This usually means that they must share common elements. Universities will often require that all pages use a banner that includes the name or seal of the university, or both. You may also prefer that the pages display other common elements like specific tiled backgrounds, color schemes (including specific colors for hyperlinked items), and footers. An alternate approach would be not to require the use of such elements but that, if they are used, they be used consistently. That is, a page may choose not to use the university's seal, but if it does, it must use a specific version and in specific dimensions.
- *Arrangements of elements on the page.* You might also require or recommend that elements be laid out in particular ways on the page. For example, if you allow the use of frames, you might specify that certain elements always be on the left margin of the page, or that a graphic that is used consistently on other pages as a footer graphic is always used as a footer. A common stipulation is that graphics be formatted to run left of any text or above the accompanying text; however, because the placement of graphics distorts text-only displays, this may be a technical rather than purely aesthetic issue.
- *Tastefulness and appropriateness.* This, of course, is anybody's call, and good luck getting the policy development committee to agree on what is tasteful and appropriate. But if you should reach consensus, you may wish to make a statement describing material that will be considered inappropriate. Your greatest concern may be sexual materials, but there are other topics that may offend many people on campus that don't have anything to do with sex—such

as tasteless jokes, racially offensive speech, scatological speech, violence, and occult materials. Refer to the next section of this chapter, which deals with attempting to regulate content on the Web page, and be sure to tread lightly on First Amendment issues. If you do intend to patrol and regulate pages of appropriateness, be sure to have in place a set of criteria that carefully describe what is not acceptable to include in a Web page located on the library, school, or university server.

Content

Perhaps the most significant discussion you will have regarding Web policy will be what to allow in terms of content. Again, this is dangerous ground, where the institution must proceed with caution lest it infringe First Amendment rights. There are, however, certain content issues that can and must be addressed.

- *Spelling, grammar, usage.* Although having a penalty for noncompliance is questionable, it is wise to state for the record that you expect Web pages to conform to standards of accuracy in the use of language, including spelling and grammar. In some cases you may need to go further and require that longer articles or citations of other articles conform to a standard usage manual such as *The Chicago Manual of Style* or the *MLA Handbook* (Modern Language Association). Incidentally, there is an increasing body of published material that instructs users in standard procedures for the citation of online sources, for example *Electronic Styles: A Handbook for Citing Electronic Information* by Xia Li and Nancy B. Crane.

- *Factual information.* Your policy may explicitly state that anyone posting information to their Web pages must make every reasonable effort to ensure that the information published on the page is accurate. The most pressing reason is that if any harm or loss occurs to an individual as a result of information obtained via the university, school, or library Web page, the institution may be held liable. Regardless of this potential for trouble, however, your standards should dictate that hosted pages have accurate information, a particularly important point for departmental as well as individual pages.

- *Political speech (disclaimers).* Address the inclusion of political speech on sponsored Web pages. It would be problematic and ill advised for you to write an outright prohibition on the publication of political speech online, but you can require that personal and departmental Web pages carry a disclaimer regarding the opinions expressed on the page. The Brown University Student Handbook states, for example, "Administrative officers, faculty, students and staff of Brown University are free to express their individual and collective political views, whether on or off campus; PROVIDED that it is made clear that they are not speaking for or in the name of Brown University" (*www.brown.edu/webmaster/TM009.html*). It is important to note that this statement comes from a document that is not specific to online speech. Most colleges and universities have policies of this sort that govern all speech on campus or off that is sponsored or supported by the institution, so check for any institutional policies before writing your statement.

People sometimes give controversial opinions on the Internet. If you offer students, faculty, or library patrons the opportunity to express themselves online, sooner or later someone else is likely to take offense. As with other forms of access, to impose restrictions on certain types of speech can leave you vulnerable to a lawsuit on the grounds that you have violated First Amendment rights. If you are considering initiating a service for users to put their Web pages on your server, be sure to talk over these issues with your board and others. Make sure that they understand and adopt your Web guidelines as well as any procedures governing the review and approval of Web pages. Have procedures in place for review of challenged materials on Web pages, and make sure that the board understands and concurs with these. As with any other potentially controversial material, the more of your policy and procedures that you can spell out *before* you have a problem, the easier it will be to cope with a challenge.

- *Confidentiality.* Of course, you have an obligation to protect the confidentiality of members of your student body or faculty. For this reason, consider a policy that prohibits the use of full names, phone numbers, home addresses, or other contact information on Web pages. If you find, however, that someone wishes to use their entire name, be sure they furnish you with a written release to publish this information.
- *Respecting intellectual property.* Safeguards for protecting copyrighted material should be part of the Web policy. All Web designers need to know that they cannot post copyrighted materials to their pages without securing written permission and stating the permissions online. Copyrighted materials, of course, include graphics and software as well as textual materials.

- *Illegal activities.* Copyright violations are one of several potentially illegal activities that can occur on Web pages, others including the display of obscene materials—including child pornography—that are prohibited by state or federal statutes, the sale and distribution of controlled substances, libelous or slanderous statements, and the use of the Web page to convey threats toward individuals. The use of institutional resources to conduct illegal activities creates a liability for the library, school, or university, so most Web policies address such illegal activities. The consequence for such activity is usually loss of network privileges as well as the potential for criminal prosecution or civil action.

Review Procedures

Your Web policy should give the terms by which you will review, approve, and enforce Web guidelines. Most Web pages go through some sort of committee review before they are mounted on the server or made live to catch any deviations from the standards and require that they be corrected before the page can be launched. It can also be a good idea to have a periodic review of Web pages once they are live, to ensure that they continue to meet standards for WWW development as set forward in your policy.

Sample Policies

The policies in Figure 8–1 and 8–2 nicely illustrate the distinction that can be drawn between recommended and required policies. The required elements (standards) are very brief and consist mainly of core elements that the college expects to find on every page, including the actual HTML code for that part of the page so that designers can cut and paste the codes from the online policy into the code for the page.

Figure 8–1	SAMPLE SCHOOL WEB POLICY

Winona School District 861
Winona, Minnesota 55987
Creating and Placing Web Pages
Board Adopted Policy: 04-22-96
School District Code 832.5

The availability of Internet access in District 861 schools provides an opportunity for students and staff to contribute to the School District's presence on the World Wide Web. The District's Web sites provide information to the world about school curriculum, instruction, school-authorized activities, and other general information relating to our schools and our District's mission. Internet access for the creation of Web pages is provided by District media specialists and the District network specialist. Creators of Web pages need to familiarize themselves with and adhere to the following policies and responsibilities. Failure to follow these policies or responsibilities may result in the loss of authoring privileges or other more stringent disciplinary measures.

CONTENT STANDARDS

Building and district administrators, with input from media specialists and the network specialist, are responsible for Web page approval.

SUBJECT MATTER

All subject matter on Web pages should relate to curriculum, instruction, school-authorized activities, general information that is appropriate and of interest to others, or it should relate to the School District, or the schools within the District. Therefore, neither staff nor students may publish personal home pages as part of the District Web Sites, or home pages for other individuals or organizations not directly affiliated with the District. Staff or student work may be published only as it relates to a class project, course, or other school-related activity.

QUALITY

All Web page work must be free of spelling and grammatical errors. Documents may not contain objectionable material or point (link) directly to objectionable material. Objectionable material is defined as material that does not meet the standards for instructional resources specified in District policies. Regarding the question of quality or propriety of Web page material, appearance, or content, the judgment of the media specialists, network specialist, building or district administrators will prevail.

OWNERSHIP AND RETENTION

All Web pages on the District's server(s) are property of the School District. Web pages will be deleted when a student graduates or moves unless prior arrangements have been made with the media specialist or the network specialist.

Figure 8–1	(Continued)

STUDENT SAFEGUARDS

- Web page documents may include only the first name and the initial of the student's last name.
- Documents may not include a student's phone number, address, names of other family members, or names of friends.
- Published e-mail addresses are restricted to staff members or to a general group e-mail address where arriving e-mail is forwarded to a staff member.
- Decisions on publishing student pictures (video or still) and audio clips are based on the supervising teacher's judgment. The teacher must first check with the school office or the District office to determine if the student's parents/guardians have objected to such publication through the regular Data Privacy restriction process.
- Web page documents may not include any information which indicates the physical location of a student at a given time, other than attendance at a particular school, or participation in activities.

SCHOOL BOARD POLICIES

All documents on District 861 server(s) must conform to School Board Policies and regulations as well as established school guidelines. Copies of Board Policies are available in all school offices. Persons developing or maintaining Web documents are responsible for complying with these and other policies. Some of the relevant issues and related Board Policies include the following:

- Electronic transmission of materials is a form of copying. As specified in District Policy, no unlawful copies of copyrighted materials may be knowingly produced or transmitted via the District's equipment, including its Web server(s).
- Documents created for the Web and linked to District Web pages will meet the criteria for use as an instructional resource.
- Any links to District Web pages that are not specifically curriculum-related will meet the criteria established in the District Internet Authorized Use Policy (AUP). Any other non-curricular materials should be limited to information about other youth activities, agencies, or organizations which are known to be non-sectarian, exclusively devoted to community interests or child welfare, are non-profit, and non-discriminatory. Web page links may not include entities whose primary purpose is commercial or political advertising.
- All communications via the District Web pages will comply with the District Internet Authorized Use Policy (AUP) and the District Code of Conduct Policy. Offensive behavior that is expressly prohibited by this policy includes religious, racial, and sexual harassment and/or violence.
- Any student information communicated via the District Web pages will comply with District 861 policies on Data Privacy and Public Use of School Records.
- Any deliberate tampering with or misuse of District network services or equipment will

Figure 8–1	(Continued)

be considered vandalism and will be handled in accordance with the District Internet Authorized Use Policy (AUP), the District Code of Conduct, and other related policies.

TECHNICAL STANDARDS AND CONSISTENCY

Each Web page added to the District Web site(s) must contain certain elements which will provide general consistency for District Web pages.

- At the bottom of the Web page, there must be an indication of the date of the last update to that page and the name or initials of the person(s) responsible for the page or update. It shall be that person's responsibility to keep the Web page current.
- At the bottom of the Web page, there must be a link that returns the user to the appropriate point(s) in the District Web pages. A template will be provided for all users.
- Additional consistency standards will be developed by the District as the need arises.
- All Web pages must be submitted to a District media specialist or the District network specialist for review prior to their placement on the District server(s). In the absence of a District media specialist, the building administrator or designee shall review the Web page.
- No computers other than the assigned building Web servers shall be configured as Web/FTP servers.
- Users must exhibit care when creating Web pages with extensive tiled backgrounds or large graphics. Such files require extensive download time, are frustrating for modem users, and slow down the file servers. As a general rule, a Web page should not take longer than one minute to download over a 14.4K modem connection. Graphics files shall be under 60K in size unless a special situation exists that requires a larger graphic.
- The authorized teacher who is publishing the final Web page(s) for herself or himself, or for a student, will edit and test the page(s) for accuracy of links, and check for conformance with standards outlined in this policy.
- Web pages may not contain links to other Web pages not yet completed. If additional pages are anticipated, but not yet developed, the text that will provide such a link should be included. However, the actual link to said page(s) may not be made until the final page is actually in place on the District server(s).
- All Web pages must be given names which clearly identify them. The names of all documents shall coincide with current District naming practices and structures.
- Any graphics, sounds, or video used on Web pages must conform to the format currently used or approved by the District.
- Web pages may not contain any student e-mail address links, any survey-response links, or any other type of direct-response links.
- Final decisions regarding access to active Web pages for editing content or organization will rest with the building principal, with input from the media specialist and/or the network specialist.
- All Web pages shall be linked to other District pages in relation to their current location

Figure 8–1	(Continued)

on the server(s).

OTHER

- Material on Web pages reflect an individual's thoughts, interests, and activities. Such Web pages do not, in any way, represent individual schools or District 861, nor are they endorsed or sanctioned by the individual school or the District. Concern about the content of any page(s) created by students or staff should be directed to the building principal of that school or to that school's media specialist.
- Given the rapid change in technology, some of the technical standards outlined in this policy may require change throughout the year. Such changes will be made by the District network specialist with approval of the Superintendent. This Web Page Policy will be updated on an annual basis, or more frequently if required.

Source: Winona (MN) School District (*wms.luminet.net/wmstechnology/861.WebPagesPolicy. html*)

Figure 8–2	SAMPLE COLLEGE WEB POLICY

SENECA COLLEGE WEB DOCUMENT STANDARDS

All of the following requirements must be met if a Web page is to be linked to the Seneca Web top level and organizational pages.

Seneca Specific

All Web pages must be clearly marked as originating at Seneca College and must have a link to the Seneca Home Page.

Accountability

All pages must have the name and e-mail address of the person responsible for its contents clearly marked on it.

Seneca Graphics

The use of Seneca graphics and symbols must be limited to those images located in the Seneca graphics directory. This applies to all documents anywhere on any Seneca Web server. They can be retrieved by clicking on the desired one with the right mouse button (in Netscape). Document creators are reminded that Seneca graphics and images are owned by the College and they are not free to alter them in any way.

Headers

Each page should begin with a header of the form:

`<HTML><HEADER><TITLE>Seneca College: page title</TITLE></HEADER><BODY>`

The title of the page should begin with the words Seneca College, as shown.

Footers

All pages should have a footer that includes at least the name and Email address of the person responsible, a link to the Seneca home page and the date the page was last modified. It should look like this:

`<HR><FONT SIZE=2>Maintained by:<A HREF="MAILTO:author's Email address">author's name</A>, <A HREF="HTTP://WWW.SENECAC.ON.CA/">Seneca College</A>, updated: date</BODY></HTML>`

SENECA COLLEGE HTML GUIDELINES

It is strongly recommended that the following guidelines be followed in order to maintain a consistent appearance for College Web pages.

Backgrounds

Many Seneca pages, like this one, have plain white backgrounds by using the tag: `<body bgcolor="FFFFFF">`. Others use tiled background .gif files. You can view and retrieve the approved background tiles from the Seneca backgrounds directory. Use of these backgrounds is desirable to maintain a consistent appearance for Seneca information. If you have other backgrounds which you would like included in this directory, please ask the Webmaster.

Figure 8–2	(Continued)

Icon Graphics

For a consistent look to Seneca's Web pages, it is suggested that icon graphics be used from the Seneca icon graphics directory.

Blinking

Most people find use of the blink tag annoying. Please use it with discretion.

Grammar and Spelling

All pages should be properly spell-checked and grammatically correct.

Headings within Documents

All headings within a document should be H2 or H3. H1 is generally too large.

All documents should begin with a visible title (as well as the <title> tag) enclosed in the H2 tags.

If you use a graphic as the visible title, the graphic used must include text that states the title of the document and you should use ALT="heading" in the IMAGE tag so that non-graphical browsers can see the title.

"Under Construction"

Links to pages that are empty of content except for "Watch this space" messages are discouraged. Better practice is to not construct the link until the content is in place. Little "under construction" icons are also discouraged.

Versions of HTML

There are many extensions to HTML proposed and working in the marketplace today. There is every reason to suppose that the situation will remain very dynamic. Seneca WWW documents should be created using HTML that reflects current market conditions and does not exclude a large class of users from viewing document content. At the present time, it would appear that writing for Netscape HTML extensions supported by the current non-beta release is a good choice. If you are experimenting with HTML extensions beyond the released standard, it is wise to inform the reader.

File Size

If you are linking to files such as graphics, audio or video clips, you should indicate the file size. If the file is a non-HTML document or something that requires a non-standard viewer, you should include information or a link to where the viewer can be obtained.

Page Size

Many people are discouraged by pages which take a long time to load. You should remember that use of 14.4 KBPS modems are common. Try to keep your pages less than 80 KB including all graphics. It would be wise to split up pages which are larger, or use smaller graphics.

Source: Seneca College of Applied Arts and Technology (*www.senecac.on.ca/standard/web-sag.htm*)

REFERENCES

Li, Xia and Nancy B. Crane. *Electronic Styles: A Handbook for Citing Electronic Information.* Medford, N.J.: Information Today, 1996.

Modern Language Association. *MLA Handbook.* New York: Modern Language Association, 1995.

University of Chicago Press. *The Chicago Manual of Style*, 14th ed. Chicago, Ill: University of Chicago Press, 1993.

9

Next Steps: After the Policy Is Written

Your policy is finally written. What next? Remember that policy development is an ongoing process, not a product, so now you begin to evaluate your policy. If your library is like others, the Internet is a pretty new service, which means that your policy charted territory that was new to you, your library board, staff, and patrons. The policy that you developed—regardless of how carefully you thought it through or how many colleagues you consulted—was only your best guess for what would work in your situation. After implementation you will find that some policies work very well, but others don't. Maybe it was the right call to require sign ups, but the time limits you imposed were too long or too short. Perhaps you received enough complaints from patrons about your filtering policy that you can approach the board with the suggestion that some machines be unfiltered. Or maybe so many people requested the option to send e-mail that you have reconsidered your ban on allowing mail from your workstation browsers.

These decisions must be made according to the best information you have available. But what information do you use, and how do you go about gathering it? The variety of sources of information include:

- *Patron comments.* Gathered either verbally across the circulation desk, on response cards, via correspondence, or overheard in the library, take every opportunity you can to hear what your patrons think, and evaluate your policies accordingly.
- *Staff feedback.* Your staff are those most closely in touch with the

implementation of the policy and will tell you when things are not appropriate or could work better. It is from staff that you are most likely to hear that a given policy is unenforceable, creates undue pressure on the staff, is impractical, or leads to unnecessary conflict between the staff and the public.

- *Data.* One of the most elusive elements in policy regarding the Internet has been actual data. Nevertheless, there are statistics you can collect that will help you to evaluate your policies. Among them are the numbers of people who sign up to use the machines by day and hour, and by location of workstation. These data will help you review such issues as whether you need to require sign ups at all times and where you can most effectively locate machines. Software exists that allows you to log the number of items selected on a Web page so that you can monitor which of your preselected sites are most useful and develop your page accordingly. Staff who serve as intermediaries in the provision of reference services via the Internet can log their questions and answers to inform you how patrons use the service.

- *Changing technology.* Your policy will have to adapt to changes in the technological environment of your library. More sophisticated software, more powerful machines, and the advent of new Internet protocols and plug-in software will change what your library can offer via the Internet. With every new service will come the need for new or revised policy.

How will you rewrite the policy? You may wish to draft a group of citizens or faculty or parents to serve as a blue-ribbon policy committee, or perhaps use a subcommittee of your library board. You may charge staff to recommend changes in the policy, or ask each member of the staff to identify one element of the policy that they would change if they had the opportunity. In the end, remember that, any modification in your policy should be submitted to the governing authority for ultimate review and adoption.

Over time, with some attention and flexibility on the part of library managers, staff, and board, your Internet policy will become a finely tuned document that balances the needs of patrons and staff, asserts the values of the institution, shields the library from liability, and provides a framework for the most effective possible use of the Internet.

Appendix A

Sample Internet Policies

The following policies demonstrate the range of possibilities for length and depth of coverage for public, academic, and school library Internet policies. All are available on the Web.

CARNEGIE-STOUT PUBLIC LIBRARY (DUBUQUE, IOWA)

This policy is typical of the very brief access-and-disclaimer statement used by many libraries. The point of this policy is to state the library's policy on open access and to warn patrons that there are materials on the Internet that they may find offensive or that may convey inaccurate information. It does not address acceptable or restricted use or any procedures regarding time limits, sign up, guided use, and the like.

CARNEGIE-STOUT PUBLIC LIBRARY

360 West 11th Street, Dubuque, Iowa 52001 • 1-319-589-4225

INTERNET DISCLAIMER

The Internet is a global electronic network which enables the library to provide information to patrons beyond the library's collection. It includes useful ideas, information, and opinions from around the world. In offering Internet access, the library staff cannot control:

- the accuracy and validity of the information.
- the availability of links users would like to visit. Sites frequently change addresses or close down and some sites may limit access to affiliated or authorized users.
- the materials you may find offensive.

Many sites carry information you may find controversial, indecent, or inappropriate. Users are responsible for the access points they reach. Parents are encouraged to work with and supervise their minor children's Internet sessions.

SPOKANE (WASHINGTON) PUBLIC LIBRARY

This is a very nice example of a middle-length, public-library policy that addresses access, physical arrangement, security, appropriate use, and guided-use issues. Though no issue is presented in great detail, most key issues are addressed along with basic protections and guidance. This is a policy on which more detailed staff procedures can be built.

SPOKANE PUBLIC LIBRARY COMPUTER AND INTERNET USAGE POLICY

Adopted by the Spokane Public Library Board of Trustees on June 20, 1995.

1. Access to Internet Resources

1.1—The mission of the Spokane Public Library is to ensure that the people of the City of Spokane have the right and means to free and open access to ideas and information which are fundamental to a democracy. The Library will protect intellectual freedom, promote literacy, encourage lifelong learning, and provide library materials and information services.

1.2—Throughout its history the Spokane Public Library has made information available in a variety of formats, from print to audiovisual materials. The Library's computer system provides the opportunity to integrate electronic resources from information networks around the world with the Library's other resources.

1.3—The Internet, as an information resource, enables the Library to provide information beyond the confines of its own collection. It allows access to ideas, information and commentary from around the globe. Currently, however, it is an unregulated medium. As such, while it offers access to a wealth of material that is personally, professionally, and culturally enriching to individuals of all ages, it also enables access to some material that may be offensive, disturbing and/or illegal.

1.4—In introducing the Internet as an information resource, the Spokane Public Library's goal is to enhance its existing collection in size and depth and as a public access agency give opportunity to any citizen who wishes to participate in navigating the Internet, both in the Library and at home through Dial-In service.

1.5—Library staff will identify specific starting points for searches on the Library's home page which are appropriate to the Library's mission and service roles. The Library cannot control or monitor other material which may be accessible from Internet sources. It is not possible to apply the same selection criteria which are used for other materials.

1.6—When feasible, the Library will implement software and hardware control mechanisms to prohibit information which the Library has determined to be inconsistent with its Mission and service roles. Such controls will be implemented to the extent feasible given budgeting and programming limitations. The Library cannot successfully control or monitor the vast amount of material accessible from computers and networks via the Internet. Individual users must accept responsibility for determining content in the event the Library is unable to determine the suitability.

2. In-Library Access

2.1—The Library upholds and affirms the right of each individual to have access to constitutionally protected material. The Library also affirms the right and responsibility of parents to determine and monitor their children's use of Library materials and resources.

2.2—The Library will provide Internet stations in the Downtown Children's Room, reserved for youth and will mount a Kids Page with appealing and age-appropriate reading levels.

Library staff is available to provide assistance and to help identify appropriate sites. The user, however, is the selector in using the Internet with individual choices and decisions.

3. **Conditions and Terms of Use in the Library**

3.1—In an effort to ensure that the use of this medium is consistent with the Mission of the Spokane Public Library the following regulations shall apply:

3.1.2—Designated Internet stations will be located where they can be monitored by staff for assistance and security.

3.1.3—The Library reserves the right to require all prospective users to attend an orientation session as a condition for access to the Library Internet stations. Orientation will include training in the use of software and hardware, and guidelines for the responsible care of Library equipment.

3.1.4—Prospective users will sign an Internet Use Contract. Youth under 18 years of age will be required to have parental or guardian permission to access the Internet. While the Library will make every effort to ensure that the use of the Internet is consistent with the Mission statement, parents are encouraged to work closely with their children in selecting material that is consistent with personal and family values and boundaries.

3.1.5—The Library will establish procedures that will make Internet stations available on a first come, first served appointment basis.

3.1.6—Internet use will be managed in a manner consistent with the Library's Rules of Conduct which have been adopted and are posted in the Library.

3.1.7—Failure to use the Internet stations appropriately and responsibly, as defined in the training session and on the application form, may result in revocation of Internet use privileges.

Reprinted courtesy Spokane Public Library.

HOUSTON (TEXAS) PUBLIC LIBRARY

One of the first public library Internet policies to be posted on the Web, the Houston policy provides another example of a well-written, middle-length policy statement that provides a good amount of information about adult supervision, filtering policies, acceptable and restricted use, and protocols offered.

HOUSTON PUBLIC LIBRARY INTERNET USE POLICY AND GUIDELINES

This policy applies to all users of Houston Public Library computers or networks. If you have any questions about the policy or what it means, please contact a librarian for more information.

PURPOSE

To fulfill our mission, Houston Public Library provides access to a broad range of information resources, including those available through the Internet. We make this service available as part of our mission to offer a broadly defined program of informational, educational, recreational and cultural enrichment opportunities for Houstonians of all ages and backgrounds.

The Library only assumes responsibility for the information provided on the home page and the supporting web pages resident on this server. Houston Public Library does not monitor and has no control over the information accessed through the Internet. The Internet offers access to many valuable local, national, and international sources of information. However, not all sources on the Internet provide accurate, complete, or current information. A good information consumer evaluates the validity of information found. Restriction of a child's access to the Internet is the responsibility of the parent or guardian; the Library does not have the right or responsibility to act in loco parentis. For more information on children and the Internet, see *Child Safety on the Information Highway* produced by the National Center for Missing and Exploited Children and Interactive Service Organization.

RESPONSIBILITIES OF USERS

Supervising children's use

It is the library's policy that parents or legal guardians must assume responsibility for deciding what library resources are appropriate for their children. There will be some resources which parents may feel are inappropriate for their children. Parents should let their children know if there are materials which they do not want them to use. Parents should supervise their child's Internet sessions. Some library computers are designated as Children's Workstations. These workstations use filtering software to access the Internet. No filtering software can control access to all materials that an individual may deem inappropriate. Parents should instruct children in the Rules for Online Safety recommended by the National Center for Missing and Exploited Children. These rules are repeated for children who access the Library's Kids' Page.

Choosing and evaluating sources

The Internet is a global entity with a highly diverse user population and information content. Library patrons use it at their own risk. The Library cannot censor access to materials or protect users from materials they may find offensive. In choosing sources to link to our home page, we follow generally accepted library practices. Beyond this, we do not monitor or control information accessible through the Internet and do not accept responsibility for its content. We are not responsible for changes in content of the sources to which we link, nor for the content of sources accessed through secondary links.

As with printed information, not all sources on the Internet provide accurate, complete, or current information. Users should evaluate Internet sources just as they do printed publications, questioning the validity of the information provided.

Rules governing use

Please limit your time on the workstation to twenty minutes when others are waiting to use it. Users may not:

1. Use the workstations to gain access to the Library's networks or computer systems or to any other network or computer system.
2. Obstruct other people's work by consuming gratuitously large amounts of system resources or by deliberately crashing any Library computer system.
3. Make any attempt to damage computer equipment or software.
4. Make any attempt to alter software configurations.
5. Make any attempt to cause degradation of system performance.
6. Use any Library workstation for any illegal or criminal purpose.
7. Violate copyright laws or software licensing agreements in their use of Library workstations.
8. Engage in any activity which is deliberately and maliciously offensive, libelous, or slanderous.
9. Install or download any software.

Violations may result in loss of access. Unlawful activities will be dealt with in a serious and appropriate manner.

INTERNET FUNCTIONS SUPPORTED

The Library provides a graphical browser at the Central Library and Regional Libraries and is expanding to branch libraries. Library branches have at least Lynx access to the web at this time. The Library does not provide electronic mail accounts, Internet Relay Chat, or Newsgroups.

Printing and downloading are not currently available at all sites, but the library is expanding these services.

COPYRIGHT

U.S. copyright law (Title 17, U.S. Code) prohibits the unauthorized reproduction or distribution of copyrighted materials, except as permitted by the principles of "fair use". Users may not copy or distribute electronic materials (including electronic mail, text, images, programs or data) without the explicit permission of the copyright holder. Any responsibility for any consequences of copyright infringement lies with the user; the Library expressly disclaims any liability or responsibility resulting from such use.

The Library expressly disclaims any liability or responsibility arising from access to or use of information obtained through its electronic information systems, or any consequences thereof.

Houston Public Library
500 McKinney
Houston, Texas 77002
(713) 247-2222
(713) 236-1313—Reference Service

Last modified: March 30, 1998 at 13:15—policy.html
Reprinted courtesy Houston Public Library.

JERVIS PUBLIC LIBRARY (ROME, NEW YORK)

This interesting policy mainly addresses the question of freedom of access (especially children's access), but does so in a unique and informative manner.

JERVIS PUBLIC LIBRARY (ROME, NEW YORK)

INTERNET ACCESS POLICY

The Internet and the Library's Mission: The Internet is a growing global electronic network to which Jervis offers access as part of its mission to provide a wide variety of services. All Mid-York Library System libraries have been awarded Electronic Doorway Library status by the NYS Dept. of Education & Board of Regents which urge such access for all. The library's endorsement of the Library Bill of Rights, Freedom to Read, and Free Access to Libraries for Minors applies as well to electronic information. Public Internet access, both graphical and text-only, is provided via the Mid-York System. Mid-York and Jervis do not provide e-mail accounts, file transfer, or other Internet services beyond the capabilities of the hardware and software, as configured.

The Nature of Information on the Internet: The Internet is not controlled or governed by any single entity, hence, Jervis cannot verify accuracy, timeliness, usefulness, validity of information, availability of sites, or content of information found on the Internet. As with other sources, patrons themselves must evaluate the information. Availability of networked information via library terminals does not constitute the library's endorsement of the information. If a patron believes information obtained via terminals is inaccurate, illegal, or offensive, the patron is advised to contact the original producer or distributor.

Statement of Parental/Guardian Responsibility: Jervis Board of Trustees' policy is that parents or legal guardians are responsible for deciding what library resources are appropriate for their minor children. As with other library resources, supervision or restriction of a child's access to the Internet remains the responsibility of a parent or guardian. Children also bear responsibility in using library resources properly. More information on children and the Internet can be found in Librarian's Guide to Cyberspace for Parents and Kids by the American Library Association, Child Safety on the Information Highway by the National Center for Missing and Exploited Children, Free Access to Libraries for Minors, and other materials available at the library. Jervis maintains a web site at *http://www.borg.com/~jervis* that includes a children's web page which provides links to numerous Internet sites parents or guardians may find appropriate and useful for their children.

Appropriate Use & Disclaimer: All users of electronic resources are to act in a responsible and ethical manner, consistent with policies of the library and, for minors, consistent also with parental or legal guardian guidance. In accordance with federal and state laws and regulations, patrons are not permitted to use terminals for any illegal or criminal purpose, including, but not limited to, accessing legally obscene materials, harassment or stalking, unauthorized access to computer systems, or in a manner disruptive of other people's work. Legal references are available at the library. The library expressly disclaims any liability or responsibility arising from access to or use of information obtained through electronic information systems; and encompassing any activities by a user found to be illegal, or any consequences thereof. Patrons who violate policies risk losing their right to access the Internet and other electronic sources via library equipment.

Access and Privacy Restrictions: It is likely that the number of terminals will never equal demand. Access restrictions are essential for equitable and orderly use. A maximum of two people may use a terminal. The library reserves the right to enforce a time allowance per session, including printing, and to charge for printing. Due to the locations and configuration of the terminals, patrons' privacy is not ensured.

Staff Internet Assistance: Librarians will show patrons how to access the Internet and explain basic navigational commands. Lengthy one-on-one tutorials are not possible due to staffing constraints.

This policy may be revised from time to time by resolution of the Board of Trustees.

Revised and approved by the Board of Trustees 2/12/98

Reprinted courtesy Jervis Public Library.

UNIVERSITY OF PENNSYLVANIA (PHILADELPHIA, PENNSYLVANIA)

This rather lengthy academic policy is very thorough and contains a number of interesting features including a tiered system of priorities for networking uses, links to a number of other resources, a clear delineation of acceptable and prohibited uses, and an appendix of related materials including applicable state and federal laws.

PENN COMPUTING

POLICY

The overarching policy governing computing and networking at Penn is the Policy on Acceptable Use of Electronic Resources. The policy is reprinted in its entirety below. Faculty, staff, and students are urged to review and understand the contents of this policy. Violations of the policy may result in sanctions up to and including termination or expulsion.

POLICY ON ACCEPTABLE USE OF ELECTRONIC RESOURCES

Summary

This policy defines the boundaries of "acceptable use" of limited University electronic resources, including computers, networks, electronic mail services and electronic information sources, as detailed below. It includes by reference a self-contained compilation of specific rules that can be modified as the electronic information environment evolves.

The policy is based on the principle that the electronic information environment is provided to support University business and its mission of education, research and service. Other uses are secondary. Uses that threaten the integrity of the system; the function of non-University equipment that can be accessed through the system; the privacy or actual or perceived safety of others; or that are otherwise illegal are forbidden.

By using University electronic information systems you assume personal responsibility for their appropriate use and agree to comply with this policy and other applicable University policies, as well as City, State and Federal laws and regulations, as detailed below.

The policy defines penalties for infractions, up to and including loss of system access, employment termination or expulsion. In addition some activities may lead to risk of legal liability, both civil and criminal.

Users of electronic information systems are urged in their own interest to review and understand the contents of this policy.

Purposes

The University of Pennsylvania makes computing resources (including, but not limited to, computer facilities and services, computers, networks, electronic mail, electronic information and data, and video and voice services) available to faculty, students, staff, registered guests, and the general public to support the educational, research and service missions of the University.

When demand for computing resources may exceed available capacity, priorities for their use will be established and enforced. Authorized faculty and staff may set and alter priorities for exclusively local computing/networking resources. The priorities for use of University-wide computing resources are:

Highest: Uses that directly support the educational, research and service missions of the University.

Medium: Other uses that indirectly benefit the education, research and service missions of the University, as well as and including reasonable and limited personal communications.

Lowest: Recreation, including game playing.

Forbidden: All activities in violation of the General Standards or prohibited in the *Specific Rules* interpreting this policy.

The University may enforce these priorities by restricting or limiting usages of lower priority in circumstances where their demand and limitations of capacity impact or threaten to impact usages of higher priority.

Implied consent

Each person with access to the University's computing resources is responsible for their appropriate use and by their use agrees to comply with all applicable University, School, and departmental policies and regulations, and with applicable City, State and Federal laws and regulations, as well as with the acceptable use policies of affiliated networks and systems (See Appendices to *Specific Rules*).

Open Expression in the Electronic Information Environment: The rights to freedom of thought, inquiry and expression, as defined in the University's Guidelines on Open Expression, are paramount values of the University community. The University's commitment to the principles of open expression extends to and includes the electronic information environment, and interference in the exercise of those rights is a violation of this policy and of the Guidelines on Open Expression. As provided in the Guidelines, in case of conflict between the principles of the Guidelines on Open Expression and this or other University policies, the principles of the Guidelines take precedence.

General Standards for the Acceptable Use of Computer Resources: Failure to uphold the following General Standards for the Acceptable Use of Computer Resources constitutes a violation of this policy and may be subject to disciplinary action.

The General Standards for the Acceptable Use of Computer Resources require:

- Responsible behavior with respect to the electronic information environment at all times;
- Behavior consistent with the mission of the University and with authorized activities of the University or members of the University community;
- Respect for the principles of open expression;
- Compliance with all applicable laws, regulations, and University policies;
- Truthfulness and honesty in personal and computer identification;
- Respect for the rights and property of others, including intellectual property rights;
- Behavior consistent with the privacy and integrity of electronic networks, electronic data and information, and electronic infrastructure and systems; and
- Respect for the value and intended use of human and electronic resources.

Enforcement and Penalties for Violation: Any person who violates any provision of this policy, of the *Specific Rules* interpreting this policy, of other relevant University policies, or of applicable City, State, or Federal laws or regulations may face sanctions up to and including termination or expulsion. Depending on the nature and severity of the offense, violations can be subject to disciplinary action through the Student Disciplinary System or disciplinary procedures applicable to faculty and staff.

It may at times be necessary for authorized systems administrators to suspend someone's access to University computing resources immediately for violations of this policy, pending interim resolution of the situation (for example by securing a possibly compromised account and/ or making the owner of an account aware in person that an activity constitutes a violation). In the case of egregious and continuing violations suspension of access may be extended until final resolution by the appropriate disciplinary body.

System owners, administrators or managers may be required to investigate violations of this policy and to ensure compliance.

Amendment

Formal amendment of the General Standards of Acceptable Use of Computing Resources or other aspects of this policy may be promulgated by the Provost following consultation with the University Council Committee on Communications, publication "For Comment" in *Almanac,* a reasonable waiting period, and publication "Of Record" in *Almanac.*

Interpreting this policy

As technology evolves, questions will arise about how to interpret the general standards expressed in this policy. The Vice Provost for Information Systems and Computing shall, after consultation with the University Council Committee on Communications, and subject to the same waiting period and publication provisions as above, publish specific rules interpreting this policy.

Waiver

When restrictions in this policy interfere with the research, educational or service missions of the University, members of the University community may request a written waiver from the Vice Provost for Information Systems and Computing (or designee).

Further information

For further information about University computing regulations or Commonwealth of Pennsylvania and Federal computing laws, contact the University Information Security Officer at (215) 898-2172, or send e-mail to: security@isc.upenn.edu.

SPECIFIC RULES INTERPRETING THE POLICY ON ACCEPTABLE USE OF ELECTRONIC RESOURCES

The following specific rules apply to all uses of University computing resources. These rules are not an exhaustive list of proscribed behaviors, but are intended to implement and illustrate the General Standards for the Acceptable Use of Computer Resources, other relevant University policies, and applicable laws and regulations. Additional specific rules may be promulgated for the acceptable use of individual computer systems or networks by individual Schools, departments, or system administrators.

Content of communications

- Except as provided by applicable City, State, or Federal laws, regulations or other University policies, the content of electronic communications is not by itself a basis for disciplinary action.
- Unlawful communications, including threats of violence, obscenity, child pornography, and harassing communications (as defined by law), are prohibited.

- The use of University computer resources for private business or commercial activities (except where such activities are otherwise permitted or authorized under applicable University policies), fundraising or advertising on behalf of non-University organizations, or the reselling of University computer resources to non-University individuals or organizations, and the unauthorized use of the University's name, are prohibited. The Vice Provost for Information Systems (or designee) may specify rules and specific forums where limited use of University resources for non-recurring exchange and sale of personal items is permitted.

Identification of users

Anonymous and pseudonymous communications are permitted except when expressly prohibited by the operating guidelines or stated purposes of the electronic services to, from, or through which the communications are sent. However, when investigating alleged violations of the Guidelines on Open Expression, the Committee on Open Expression may direct the University's Information Security Officer, or an authorized system administrator, to attempt to identify the originator of anonymous/pseudonymous messages, and may refer such matters to appropriate disciplinary bodies to prevent further distribution of messages from the same source.

The following activities and behaviors are prohibited:

- Misrepresentation (including forgery) of the identity of the sender or source of an electronic communication;
- Acquiring or attempting to acquire passwords of others;
- Using or attempting to use the computer accounts of others;
- Alteration of the content of a message originating from another person or computer with intent to deceive; and
- The unauthorized deletion of another person's news group postings.

Access to computer resources

The following activities and behaviors are prohibited:

- The use of restricted-access University computer resources or electronic information without or beyond one's level of authorization;
- The interception or attempted interception of communications by parties not explicitly intended to receive them;
- Making University computing resources available to individuals not affiliated with the University of Pennsylvania without approval of an authorized University official;
- Making available any materials the possession or distribution of which is illegal;
- The unauthorized copying or use of licensed computer software;
- Unauthorized access, possession, or distribution, by electronic or any other means, of electronic information or data that is confidential under the University's policies regarding privacy or the confidentiality of student, administrative, personnel, archival, or other records, or as defined by the cognizant Data Steward;
- Intentionally compromising the privacy or security of electronic information; and
- Intentionally infringing upon the intellectual property rights of others in computer programs or electronic information (including plagiarism and unauthorized use or reproduction).

Operational integrity

The following activities and behaviors are prohibited:

- Interference with or disruption of the computer or network accounts, services, or equipment of others, including, but not limited to, the propagation of computer "worms" and "viruses", the sending of electronic chain mail, and the inappropriate sending of "broadcast" messages to large numbers of individuals or hosts;
- Failure to comply with requests from appropriate University officials to discontinue activities that threaten the operation or integrity of computers, systems or networks, or otherwise violate this policy;
- Revealing passwords or otherwise permitting the use by others (by intent or negligence) of personal accounts for computer and network access;
- Altering or attempting to alter files or systems without authorization;
- Unauthorized scanning of networks for security vulnerabilities;
- Attempting to alter any University computing or networking components (including, but not limited to, bridges, routers, and hubs) without authorization or beyond one's level of authorization;
- Unauthorized wiring, including attempts to create unauthorized network connections, or any unauthorized extension or re-transmission of any computer or network services;
- Intentionally damaging or destroying the integrity of electronic information;
- Intentionally disrupting the use of electronic networks or information systems;
- Intentionally wasting human or electronic resources; and
- Negligence leading to the damage of University electronic information, computing/networking equipment and resources.

APPENDICES

Relevant University policies

This Acceptable Use Policy incorporates and supersedes the earlier Policy on <u>Ethical Behavior with Respect to the Electronic Information Environment</u>. The use of computing resources is also required to conform to the following University policies:

- <u>Code of Student Conduct</u>
- <u>Guidelines on Open Expression</u>

In addition, specific policies of the University's Schools, departments, computer systems and networks, and other general University policies and regulations are also applicable to the use of computer resources. These policies include, but are not limited to, the following:

- <u>Patent Policy</u>
- <u>Copyright Policy</u>
- <u>Computer Software Policy</u>
- <u>Policy on the Uses of University Resources</u>
- <u>Policy on Confidentiality of Student Records and Information</u>
- <u>Policy Regarding Faculty Misconduct in Research</u>
- <u>Policy on Privacy of Electronic Information</u>

- Code of Academic Integrity
- Protocols for human subjects research: any research involving human subjects must be approved by the Committee on Studies Involving Human Beings — Acceptable Use Policies of individual Schools, departments, computer systems, and networks — Guidelines for administrators of University e-mail systems.

Applicable laws

Computer and network use is also subject to Pennsylvania and Federal laws and regulations. Suspected violations of applicable law are subject to investigation by University and law enforcement officials. Among the applicable laws are:

- *Federal Copyright Law:* U.S. copyright law grants authors certain exclusive rights of reproduction, adaptation, distribution, performance, display, attribution and integrity to their creations, including works of literature, photographs, music, software, film and video. Violations of copyright laws include, but are not limited to, the making of unauthorized copies of any copyrighted material (such as commercial software, text, graphic images, audio and video recordings) and distributing copyrighted materials over computer networks or through other means.
- *Federal Wire Fraud Law:* Federal law prohibits the use of interstate communications systems (phone, wire, radio, or television transmissions) to further an illegal scheme or to defraud.
- *Federal Computer Fraud and Abuse Law:* Federal law prohibits unauthorized access to, or modification of information in computers containing national defense, banking, or financial information.
- *Federal and Pennsylvania Child Pornography Laws:* Federal and Pennsylvania laws prohibit the creation, possession, or distribution of graphic depictions of minors engaged in sexual activity, including computer graphics. Computers storing such information can be seized as evidence.
- *Pennsylvania Computer Crime Law:* Pennsylvania law prohibits access to any computer system or network with the intent to interrupt an organization, or to perpetrate a fraud including the intentional and unauthorized publication of computer passwords.
- *Pyramid schemes/Chain Letters:* It is a violation of the Federal Postal Lottery Statute to send chain letters which request sending money or something of value through the U.S. mail. Solicitations through electronic messaging are also illegal, if they require use of U.S. mail for sending money/something of value.
- *Defamation:* Someone may seek civil remedies if they can show that they were clearly identified as the subject of defamatory messages and suffered damages as a consequence. Truth is a defense against charges of defamation.
- *Common law actions for invasion of privacy:* Someone may take seek civil remedies for invasion of privacy on several grounds.
- *Public disclosure of private facts:* the widespread disclosure of facts about a person, even when true, may be deemed harmful enough to justify a lawsuit.
- *False light:* a person wrongfully attributes views or characteristics to another person in

ways that damage that person's reputation.
- *Wrongful intrusion:* the law often protects those areas of a person's life in which they can reasonably expect they will not be intruded upon.

Related resources
- Information Security and Privacy
- Computing and networking policies and laws

Comments and Questions
Certifying authority: Vice Provost, ISC
URL: http://www.upenn.edu/computing/policy/
Last modified: 9 September 1997

COLLEGE OF THE HOLY CROSS (WORCESTER, MASSACHUSETTS)

Holy Cross, a small liberal arts college, has developed an access policy that addresses Web publishing, e-mail use, and system security. The policy provides for a complaints and appeals process, and includes an unusually thorough copyright protection statement.

DRAFT

COLLEGE OF THE HOLY CROSS
ENTERPRISE INTERNET POLICY

- Purpose of this Document
- Internal vs. External Use
- Publishing on the CWIS
- Editorial Policy
- Accountability
- Support
- Disclaimers
- Amendments
- Complaints or Violations of Policy
- Appeals Process
- Required Information
- E-mail and other Communication Privileges
- Passwords
- Privacy Issues
- Copyright and Use of Images
- Virus Precautions
- Inappropriate/Appropriate Material
- Netiquette Guidelines

Purpose of this document

This document describes the policies under which the Campus Wide Information System (CWIS) will be managed. The CWIS is established to improve electronic access to institutional information related to educational purposes and College activities, to provide tools for the College community to aid in the exploration of emerging technologies and to provide a user friendly gateway to the Internet. The CWIS is available to members of the campus community and, to a limited extent, off-campus users of the Internet. The privilege of contributing to the CWIS is extended to those in compliance with the College Computer Use Policy.

Internal vs. External Use

The College CWIS permits access to information by users both internal and external to the College community. Some information may be restricted to internal use only. Because placement of information on the CWIS for use by external users presents a view of the College to the outside world, additional requirements must be met. Contributions for external use may be subject to review by the College to ensure consistency with College policies.

Publishing on the CWIS

All recognized College organizations are allowed and encouraged to publish pages on the CWIS. Academic departments, administrative offices, and student groups may request access to resources necessary for Web development.

All personal pages on the campus network are subject to the College policies and the editorial policies defined herein. Currently, individuals may apply for space on the College servers for their page development. An application is available at *http://www.holycross.edcu/departments/ its/webapp.html*. For further information, please read the Guide to Writing for the Web and Creating Pages on the Holy Cross Web FAQ.

Editorial Policy

Publication of material that violates College policy, as stated in the Student Handbook, Student Computer Use, Use of Information Technology Services, Harassment on Campus and the Safety and Security Report or any other College policy documents is prohibited.

The College pages utilize a standard header and footer to maintain a consistent look and feel throughout the College's Web site. The template also adds a copyright statement and a mailto: link pointing to the author of the page. The template, in its simplest form, provides a standard framework for the development of College pages, and, more importantly, lends to the site's ease of use with consistent navigation tools, background color and text formatting.

Academic departments and administrative offices should use the College Template as a structural and design basis for their Web pages. Since the template carries the College name and implies an official connection to the College, the College reserves the right to deny any group or individual use of the College Template, including the header and footer images. The header and footer of the Template should not be modified except to update the e-mail address of the page's owner, the Copyright date and/or the last modified date.

Accountability

College pages, like all Web pages, provide links to sites across the Internet. Users should be aware that the College does not control the content (including decency and legality) of pages external to the College.

The College expects publishers of information over the campus network to accept full editorial responsibility for their documents. Web pages on the CWIS must abide by federal copyright laws and all applicable laws relating to public expression.

All pages must include an e-mail address for the person or persons responsible for the publication of the document. Running a Web site involves the continuing development of new pages and the updating of old pages. Linking pages from the CWIS implies an obligation to maintain and update those pages. Pages that are not maintained or reviewed may be removed from the system by the Web Development Team.

Support

The College fully supports all pages created under the direction of the Web Development Team. Limited resources restrict support for the independent publication of documents on the CWIS. Please read the Guide to Writing for the Web and Creating Pages on the Holy Cross Web FAQ or contact the Webmaster for more information.

Disclaimers

The College does not accept any responsibility or liability for information found on personal home pages. Personal home page authors are solely responsible for the content and organization of information they post, even if such information is accessed through College servers.

Amendments

The CWIS Policy Board reserves the right to amend these policies and procedures. Comments or suggestions about this document may be directed to the Web Coordinator.

Complaints or Violations of Policy

The College reserves the right to deny access to the CWIS to any Personal home page author providing inappropriate material or information through the College CWIS.

Complaints about the content of material on the CWIS should be directed to the Web Coordinator who will notify the contributor(s) of problems or policy violations.

The College also reserves the right to disable access to pages which are causing a negative impact on server or network performance. In such an event, the CWIS Manager will make a reasonable attempt to notify the responsible contributor before disabling access.

Violations of the rules can subject the offender to College disciplinary actions and in some cases, to state or federal prosecution.

Appeals Process

Individuals whose access to the CWIS has been suspended may appeal the decision.

Required Information

Contributions to the College CWIS must contain the following information:
- name and e-mail address of contributor
- author of the document (if different from contributor)
- maintainer of the document (if different from contributor)
- page title and description
- most recent revision date of material
- expiration date of material (if applicable)
- any known problems with the material or links

Electronic mail (email) and other Communication Privileges

Electronic mail is a fast, convenient form of communication. It is easy to send electronic mail to multiple recipients by using a mailing list. However, this ability to send messages to many people makes it easy to misuse the system. The general rule is: *use email to communicate with other specific users, not to broadcast announcements to the user community at large.*

For example, while it is appropriate to use email to have an interactive discussion with a set of people (even 20 or more users) or to use email to send a single copy of an announcement to some "bulletin board" facility with a wide readership (e.g. Network News, or an event), it is not appropriate to use email as a way to broadcast information directly to a very large number of people (e.g., an entire class). This is true whether you include the recipient usernames individually or by using a mailing list: *under no circumstance should you use the email system to get a general announcement out to some large subset of the College community.*

These guidelines are not based on etiquette alone: *the mail system has a finite capacity to process email messages.* When a user sends out an announcement to a huge list of recipients, the mail servers may get overloaded, disks may fill up, and staff intervention may be required. The overall result is a negative impact on the quality of service provided for all users.

Finally, the proliferation of electronic chain letters is especially abusive of the mail system and the network. Chain letters waste valuable computing resources, and may be considered harassing.

Creating or forwarding chain letters may subject you to College disciplinary proceedings. Creating or forwarding chain letters is strictly prohibited.

Password(s)

While you should feel free to let others know your username (this is the name by which you are known to the whole Internet user community), you should never let anyone know your account passwords. This includes even trusted friends and computer system administrators (e.g., Information Technology Services staff).

Giving someone else your password is like giving them a signed blank check or your charge card. You should never do this, even to "lend" your account to them temporarily. Anyone who has your password can use your account, and whatever they do that affects the system will be traced back to your username. *If your username or account is used in an abusive or otherwise inappropriate manner, you can be held responsible.*

Every student, faculty member or on-campus staff person who wants an account of his or her own can have one. If your goal is permitting other users to read or write some of your files, there are ways of doing this without giving away your password. There is never any reason to tell anyone your password.

For information about how to manage the security of your account, including advice on how to choose a good password, how to change passwords, and how to share information without giving away your password, contact the <u>Help Desk</u> in Fenwick B-22, x-3548.

Privacy Issues

The Electronic Communications Privacy Act (18 USC 2510 et seq., as amended) and other federal laws protect the privacy of users of wire and electronic communications.

Security mechanisms for protecting information from unintended access, from within the system or from the outside, are minimal. These mechanisms, by themselves, are not sufficient for a large community in which protection of individual privacy is as important as sharing. Users must therefore supplement the system's security mechanisms by using the system in a manner that preserves the privacy of themselves and others. All users should make sure that their actions don't violate the privacy of other users, if even unintentionally.

Some specific areas to watch for include the following:

- Don't try to access the files or directories of another user without clear authorization from that user.
- Don't try to intercept or otherwise monitor any network communications not explicitly intended for you. These include logins, e-mail, user-to-user dialog, and any other network traffic not explicitly intended for you.

- Unless you understand how to protect private information on a computer system, don't use the system to store personal information about individuals which they would not normally disseminate freely about themselves (e.g., grades, address information, etc.).
- Don't make any personal information about individuals publicly available without their permission. This includes both text and number data about the person (biographical information, phone numbers, etc.), as well as representations of the person (graphical images, video segments, sound bites, etc.). For instance, it is not appropriate to include a picture of someone on a World Wide Web page without that person's permission. (Depending on the source of the information or image, there may also be copyright issues involved.)
- Don't create any shared programs that secretly collect information about their users. This means, for example, that you may not collect information about individual users without their consent.

Copyright and Use of Images

All network publishers should be aware of US laws governing copyrights. Any violation of copyright or any other law is the sole responsibility of the web page creator. It is safest to assume that copyright laws which apply to printed material also apply to online publishing.

Only those images for which the College owns copyright privileges or for which it has been granted permission for electronic use may be reproduced on the CWIS. Contributors may not scan or use images from College publications without prior permission from the College or from other publications without prior permission from the copyright holder(s).

Many computer programs, and related materials such as documentation, are owned by individual users or third parties, and are protected by copyright and other laws, together with licenses and other contractual agreements. You must abide by these legal and contractual restrictions, because to do otherwise may subject you to civil or criminal prosecution.

Copyright-related restrictions may include (but are not necessarily limited to) prohibitions against:

- copying programs or data
- reselling programs or data
- redistributing or providing facilities for redistributing programs or data
- using programs or data for non-educational purposes
- using programs or data for financial gain
- using programs or data without being among the individuals or groups licensed to do so
- publicly disclosing information about programs (e.g., source code) without the owner's authorization

The above prohibitions focus on computer software, but copyright laws apply to all material on the CWIS. For example, it is inappropriate to copy any material owned by others from any source (e.g., cartoons, photographs, articles, poems, graphics scanned from a magazine, etc.) without permission of the owner. You should assume that all materials are copyrighted unless a disclaimer or waiver is explicitly provided. (This is particularly true on the World Wide Web; to include information from some other source on a Web page, link to it, don't copy it. In some cases, even this action may violate copyright or licensing agreements by enabling illegal redistribution of programs or data. If you're unsure, ask the owner.)

Virus Precautions

Software obtained via bulletin boards, shareware outlets, etc., should not be used on computers containing critical data. While the likelihood of infection by a "computer virus" may seem remote, it is still a possibility and a risk that cannot be taken with computers whose operations manipulate crucial information.

Inappropriate/Appropriate Material

The following materials may not be placed on the College CWIS:

- use of the CWIS for the purpose of private financial gain not relevent to the mission of the College
- material in violation of the College Computer Use Policy
- private or confidential information (directory information without permission, student records or addresses, etc.)
- use of CWIS to intimidate/harass any group or individual
- use of CWIS to voice obscene or threatening messages
- use of CWIS to engage in any illegal activity

The following materials may be considered suitable for presentation on the CWIS:

- policy documents, reports, procedures
- course descriptions and schedules
- instructional materials
- computer-based tutorials
- computing and library resources
- campus calendars and events
- departmental/student organization information
- descriptions of available services and resources

The above policy information was adapted with permission from materials at Bowdoin College and WPI

Submitted to: Information Technology Committee

The Crossway
By ITS Staff
Send Questions & Comments to *webmaster@holycross.edu*
Copyright © 1996 College of the Holy Cross
Last Modified: September 3, 1996

Reprinted courtesy College of Holy Cross.

ALPINE SCHOOL DISTRICT (AMERICAN FORK, UTAH)

This school policy is a concise statement of acceptable and unacceptable uses of the district's Internet and WAN resources. Note that this policy states that access will be filtered but urges further caution in Internet use, and that students are not allowed to use the Internet unsupervised. Alpine School District also requires students to have parental permission to use the Internet.

ALPINE SCHOOL DISTRICT

Rules & Regulations No. 5225
(Ref:) Policy No. 5225
Students

1.0   Internet/Wide Area Network Acceptable Use

    1.1   All use of the District Wide Area Network or Internet (both hereafter referred to as Internet) must be in support of public education and educational research.

        1.1.1   Any use of Internet for illegal or inappropriate purposes or to access materials that are objectionable in a public school environment, or in support of such activities, is prohibited. Language that is deemed to be vulgar is also prohibited.

            1.1.1.1 Illegal activities is defined as a violation of local, state, and/or federal laws. Objectionable is defined as materials that are identified as such by the rules and policies of the Utah State Board of Education that relate to curriculum materials and textbook adoption.

            1.1.1.2 Use of Internet to defame or demean any person is prohibited.

        1.1.2   Internet services provided by the school district are not intended for personal and private use.

    1.2   Public school student use may be permitted provided the student receives written parental permission and proper supervision is maintained by school officials. Students shall not use the Internet unsupervised.

    1.3   No student is to be identified over Internet by full name, photograph, etc. without specific written permission from the parent or legal guardian. Additionally, private information covered under GRAMA and/or FERPA, such as home address, telephone number, etc., shall not be published over the Internet without specific written parental permission.

    1.4   Alpine School District shall maintain a filtered access point for the Internet. While the district provides a filtered access point to the Internet, sites accessible via the Internet may contain material that is illegal, defamatory, inaccurate or potentially offensive to some people. Users are expected to use appropriate judgment in selecting and viewing Internet sites.

    1.5   Alpine School District shall be the final authority on use of the network and the issuance of public education user accounts.

        1.5.1   Elementary students shall not have school-based personal electronic mail.

        1.5.2   Upon recommendation of school administration and permission of parents, secondary students may have personal electronic mail.

    1.6   Appropriate disciplinary action shall be taken against any student who willfully and knowingly violates the Acceptable Use Policy.

November 11, 1997

ALPINE SCHOOL DISTRICT

Procedure No. 5225
(Ref:) Policy No. 5225
(Ref:) Policy No. 5225

STUDENTS

ALPINE SCHOOL DISTRICT
STUDENT PERMISSION TO USE INTERNET

STUDENT SECTION

Student Name_____Grade _____
(Last)   (First)   (Middle)

Social Security Number_____

School _____

Purposes (s) for which you wish to use the Internet:

I have read the Alpine School District Acceptable Use Policy and <u>Rules & Regulations</u> (No. 5525) and agree to abide by their provisions. I understand that violation of the use provisions stated in the Policy and Rules may constitute suspension or revocation of network privileges and/or disciplinary action.

Student's Signature _____ Date _____

SPONSORING PARENT OR GUARDIAN (REQUIRED)

I have read the Alpine School District Acceptable Use Policy and <u>Rules & Regulations</u> (No. 5225). I understand that administrators of the Alpine School District network have taken reasonable precautions to ensure that controversial material is not accessible. Nevertheless, I understand that materials which may be offensive to some may still be available and have discussed with my student appropriate use of such materials. I hereby give my permission for my child to use Internet service at school under appropriate supervision.

Parent's Signature _____ Date _____

Address _____ Phone_____

Approved by _____
(School Adminstrator)

COMMUNITY HIGH SCHOOL (ANN ARBOR, MICHIGAN)

This school has created a policy that covers most essential elements including a reaffirmation of an Internet code of conduct, statements of acceptable and restricted behavior, and guidelines for Web publishing.

COMMUNITY HIGH SCHOOL INTERNETWORK POLICY STATEMENT

A. Mission
B. Rights and Responsibilities
C. Code of Conduct
D. Access to Accounts
E. Usage Guidelines
F. Content Guidelines
G. Consent and Waiver Form

MISSION

The mission of the Community High School Internetwork initiative is to improve learning and teaching through interpersonal communication, student access to information, research, teacher training, collaboration and dissemination of successful educational practices, methods, and materials.

RIGHTS AND RESPONSIBILITIES

Community High School will be connected to the Internet through the National Science Foundation (NSF) and the University of Michigan Digital Library Initiative (UMDL). This connection will provide access to local, national and international sources of information and collaboration vital to intellectual inquiry in a democracy. In return for this access, every Digital Library user has the responsibility to respect and protect the rights of every other user in our community and on the Internet. In short, account holders are expected to act in a responsible, ethical and legal manner, in accordance with the Community High School Internet Code of Conduct, the missions and purposes of the other networks they use on the Internet, and the laws of the states and the United States.

COMMUNITY HIGH SCHOOL INTERNET CODE OF CONDUCT

The Internet Code of Conduct applies to all users of the CHS network. It reads:
"I will strive to act in all situations with honesty, integrity and respect for the rights of others and to help others to behave in a similar fashion. I will make a conscious effort to be of service to others and to the community. I agree to follow the access, usage, and content rules as put forth in the *Community High School Internetwork Policy Statement*."

ACCESS TO ACCOUNTS

A UMDL sponsored Internet account is a privilege offered each academic year to the following:
1. All Community High School Foundations of Science students, and their parent(s) or guardian(s).
2. All educators who are working with Foundations students, including classroom teachers, support personnel, administrators, tutors, music staff, specialists and mentors.
3. Educators and students from other educational institutions who are working in partnership with Community High School for specific purposes over a limited period of time.

USAGE GUIDELINES

The Internet account holder is held responsible for his/her actions and activity within his/her account. Unacceptable uses of the network will result in the suspension or revoking of these privileges. Some examples of such unacceptable use are:

1. Using the network for any illegal activity, including violation of copyright or other contracts;
2. Using the network for financial or commercial gain;
3. Degrading or disrupting equipment, software or system performance;
4. Vandalizing the data of another user;
5. Wastefully using finite resources;
6. Gaining unauthorized access to resources or entities;
7. Invading the privacy of individuals;
8. Using an account owned by another user;
9. Posting personal communications without the original author's consent;
10. Posting anonymous messages;
11. Downloading, storing or printing files or messages that are profane, obscene, or that use language that offends or tends to degrade others;
12. Violating the Content Guidelines as outlined below.

CONTENT GUIDELINES

Students will be allowed to produce materials for electronic publication on the Internet. Network administrators will monitor these materials to ensure compliance with content standards. The content of student materials is constrained by the following restrictions:

1. No personal information about a student will be allowed. This includes home telephone numbers and addresses as well as information regarding the specific location of any student at any given time.
2. All student works must be signed with the student's full name.
3. Individuals in pictures, movies or sound recordings may be identified only by initials (e.g. JQP for John Q. Public). Absolutely no first or last names may appear in reference to individuals in any image, movie, or sound recording.
4. No text, image, movie or sound that contains pornography, profanity, obscenity, or language that offends or tends to degrade others will be allowed.

COMMUNITY HIGH SCHOOL INTERNETWORK CONSENT AND WAIVER FORM

The consent forms are standard University of Michigan CAEN network access documents which have been slightly modified for use with the UMDL project. By signing the *UMDL Conditions of Use* and *Account Request* forms, the requester and his/her parent(s) or guardian(s) agree to abide by the restrictions outlined in this policy. The student and his/her parent(s) or guardian(s) should discuss these rights and responsibilities. Ultimately, parent(s) and guardian(s) of minors are responsible for setting and conveying the standards that their child or ward should follow. To that end, Community High School supports and respects each family's right to decide whether or not to apply for Internet access.

The UMDL is an experimental system being developed to support Community High School's educational responsibilities and mission. The specific conditions and services being offered may change from time to time. Community High School makes no warranties with respect to Internet service or content. Further, the requester and his/her parent(s) or guardian(s) should be aware that Community High School does not have control of the information on the Internet, nor can it provide barriers to account holders accessing the full range of information available. Other sites accessible via the Internet may contain material that is illegal, defamatory, inaccurate or potentially offensive to some people. Similarly, while Community High School supports the privacy of electronic mail, account users must assume that this cannot be guaranteed.

Community High School believes that the benefits to educators and students from access to the Internet, in the form of information resources and opportunities for collaboration, far exceed any disadvantages of access. We hope you and your student will join us on the Internet.

Appendix B

National and State Library Association Policies

The following are policy documents on freedom of access and Internet access from the American Library Association (ALA) and state library associations. The first two publications are the Library Bill of Rights and the Freedom to Read statement, both of which predate the Internet by decades—they were first adopted by the ALA in 1948 and 1953, respectively. These policies have subsequently formed the core of local library policies in thousands of communities in the United States. These and other ALA policy statements are available on the ALA Office of Intellectual Freedom Web site *www.ala.org/alaorg/oif/freeread.html.*

LIBRARY BILL OF RIGHTS

The American Library Association affirms that all libraries are forums for information and ideas, and that the following basic policies should guide their services.

I. Books and other library resources should be provided for the interest, information, and enlightenment of all people of the community the library serves. Materials should not be excluded because of the origin, background, or views of those contributing to their creation.

II. Libraries should provide materials and information presenting all points of view on current and historical issues. Materials should not be proscribed or removed because of partisan or doctrinal disapproval.

III. Libraries should challenge censorship in the fulfillment of their responsibility to provide information and enlightenment.

IV. Libraries should cooperate with all persons and groups concerned with resisting abridgment of free expression and free access to ideas.

V. A person's right to use a library should not be denied or abridged because of origin, age, background, or views.

VI. Libraries which make exhibit spaces and meeting rooms available to the public they serve should make such facilities available on an equitable basis, regardless of the beliefs or affiliations of individuals or groups requesting their use.

Adopted June 18, 1948.
Amended February 2, 1961, and January 23, 1980,
inclusion of "age" reaffirmed January 23, 1996,
by the ALA Council.
www.ala.org/work/freedom/lbr.html
Copyright © 1997 by American Library Association.

Reprinted by permission of the American Library Association

THE FREEDOM TO READ

The freedom to read is essential to our democracy. It is continuously under attack. Private groups and public authorities in various parts of the country are working to remove books from sale, to censor textbooks, to label "controversial" books, to distribute lists of "objectionable" books or authors, and to purge libraries. These actions apparently rise from a view that our national tradition of free expression is no longer valid; that censorship and suppression are needed to avoid the subversion of politics and the corruption of morals. We, as citizens devoted to the use of books and as librarians and publishers responsible for disseminating them, wish to assert the public interest in the preservation of the freedom to read.

We are deeply concerned about these attempts at suppression. Most such attempts rest on a denial of the fundamental premise of democracy: that the ordinary citizen, by exercising critical judgment, will accept the good and reject the bad. The censors, public and private, assume that they should determine what is good and what is bad for their fellow-citizens.

We trust Americans to recognize propaganda, and to reject it. We do not believe they need the help of censors to assist them in this task. We do not believe they are prepared to sacrifice their heritage of a free press in order to be "protected" against what others think may be bad for them. We believe they still favor free enterprise in ideas and expression.

We are aware, of course, that books are not alone in being subjected to efforts at suppression. We are aware that these efforts are related to a larger pattern of pressures being brought against education, the press, films, radio and television. The problem is not only one of actual censorship. The shadow of fear cast by these pressures leads, we suspect, to an even larger voluntary curtailment of expression by those who seek to avoid controversy.

Such pressure toward conformity is perhaps natural to a time of uneasy change and pervading fear. Especially when so many of our apprehensions are directed against an ideology, the expression of a dissident idea becomes a thing feared in itself, and we tend to move against it as against a hostile deed, with suppression.

And yet suppression is never more dangerous than in such a time of social tension. Freedom has given the United States the elasticity to endure strain. Freedom keeps open the path of novel and creative solutions, and enables change to come by choice. Every silencing of a heresy, every enforcement of an orthodoxy, diminishes the toughness and resilience of our society and leaves it the less able to deal with stress.

Now as always in our history, books are among our greatest instruments of freedom. They are almost the only means for making generally available ideas or manners of expression that can initially command only a small audience. They are the natural medium for the new idea and the untried voice from which come the original contributions to social growth. They are essential to the extended discussion which serious thought requires, and to the accumulation of knowledge and ideas into organized collections.

We believe that free communication is essential to the preservation of a free society and a creative culture. We believe that these pressures toward conformity present the danger of limiting the range and variety of inquiry and expression on which our democracy and our culture depend. We believe that every American community must jealously guard the freedom to publish and to circulate, in order to preserve its own freedom to read. We believe that publishers and librarians have a profound responsibility to give validity to that freedom to read by making it possible for the readers to choose freely from a variety of offerings.

The freedom to read is guaranteed by the Constitution. Those with faith in free people will stand firm on these constitutional guarantees of essential rights and will exercise the responsibilities that accompany these rights.

We therefore affirm these propositions:

1. **It is in the public interest for publishers and librarians to make available the widest diversity of views and expressions, including those which are unorthodox or unpopular with the majority.**

Creative thought is by definition new, and what is new is different. The bearer of every new thought is a rebel until that idea is refined and tested. Totalitarian systems attempt to maintain themselves in power by the ruthless suppression of any concept which challenges the established orthodoxy. The power of a democratic system to adapt to change is vastly strengthened by the freedom of its citizens to choose widely from among conflicting opinions offered freely to them. To stifle every nonconformist idea at birth would mark the end of the democratic process. Furthermore, only through the constant activity of weighing and selecting can the democratic mind attain the strength demanded by times like these. We need to know not only what we believe but why we believe it.

2. **Publishers, librarians and booksellers do not need to endorse every idea or presentation contained in the books they make available. It would conflict with the public interest for them to establish their own political, moral or aesthetic views as a standard for determining what books should be published or circulated.**

Publishers and librarians serve the educational process by helping to make available knowledge and ideas required for the growth of the mind and the increase of learning. They do not foster education by imposing as mentors the patterns of their own thought. The people should have the freedom to read and consider a broader range of ideas than those that may be held by any single librarian or publisher or government or church. It is wrong that what one can read should be confined to what another thinks proper.

3. **It is contrary to the public interest for publishers or librarians to determine the acceptability of a book on the basis of the personal history or political affiliations of the author.**

A book should be judged as a book. No art or literature can flourish if it is to be measured by the political views or private lives of its creators. No society of free people can flourish which draws up lists of writers to whom it will not listen, whatever they may have to say.

4. **There is no place in our society for efforts to coerce the taste of others, to confine adults to the reading matter deemed suitable for adolescents, or to inhibit the efforts of writers to achieve artistic expression.**

To some, much of modern literature is shocking. But is not much of life itself shocking?

We cut off literature at the source if we prevent writers from dealing with the stuff of life. Parents and teachers have a responsibility to prepare the young to meet the diversity of experiences in life to which they will be exposed, as they have a responsibility to help them learn to think critically for themselves. These are affirmative responsibilities, not to be discharged simply by preventing them from reading works for which they are not yet prepared. In these matters taste differs, and taste cannot be legislated; nor can machinery be devised which will suit the demands of one group without limiting the freedom of others.

5. **It is not in the public interest to force a reader to accept with any book the pre-judgment of a label characterizing the book or author as subversive or dangerous.**

The ideal of labeling presupposes the existence of individuals or groups with wisdom to determine by authority what is good or bad for the citizen. It presupposes that individuals must be directed in making up their minds about the ideas they examine. But Americans do not need others to do their thinking for them.

6. **It is the responsibility of publishers and librarians, as guardians of the people's freedom to read, to contest encroachments upon that freedom by individuals or groups seeking to impose their own standards or tastes upon the community at large.**

It is inevitable in the give and take of the democratic process that the political, the moral, or the aesthetic concepts of an individual or group will occasionally collide with those of another individual or group. In a free society individuals are free to determine for themselves what they wish to read, and each group is free to determine what it will recommend to its freely associated members. But no group has the right to take the law into its own hands, and to impose its own concept of politics or morality upon other members of a democratic society. Freedom is no freedom if it is accorded only to the accepted and the inoffensive.

7. **It is the responsibility of publishers and librarians to give full meaning to the freedom to read by providing books that enrich the quality and diversity of thought and expression. By the exercise of this affirmative responsibility, they can demonstrate that the answer to a bad book is a good one, the answer to a bad idea is a good one.**

The freedom to read is of little consequence when expended on the trivial; it is frustrated when the reader cannot obtain matter fit for that reader's purpose. What is needed is not only the absence of restraint, but the positive provision of opportunity for the people to read the best that has been thought and said. Books are the major channel by which the intellectual inheritance is handed down, and the principal means of its testing and growth. The defense of their freedom and integrity, and the enlargement of their service to society, requires of all publishers and librarians the utmost of their faculties, and deserves of all citizens the fullest of their support.

We state these propositions neither lightly nor as easy generalizations. We here stake out a lofty claim for the value of books. We do so because we believe that they are good, possessed of enormous variety and usefulness, worthy of cherishing and keeping free. We realize that the application of these propositions may mean the dissemination of ideas and manners of expression that are repugnant to many persons. We do not state these propositions in the comfortable belief that what people read is unimportant. We believe rather that what people read is deeply important; that ideas can be dangerous; but that the suppression of ideas is fatal to a democratic society. Freedom itself is a dangerous way of life, but it is ours.

This statement was originally issued in May of 1953 by the Westchester Conference of the American Library Association and the American Book Publishers Council, which in 1970 consolidated with the American Educational Publishers Institute to become the Association of American Publishers.

Adopted June 25, 1953; revised January 28, 1972, January 16, 1991, by the ALA Council and the AAP Freedom to Read Committee.

A Joint Statement by: *American Library Association* & *Association of American Publishers*
Subsequently Endorsed by:
- American Booksellers Association
- American Booksellers Foundation for Free Expression
- American Civil Liberties Union
- American Federation of Teachers AFL-CIO
- Anti-Defamation League of B'nai B'rith
- Association of American University Presses
- Children's Book Council
- Freedom to Read Foundation
- International Reading Association
- Thomas Jefferson Center for the Protection of Free Expression
- National Association of College Stores
- National Council of Teachers of English
- PEN American Center
- People for the American Way
- Periodical and Book Association of America
- Sexuality Information and Education Council of the United States
- Society of Professional Journalists
- Women's National Book Association
- The YWCA of the USA

www.alaorg/oif/freeread.html

ACCESS TO ELECTRONIC INFORMATION, SERVICES, AND NETWORKS

AN INTERPRETATION OF THE LIBRARY BILL OF RIGHTS

Introduction

The world is in the midst of an electronic communications revolution. Based on its constitutional, ethical, and historical heritage, American librarianship is uniquely positioned to address the broad range of information issues being raised in this revolution. In particular, librarians address intellectual freedom from a strong ethical base and an abiding commitment to the preservation of the individual's rights.

Freedom of expression is an inalienable human right and the foundation for self-government. Freedom of expression encompasses the freedom of speech and the corollary right to receive information. These rights extend to minors as well as adults. Libraries and librarians exist to facilitate the exercise of these rights by selecting, producing, providing access to, identifying, retrieving, organizing, providing instruction in the use of, and preserving recorded expression regardless of the format or technology.

The American Library Association expresses these basic principles of librarianship in its *Code of Ethics* and in the *Library Bill of Rights* and its Interpretations. These serve to guide librarians and library governing bodies in addressing issues of intellectual freedom that arise when the library provides access to electronic information, services, and networks.

Issues arising from the still-developing technology of computer-mediated information generation, distribution, and retrieval need to be approached and regularly reviewed from a context of constitutional principles and ALA policies so that fundamental and traditional tenets of librarianship are not swept away.

Electronic information flows across boundaries and barriers despite attempts by individuals, governments, and private entities to channel or control it. Even so, many people, for reasons of technology, infrastructure, or socio-economic status do not have access to electronic information.

In making decisions about how to offer access to electronic information, each library should consider its mission, goals, objectives, cooperative agreements, and the needs of the entire community it serves.

The Rights of Users

All library system and network policies, procedures or regulations relating to electronic resources and services should be scrutinized for potential violation of user rights.

User policies should be developed according to the policies and guidelines established by the American Library Association, including *Guidelines for the Development and Implementation of Policies, Regulations, and Procedures Affecting Access to Library Materials, Services and Facilities*.

Users should not be restricted or denied access for expressing or receiving constitutionally protected speech. Users' access should not be changed without due process, including, but not limited to, formal notice and a means of appeal.

Although electronic systems may include distinct property rights and security concerns, such elements may not be employed as a subterfuge to deny users' access to information. Users have the right to be free of unreasonable limitations or conditions set by libraries, librarians, system administrators, vendors, network service providers, or others. Contracts, agreements, and licenses entered into by libraries on behalf of their users should not violate this right. Users also have a right to information, training and assistance necessary to operate the hardware and software provided by the library.

Users have both the right of confidentiality and the right of privacy. The library should uphold these rights by policy, procedure, and practice. Users should be advised, however, that because security is technically difficult to achieve, electronic transactions and files could become public.

The rights of users who are minors shall in no way be abridged.[1]

Equity of Access

Electronic information, services, and networks provided directly or indirectly by the library should be equally, readily and equitably accessible to all library users. American Library Association policies oppose the charging of user fees for the provision of information services by all libraries and information services that receive their major support from public funds (50.3; 53.1.14; 60.1; 61.1). It should be the goal of all libraries to develop policies concerning access to electronic resources in light of *Economic Barriers to Information Access: An Interpretation of the Library Bill of Rights* and *Guidelines for the Development and Implementation of Policies, Regulations and Procedures Affecting Access to Library Materials, Services and Facilities.*

Information Resources and Access

Providing connections to global information, services, and networks is not the same as selecting and purchasing material for a library collection. Determining the accuracy or authenticity of electronic information may present special problems. Some information accessed electronically may not meet a library's selection or collection development policy. It is, therefore, left to each user to determine what is appropriate. Parents and legal guardians who are concerned about their children's use of electronic resources should provide guidance to their own children.

Libraries and librarians should not deny or limit access to information available via electronic resources because of its allegedly controversial content or because of the librarian's personal beliefs or fear of confrontation. Information retrieved or utilized electronically should be considered constitutionally protected unless determined otherwise by a court with appropriate jurisdiction.

Libraries, acting within their mission and objectives, must support access to information on all subjects that serve the needs or interests of each user, regardless of the user's age or the content of the material. Libraries have an obligation to provide access to government information available in electronic format. Libraries and librarians should not deny access to information solely on the grounds that it is perceived to lack value.

In order to prevent the loss of information, and to preserve the cultural record, libraries may need to expand their selection or collection development policies to ensure preservation, in appropriate formats, of information obtained electronically.

Electronic resources provide unprecedented opportunities to expand the scope of information available to users. Libraries and librarians should provide access to information presenting all points of view. The provision of access does not imply sponsorship or endorsement. These principles pertain to electronic resources no less than they do to the more traditional sources of information in libraries.[2]

Adopted by the ALA Council, January 24, 1996
[ISBN: 8389-7830-4]

[1]See: *Free Access to Libraries for Minors: An Interpretation of the Library Bill of Rights*; *Access to Resources and Services in the School Library Media Program: An Interpretation of the Library Bill of Rights*; and *Access for Children and Young People to Videotapes and Other Nonprint Formats: An Interpretation of the Library Bill of Rights*.
[2]See: *Diversity in Collection Development: An Interpretation of the Library Bill of Rights*.
See also: *Questions and Answers on Access to Electronic Information, Services and Networks: An Interpretation of the Library Bill of Rights*.

RESOLUTION ON THE USE OF FILTERING SOFTWARE IN LIBRARIES

WHEREAS, On June 26, 1997, the United States Supreme Court issued a sweeping re-affirmation of core First Amendment principles and held that communications over the Internet deserve the highest level of Constitutional protection; and

WHEREAS, The Court's most fundamental holding is that communications on the Internet deserve the same level of Constitutional protection as books, magazines, newspapers, and speakers on a street corner soapbox. The Court found that the Internet "constitutes a vast platform from which to address and hear from a world-wide audience of millions of readers, viewers, researchers, and buyers," and that "any person with a phone line can become a town crier with a voice that resonates farther than it could from any soapbox"; and

WHEREAS, For libraries, the most critical holding of the Supreme Court is that libraries that make content available on the Internet can continue to do so with the same Constitutional protections that apply to the books on libraries' shelves; and

WHEREAS, The Court's conclusion that "the vast democratic fora of the Internet" merit full constitutional protection will also serve to protect libraries that provide their patrons with access to the Internet; and

WHEREAS, The Court recognized the importance of enabling individuals to receive speech from the entire world and to speak to the entire world. Libraries provide those opportunities to many who would not otherwise have them; and

WHEREAS, The Supreme Court's decision will protect that access; and

WHEREAS, The use in libraries of software filters which block Constitutionally protected speech is inconsistent with the United States Constitution and federal law and may lead to legal exposure for the library and its governing authorities; now, therefore, be it

RESOLVED, That the American Library Association affirms that the use of filtering software by libraries to block access to constitutionally protected speech violates the *Library Bill of Rights*.

Adopted by the ALA Council, July 2 1997
www.ala.org/alaorg/oif/filt_res.html
Copyright © 1997 by American Library Association.

Reprinted by permission of the American Library Association

STATEMENT ON LIBRARY USE OF FILTERING SOFTWARE

AMERICAN LIBRARY ASSOCIATION/INTELLECTUAL FREEDOM COMMITTEE
JULY 1, 1997

On June 26, 1997, the United States Supreme Court issued a sweeping re-affirmation of core First Amendment principles and held that communications over the Internet deserve the highest level of Constitutional protection.

The Court's most fundamental holding is that communications on the Internet deserve the same level of Constitutional protection as books, magazines, newspapers, and speakers on a street corner soapbox. The Court found that the Internet "constitutes a vast platform from which to address and hear from a world-wide audience of millions of readers, viewers, researchers, and buyers," and that "any person with a phone line can become a town crier with a voice that resonates farther than it could from any soapbox."

For libraries, the most critical holding of the Supreme Court is that libraries that make content available on the Internet can continue to do so with the same Constitutional protections that apply to the books on libraries' shelves. The Court's conclusion that "the vast democratic fora of the Internet" merit full constitutional protection will also serve to protect libraries that provide their patrons with access to the Internet. The Court recognized the importance of enabling individuals to receive speech from the entire world and to speak to the entire world. Libraries provide those opportunities to many who would not otherwise have them. The Supreme Court's decision will protect that access.

The use in libraries of software filters which block Constitutionally protected speech is inconsistent with the United States Constitution and federal law and may lead to legal exposure for the library and its governing authorities. The American Library Association affirms that the use of filtering software by libraries to block access to constitutionally protected speech violates the Library Bill of Rights.

WHAT IS BLOCKING/ FILTERING SOFTWARE?

Blocking/filtering software is a mechanism used to:

restrict access to Internet content, based on an internal database of the product, or;

restrict access to Internet content through a database maintained external to the product itself, or;

restrict access to Internet content to certain ratings assigned to those sites by a third party, or;

restrict access to Internet content by scanning content, based on a keyword, phrase or text string, or;

restrict access to Internet content based on the source of the information.

PROBLEMS WITH THE USE OF BLOCKING/FILTERING SOFTWARE IN LIBRARIES

Publicly supported libraries are governmental institutions subject to the First Amendment, which forbids them from restricting information based on viewpoint or content discrimination.

Libraries are places of inclusion rather than exclusion. Current blocking/filtering software prevents not only access to what some may consider "objectionable" material, but also blocks information protected by the First Amendment. The result is that legal and useful material will inevitably be blocked. Examples of sites that have been blocked by popular commercial blocking/filtering products include those on breast cancer, AIDS, women's rights, and animal rights.

Filters can impose the producer's viewpoint on the community.

Producers do not generally reveal what is being blocked, or provide methods for users to reach sites that were inadvertently blocked.

Criteria used to block content are vaguely defined and subjectively applied.

The vast majority of Internet sites are informative and useful. Blocking/filtering software often blocks access to materials it is not designed to block.

Most blocking/filtering software is designed for the home market. Filters are intended to respond to the preferences of parents making decisions for their own children. Libraries are responsible for serving a broad and diverse community with different preferences and views. Blocking Internet sites is antithetical to library missions because it requires the library to limit information access.

In a library setting, filtering today is a one-size-fits-all "solution," which cannot adapt to the varying ages and maturity levels of individual users.

A role of librarians is to advise and assist users in selecting information resources. Parents and only parents have the right and responsibility to restrict their own children's access—and only their own children's access—to library resources, including the Internet. Librarians do not serve in loco parentis.

Library use of blocking/filtering software creates an implied contract with parents that their children *will not* be able to access material on the Internet that they do not wish their children read or view. Libraries will be unable to fulfill this implied contract, due to the technological limitations of the software, thus exposing themselves to possible legal liability and litigation.

Laws prohibiting the production or distribution of child pornography and obscenity apply to the Internet. These laws provide protection for libraries and their users.

WHAT CAN YOUR LIBRARY DO TO PROMOTE ACCESS TO THE INTERNET?

Educate yourself, your staff, library board, governing bodies, community leaders, parents, elected officials, etc., about the Internet and how best to take advantage of the wealth of information available. For examples of what other libraries have done, contact the ALA Public Information Office at 800/545-2433, ext. 5044 or *pio@ala.org*.

Uphold the First Amendment by establishing and implementing written guidelines and policies on Internet use in your library in keeping with your library's overall policies on access to library materials. For information on and copies of the *Library Bill of Rights* and its Interpretation on Electronic Information, Services and Networks, contact the ALA Office for Intellectual Freedom at 800/545-2433, ext. 4223.

Promote Internet use by facilitating user access to Web sites that satisfy user interest and needs.

Create and promote library Web pages designed both for general use and for use by children. These pages should point to sites that have been reviewed by library staff.

Consider using privacy screens or arranging terminals away from public view to protect a user's confidentiality.

Provide information and training for parents and minors that remind users of time, place and manner restrictions on Internet use.

Establish and implement user behavior policies.

For further information on this topic, contact the Office for Intellectual Freedom at 800/545-2433, ext. 4223, by fax at (312) 280-4227, or by e-mail at *oif@ala.org*.

www.ala.org/alaorg/oif/filt_stm.html

GUIDELINES AND CONSIDERATIONS FOR DEVELOPING A PUBLIC LIBRARY INTERNET USE POLICY
JUNE 1998

INTELLECTUAL FREEDOM'S MEANING AND SCOPE

Libraries are *the* information source in our society. They link individuals with the knowledge, information, literature, and other resources people seek. It is never libraries' role to keep individuals from what other people have to say.

By providing information and ideas across the spectrum of social and political thought, and making these ideas and information available and accessible to anyone who wants or needs them, libraries allow individuals to exercise their *First Amendment* right to seek and receive all types of information, from all points of view. Materials in any given library cover the spectrum of human thought, some of which people may consider to be untrue, offensive, or even dangerous.

In the vast amount of information on the Internet, there are some materials—often loosely called "pornography"—that parents, or adults generally, do not want children to see. A very small fraction of those sexually explicit materials is actually obscenity or child pornography, materials not constitutionally protected. The rest fall within the overwhelming majority of materials on the Internet protected by the First Amendment.

Obscenity and child pornography are illegal. Federal and state statutes, the latter varying slightly depending on the jurisdiction, proscribe such materials. The U.S. Supreme Court has settled most questions about what obscenity and child pornography statutes are constitutionally sound.

According to the Court:

Obscenity must be determined using a three-part test. To be obscene, (1) the average person, applying contemporary community standards, must find that the work, taken as a whole, appeals to prurient interests; (2) the work must depict or describe, in a patently offensive way, sexual conduct as specified in the applicable statutes; and (3) the work, taken as a whole, must lack serious literary, artistic, political, or scientific value.

Child pornography may be determined using a slightly less rigorous test. To be child pornography, the work must involve depictions of sexual conduct specified in the applicable statutes and use images of children below a specified age.

Many states and some localities have "harmful to minors" laws. These laws regulate free speech with respect to minors, typically forbidding the display or dissemination of certain sexually explicit materials to children, as further specified in the laws.

According to the U.S. Supreme Court:

Materials "*harmful to minors*" include descriptions or representations of nudity, sexual conduct, or sexual excitement that appeal to the prurient, shameful, or morbid interest of minors; are patently offensive to prevailing standards in the adult community as a whole with respect to what is suitable material for minors; and lack serious literary, artistic, political, or scientific value for minors.

Knowing what materials are actually obscenity or child pornography is difficult, as is knowing, when minors are involved, what materials are actually "harmful to minors." The applicable statutes and laws, together with the written decisions of courts that have applied them in actual cases, are the only official guides. Libraries and librarians are not in a position to make those decisions for library users or for citizens generally. Only courts have constitutional authority to determine, in accordance with due process, what materials are obscenity, child pornography, or "harmful to minors."

Obscenity and child pornography statutes apply to materials on the Internet; such materials are currently being regulated there. The applicability of particular "harmful to minors" laws to materials on the Internet is unsettled, however. Because of the uncertainty, various federal and state legislative proposals are pending specifically to "protect" children from sexually explicit materials on the Internet.

INTELLECTUAL FREEDOM'S FIRST AMENDMENT FOUNDATIONS

Courts have held that the public library is a "limited public forum." "Limited" means it is a place for access to free and open communication, subject to reasonable restrictions as to the time, place, and manner for doing so. As with any public forum the government has opened for people to use for communication, the First Amendment protects people's right to use the forum without the government interfering with what is communicated there. This is the very essence of the Constitution's guarantee of freedom of speech.

In a public forum, the government is prohibited from exercising discrimination with respect to the *content* of communication, unless the government demonstrates that the restriction is necessary to achieve a "compelling" government interest and there is no less restrictive alternative for achieving that interest. This means public libraries cannot exclude books about abortion just because they discuss the subject of abortion. That would be discrimination with respect to *content*. Books can be selected on the basis of content-neutral criteria such as the quality of the writing, their position on best-seller lists, the presence or absence of other materials in the collection related to certain time periods or historical figures, and the like; they can be deselected on the basis of wear and tear, the availability of more current materials, and similar criteria. Libraries, however, cannot deliberately suppress the record of human thought on a particular subject or topic.

Filtering and other means to block content on the Internet are mechanisms that allow discrimination with respect to the *content* of communication. Filters are notoriously inept at doing what computer software engineers have designed them to do—typically, block "hard-core pornography" and other "offensive" sites on the Internet. But even at their hypothetical best, mechanisms to screen and block content on the Internet exclude far more than just obscenity and child pornography. They exclude a wide range of sexually explicit materials protected under the Constitution. For instance, materials that depict homosexual relations, variations on conventional heterosexuality, and even nudity and heterosexual relations channeled toward reproduction and family life represent distinct subjects or topics. Their suppression is discrimination with respect to the *content* of communication.

Filtering and other means to block content on the Internet only can be utilized if the government—in this case, the public library—can demonstrate both that the need is compelling and that the method chosen to achieve the purpose is the least restrictive method possible.

The lawsuit brought by the American Library Association—*American Library Ass'n v. United States Department of Justice*, consolidated with and decided by the U.S. Supreme Court under the name of *Reno v. American Civil Liberties Union*—invalidated the provisions of the Communications Decency Act of 1996 that criminalized "indecent" and "patently offensive" electronic communication. The Court did so on the ground that those provisions, suppressing speech addressed to adults, reduced the entire population only to what is fit for children. It recognized "the governmental interest in protecting children from harmful materials," but found that less restrictive means were available to achieve that interest. In the context of limiting or avoiding children's exposure to possibly "harmful" materials on library computers with Internet access, less restrictive means than the use of filters are available.

It is well documented that filtering software is over-inclusive, blocking not only sites that may have sexual content, strong language, or unconventional ideas considered harmful or offensive—but also sites having no controversial content whatsoever. Filters are known to have blocked webpages of the Religious Society of Friends (Quakers), the American Association of University Women, the Banned Books page at Carnegie Mellon University, the AIDS Quilt site, the Fileroom Project censorship database, and even the conservative Heritage Foundation. The fact that the site covering the recent Mars exploration was blocked by certain software because the URL contained "marsexpl" shows how crude the filtering technology truly is. Over-inclusive blocking violates the First Amendment rights of youth and children, as well as adults, to access constitutionally protected materials.

Adults cannot be reduced to the level of what is fit for children, and the public library, therefore, cannot restrict them to Internet-access computers with filtering software. Young adults and children also have First Amendment rights, although such rights are variable, depending on the age of the minor and other factors, including maturity, not yet settled in the law. Even though minors' First Amendment rights are not as extensive as those of adults, the public library cannot restrict them solely to computers with filtering software. Libraries favor parents' control of their children's use of the Internet. Only unfiltered Internet access accommodates both parental control and sensitive recognition of the First Amendment rights of young people.

Librarians and the strength of their commitment to professional standards and values assure that, at least through the public library, the least restrictive means available to achieve the government's interest in protecting children will be implemented.

SPECIFIC INTERNET USE POLICY PROVISIONS

The position of the American Library Association is set forth in several documents adopted by the Council, its governing body. The *Interpretation of the Library Bill of Rights* entitled *Access to Electronic Information, Services, and Networks* calls for free and unfettered access to the Internet for any library user, regardless of age. The *Resolution on the Use of Filtering Software in Libraries* and the *Statement on Library Use of Filtering Software* reiterate the U.S. Supreme Court's declaration in *Reno v. American Civil Liberties Union* that the Internet is a forum of free expression deserving full constitutional protection. The Resolution and Statement condemn as a violation of the *Library Bill of Rights* any use of filtering software by libraries that blocks access to constitutionally protected speech.

Consistent with these policies, which collectively embody the library profession's understanding of First Amendment constraints on library Internet use, the *Intellectual Freedom Committee* offers guidelines to public libraries, as follows:

- Adopt a comprehensive, written Internet use policy that, among other things, sets forth reasonable time, place, and manner restrictions. Expressly prohibit any use of library equipment to access material that is obscene, child pornography, or "harmful to minors" (consistent with any applicable state or local law).
- Communicate the relevant policies for use of Internet-access computers to all library users, and include the parents of children who may use the library without direct parental supervision. Do so in a clear and conspicuous manner sufficient to alert library users that filtering software is not utilized.
- Post notices at all Internet-access computers that use of library equipment to access the illegal materials specified in the Internet use policy is prohibited.
- Offer a variety of programs, at convenient times, to educate library users, including parents and children, on the use of the Internet. Publicize them widely.
- Offer library users recommended Internet sites. For youth and children, especially, offer them, according to age group, direct links to sites with educational and other types of material best suited to their typical needs and interests (e.g., the American Library Association's *700+ Great Sites for Kids and the Adults Who Care About Them* and its Internet guide for young adults, *TEENHoopla*).

ANSWERS TO OBJECTIONS

Various metaphors have been offered, both by opponents of free and open access in libraries, as well as proponents, to explain the use of the Internet in libraries and the impact of filtering software. Two metaphors offered by opponents and the arguments built around them deserve close examination:

The "selection" metaphor. Filtering Internet resources is tantamount to selecting materials in a library. Since libraries, opponents of unfettered Internet access say, are not constrained to select any particular materials for their collections, filtering is constitutionally unobjectionable.

This metaphor is faulty. Filtering the Internet is not selecting materials. The only selection decisions involved in use of the Internet in libraries are those as to whether, for instance, the World Wide Web will be offered with other tools based on special Internet protocols, e.g., ftp (file transfer protocol) or telnet. Selecting the World Wide Web for the library means selecting the entire resource, just as selecting *Time* means selecting the entire magazine. A library cannot select *Time* and then decide to redact or rip out the pages constituting the "American Scene" feature or the "Washington Diary." That would be censorship. It is the same with the World Wide Web. It is not an accident of terminology that the Web consists of a vast number of webpages and that browser software permits the user to bookmark those that are interesting or useful.

The "interlibrary loan" metaphor. Internet access is tantamount to interlibrary loan service. Typing a website URL into a browser's location entry box and pressing the key amounts to an interlibrary loan request that the library, opponents of unfettered access say, is free to deny.

This metaphor is faulty, too. Far more frequently than typing and entering URLs, surfers of the World Wide Web click on hot links for automatic access to the webpages they wish to see. More significantly, absent financial constraints, any public library true to its function as a public forum makes available to users any constitutionally protected material, whether that means locating the material within the library itself or obtaining it elsewhere through interlibrary loan.

As articulated by the U.S. Supreme Court in the American Library Association case culminating in *Reno v. American Civil Liberties Union*, the Internet represents a vast library. It is a virtual library already present within any public library that selects Internet access. The fundamental First Amendment question is: given the free availability of a near-infinite range of content on the Internet, can the library ever deliberately deprive a library user of the constitutionally protected materials he or she seeks? The emphatic answer of the librarian informed by principles of intellectual freedom is: absolutely not.

But what about obscenity and child pornography, as well as, when minors are involved, materials "harmful to minors"?

- As for obscenity and child pornography, prosecutors and police have adequate tools to enforce criminal laws. Libraries are not a component of law enforcement efforts naturally directed toward the source, i.e., the publishers, of such material.
- As for materials "harmful to minors," it is true that, in some jurisdictions, libraries that choose not to utilize filtering or other means to block content on the Internet may find themselves in a "bind"; under some circumstances, they may be subject to liability under "harmful to minors" laws.

Libraries should be cautioned that laws differ from state to state, and they should seek advice on laws applicable in their jurisdiction from counsel versed in First Amendment principles. In particular, they should determine whether any "harmful to minors" law applies to materials available at the library, either through Internet access or otherwise. They should specifically inquire whether they are expressly exempt from the particular "harmful to minors" laws in their jurisdiction, as libraries frequently are.

Moreover, libraries should be aware that the legal framework and context of regulation is rapidly changing; federal, state, and local governments have begun to legislate specifically in the area of library Internet use. Libraries should actively oppose proposed legislation that exposes them to new liabilities and negatively impacts intellectual freedom. As always, they should be vigilant about new regulations of free speech.

Links to non-ALA sites have been provided because these sites may have information of interest. Neither the American Library Association nor the Office for Intellectual Freedom necessarily endorses the views expressed or the facts presented on these sites; and furthermore, ALA and OIF do not endorse any commercial products that may be advertised or available on these sites.

www.ala.org/alaorg/oif/internet.html
Copyright © 1998 by American Library Association.

Reprinted by permission of the American Library Association.

STATE ASSOCIATION POLICIES

State-level library associations have begun to adopt and issue statements of their membership on the topic of Internet access and filtering. The five sample policies in this appendix are from the Minnesota, Montana New Hampshire, New Jersey, Virginia Library Associations.

As of October 28, 1998, the American Library Association's Office for Intellectual Freedom had received copies of similar resolutions from eleven states. Copies of these and more recent resolutions can be found at *www.ala.org/alaorg/oif/intr_inf.html/#iupifs*.

STATEMENT ON INTERNET ACCESS

ADOPTED BY MINNESOTA LIBRARY ASSOCIATION
OCTOBER 1998

The Minnesota Library Association believes that a democracy can only succeed if its citizens have access to the information necessary to form opinions and make decisions on issues affecting their lives. It supports the principle of open access to information and ideas, regardless of the medium in which they exist. In addition, libraries provide opportunities to access the world of information to those who would not otherwise have such access. Therefore, the Minnesota Library Association has endorsed the American Library Association's Library Bill of Rights, Code of Ethics, Freedom to Read Statement, and its interpretations of the Library Bill of Rights.

As an extension of these intellectual freedom principles, the Minnesota Library Association endorses a position of full and free access to the Internet in libraries. This position is strengthened by the Supreme Court ruling which states that communications on the Internet receive the same level of constitutional protection as books, magazines, and newspapers.

The Association recognizes the issues and concerns generated from providing full access to the Internet. The debate regarding the use of filtering devices in response to these concerns is an important one. However, filtering devices block access to constitutionally protected speech and prevent the library users from accessing materials they determine to be most suitable for themselves. Therefore, the Minnesota Library Association does not recommend the use of Internet filters in libraries and opposes attempts by federal and state governments to mandate their use.

The Minnesota Library Association respects the responsibility of all parents/legal guardians to guide their own children's use of the library, its resources and services. The Association recommends that libraries teach responsible and effective use of the Internet through handouts, online guides, training sessions, and Web pages highlighting library recommended sources. In addition, the Association encourages the management of this resource in ways that protect the privacy of Internet users.

A RESOLUTION ON THE MANDATED USE OF INTERNET FILTERS IN LIBRARIES
MONTANA STATE UNIVERITY LIBRARIES

- Whereas, in light of recent and controversial efforts by federal and state entities to impose the mandated use of Internet filters on school and public libraries, and
- Whereas, libraries provide unfettered access to information in order to maintain an informed citizenry in our democratic society, and
- Whereas, objective evaluation of existing Internet filters reveals serious and inherent flaws in such software which unintentionally block valid sites while not blocking all sites which may prove potentially offensive to someone, and
- Whereas, prior restraint on access to information may be unconstitutional, and
- Whereas, librarians in public libraries do not serve a role as in loco parentis and cannot judge what a parent may wish for his or her child, and
- Whereas, sweeping state or federal constraints circumvent the rights of local citizens to exert local control
- Therefore be it resolved that the ASLD supports the principle of free and unrestricted access to information as a foundation of an informed citizenry in a democratic society,
- And be it farther resolved that, the ASLD opposes broad mandates to restrict access to the Internet through the exclusive use of Internet filters.
- And be it further resolved that the Montana Library Association does not recommend the use of Internet filters and opposes attempts by the federal or state governments to require such use. We believe that decisions regarding use of Internet filters must remain at the local level.

Kathy Kaya
Reference Librarian
phone: 406/994-5312
Montana State University Libraries
fax: 406/994-2851
PO Box 173320
e-mail: kkayaamontana.edu
Bozeman, MT 59717-3320

NEW HAMPSHIRE LIBRARY ASSOCIATION STATEMENT ON USE OF INTERNET FILTERS

The New Hampshire Library Association supports the principle of open access to information and ideas, regardless of the medium in which they exist. The Association believes that a democracy can only succeed if its citizens have access to the information necessary to form opinions and make decisions on issues affecting their lives. The Association regards access to this information as a right of free citizens. The Association endorses the American Library Association's Code of Ethics, Freedom to Read Statement, the Library Bill of Rights, and the interpretations of the Library Bill of Rights. The Association encourages libraries to adopt policies consistent with their resources and their mission while supporting these ideals.

The New Hampshire Library Association recognizes concerns regarding access to the Internet. The use of Internet filters to restrict access has been suggested, but poses many problems for libraries. Filters block valuable information, thus preventing the library from fulfilling one of its most basic missions. Because of their inherent imperfections, and an environment that changes daily, Internet filters offer parents and caregivers a false sense of security. In addition, filters may prove unconstitutional in public institutions, since some of the information they block is constitutionally protected speech.

The New Hampshire Library Association encourages librarians to develop and promote web sites, including links to the Internet resources that best satisfy users' interests and needs, and instruct users on effective searching techniques. Libraries may want to consider acceptable use policies. In addition, they may want to consider installation of privacy screens or placing workstations away from public view to protect users' confidentiality.

The New Hampshire Library Association does not recommend the use of Internet filters in libraries, and emphatically opposes attempts by federal and state governments to set such policy for libraries.

Adopted October 14, 1998

We gratefully acknowledge the Virginia Library Association, the Rhode Island Library Association, and the North Carolina Public Library Directors Association for making their resolutions available.

RESTRICTION OF INTERNET ACCESS AND USE OF FILTERING SOFTWARE IN LIBRARIES

A STATEMENT BY THE NEW JERSEY LIBRARY ASSOCIATION

The New Jersey Library Association:
- **Affirms** the right of all users, regardless of age, to have unrestricted access to the Internet
- **Opposes** the use of filtering software to *limit* Internet access, *but*
- **Affirms** the right of libraries to make filtering software *available* to those who *deliberately choose* to use it.

Since the advent of the Internet libraries have ceased to be repositories of *selected* materials alone and have become gateways to a vast and ever-changing array of resources not selected by library employees or—for the most part—evaluated by anyone in any way. In contrast to most of the print materials in library collections the majority of Worldwide Web sites are published by their "authors" and have not been subject to the scrutiny of a publisher's editorial staff. Many of these sites provide reliable, current, readily-retrievable information, some of which is obtainable nowhere else. Unfortunately, some Web sites, not always easily distinguished from others that are more reliable, provide misinformation. Furthermore, while works intended solely to stimulate sexual excitement or solely to encourage illegal activity are seldom added to general library collections, sites intended for no other purposes abound on the Web.

Throughout the nation public officials, activists' groups, and ordinary citizens have begun to demand that libraries deny or restrict access to those sites that violate particular—and often varying—criteria. Rarely, if ever, have demands for restriction of access to particular Web sites focused on the inaccuracy of information presented. Only occasionally have they focused on ideology. Most often they have focused on erotic content—on images far more frequently than on text.

Restricting access contravenes principles long espoused by the library profession. Furthermore, legal counsel to the NJLA Executive board has warned that any publicly-supported library which denies adults access to constitutionally-protected speech on the Internet will certainly be vulnerable to legal challenges based on the First Amendment to the U.S. Constitution, and that any public library which denies or restricts minors' access to constitutionally-protected speech on the Internet may be vulnerable to similar challenges.

Some have argued that a library's decision to provide access to some Web sites but not to all does not constitute a *denial* of access but is analogous to collection development decisions. Their argument is unconvincing. Budgetary constraints and space constraints prevent libraries from acquiring everything published. Therefore, in collection development libraries must decide to expend their limited resources for some items and not for others. In contrast, restricting Internet access costs *more* than providing unrestricted access. It constitutes *deliberate* denial of access.

The shortcomings of filtering software are widely recognized. Some filtering programs automatically block access to Web sites in which certain character strings appear, inadvertently blocking access to sites that those who install the programs would deem useful as well as to sites they would deem offensive. Other programs depend upon reviewers to select sites for blocking, but give no indication of the criteria the reviewers follow. Jonathan Wallace discovered, for example, that two programs blocked access to sites inimical to filtering software. Proprietors of certain programs refuse to release lists of blocked sites. Filtering programs sometimes block access to certain sites solely because they contain links to other sites deemed objectionable. CYBERsitter, for example, blocks access to the Web site of the National Organization for Women.

Nevertheless, some library users, even if they do not wish to infringe upon the rights of others, wish to shield *themselves* and *their own children* from unintentional exposure to text and images that they deem offensive. Libraries may legitimately accommodate these users by making filtering software *available* for them to *turn on at will.* Counsel to the Executive Board has expressed the opinion that doing so in no way constitutes restriction of constitutionally-protected speech, as long as the "default" setting for the software is "off" and users must deliberately turn it on.

Libraries that make filtering software available to their users are urged to provide them with information about its limitations and about possible unforeseen consequences of its use.

Adopted by unanimous vote of the N.J.L.A. Executive Board on April 21, 1998.

Reprinted with permission of the New Jersey Library Association

VLA INTELLECTUAL FREEDOM POSITION STATEMENTS

The Intellectual Freedom Committee is pleased to announce the adoption by the Virginia Library Association, at its June 12, 1998 Council meeting, of two position statements regarding intellectual freedom.

Together these statements offer standards for the protection of intellectual freedom and first amendment rights, and serve to guide the creation of policies on open access to all forms of information, including those in electronic media.

The "Intellectual Freedom Vision Statement" and "Open Access to the Internet"—reproduced below—will be incorporated into the *Virginia Library Association Manual* and the *Intellectual Freedom Manual*.

INTELLECTUAL FREEDOM VISION STATEMENT

The Virginia Library Association supports the principle of open access to information and ideas, regardless of the medium in which they exist. The Association believes that a democracy can only succeed if its citizens have access to the information necessary to form opinions and make decisions on issues affecting their lives. The Association regards access to this information as a right of free citizens. The Association endorses the American Library Association's Code of Ethics, Freedom to Read Statement, the Library Bill of Rights, and the interpretations of the Library Bill of Rights. The Association encourages local library systems to adopt policies consistent with their resources and their mission while supporting these ideals.

OPEN ACCESS TO THE INTERNET

The position of the Virginia Library Association on Open Access to the Internet is a logical extension of its traditional commitment to any resource which has been provided to the public by libraries. The library's primary role in offering Internet resources is not to restrict them, but to offer the public user assistance in locating, interpreting and appreciating resources.

The Virginia Library Association endorses a position of open access and opposes any state or Federally mandated restrictions on or of access to the Internet. The Association encourages local library systems to adopt policies consistent with their resources and their mission while supporting these ideals.

Appendix C

Internet Policy Checklist

INTERNET POLICY CHECKLIST

The following checklist recaps most of the points discussed in this book. All are possible areas of consideration for library Internet policies. Not all have to be referenced in the policy, but they should be considered in developing policy.

Mission
___ Primary use for Internet in the library (e.g., recreational, reference, universal access)

Physical Access
___ Location of computers
___ Arrangement of monitors
___ Use of privacy screens
___ Printing from the Internet
___ Downloading from the Internet
___ Use of personal disks
___ Access to the computer's hard drive
___ Use of Internet machines for other uses
___ Filtering

Procedural Access
___ Staff and public
___ Adults and children
___ Parental permission
___ Parental accompaniment
___ Library cardholders only or everyone
___ Sign-up sheets
___ Time limits
___ Fees
___ Password access
___ Required classes or training before use

Range of Allowable Use
___ Can users send e-mail?
___ Can users play interactive games?
___ Can users enter chat rooms?
___ Can users conduct commercial business over library workstations?
___ Can users view adult materials?
___ Do users have telnet access?
___ Can users load software?

Possible Elements of Unacceptable Use

___ Viewing/downloading/printing/distributing inappropriate material

___ Copyright violations

___ Illegal activity

___ Sexual harassment

___ Misrepresentation

___ Attempts to violate system security

___ Incurring costs to the library

___ For-profit activities

Guided Use

___ Will you offer a library Web page with preselected sites?

___ Will you offer library Web page with links to parental guidance materials?

___ Will you offer Web links to special sites for children?

___ What printed materials will you provide to guide patrons in using the Internet?

___ What are the parameters of one-on-one staff assistance?

___ Will you offer informal Internet training?

___ Will you offer classes in Internet training?

___ Will you require patrons to attend an orientation before using the Internet?

Implementing the Policy

___ How will the policies and unacceptable-use statements be posted?

___ Will you post copyright warnings on the printers?

___ What are the consequences of unacceptable use?

___ Are the policies easily enforceable?

___ Are procedures sufficient to permit staff to implement policies?

___ Are the policies and procedures unambiguous?

Appendix D

The following case is an actual court opinion. It illustrates how a library can become involved in a legal battle that centers on access to sexually explicit materials on the Web and one court's ruling on whether a public library can legally develop policies that restrict patron access to Internet materials based on their content.

Although some of the heading numbers appear to be inconsistent, they follow the original as posted on the Internet.

IN THE UNITED STATES DISTRICT COURT FOR THE
EASTERN DISTRICT OF VIRGINIA
Alexandria Division

MAINSTREAM LOUDOUN, et. al.,
    Plaintiffs,

          v.   Civil Action No. 97-2049-A

BOARD OF TRUSTEES OF THE
LOUDOUN COUNTY LIBRARY,
    Defendant.

MEMORANDUM OPINION

BACKGROUND

At issue in this civil action is whether a public library may enact a policy prohibiting the access of library patrons to certain content-based categories of Internet publications. Plaintiffs are a Loudoun County non-profit organization, suing on its own behalf and on behalf of its members, and individual Loudoun County residents who claim to have had their access to Internet sites blocked by the defendant library board's Internet policy. They, along with plaintiff-intervenors ("intervenors"), individuals and other entities who claim that defendant's Internet policy has blocked their websites or other materials they placed on the Internet, allege that this policy infringes their right to free speech under the First Amendment. Defendant, the Board of Trustees of the Loudoun County Library, contends that a public library has an absolute right to limit what it provides to the public and that any restrictions on Internet access do not implicate the First Amendment.

    The background of this action is fully summarized in this Court's April 7, 1998 Memorandum Opinion and will not be repeated in depth here. On October 20, 1997, defendant passed a "Policy on Internet Sexual Harassment" ("Policy") stating that the Loudoun County public libraries would provide Internet access to its patrons subject to the following restrictions: (1) the library would not provide e-mail, chat rooms, or pornography; (2) all library computers would be equipped with site-blocking software to block all sites displaying: (a) child pornography and obscene material;[1] and (b) material deemed harmful to juveniles; (3) all library computers would be installed near and in full view of library staff; and (4) patrons would not be permitted to access pornography and, if they do so and refuse to stop, the police may be called to intervene. See Pls. Ex. 1. It is the second restriction in the Policy that lies at the heart of this action.

    To effectuate the second restriction, the library has purchased X-Stop, commercial site-blocking software manufactured by Log-On Data Corporation. While the method by which X-Stop chooses sites to block has been kept secret by its developers, see Pls. Ex. 16, Dep. of

Michael S. Bradshaw ("Bradshaw Dep.") at 12-13, it is undisputed that it has blocked at least some sites that do not contain any material that is prohibited by the Policy.[2]

If a patron is blocked from accessing a site that she feels should not be blocked under the Policy, she may request that defendant unblock the site by filing an official, written request with the librarian stating her name, the site she wants unblocked, and the reason why she wants to access the site. *See* Intervs. Ex. 21, Request to Review Blocked Site. The librarian will then review the site and manually unblock it if he determines that the site should not be blocked under the Policy. There is no time limit in which a request must be handled and no procedure for notifying the patron of the outcome of a request. *See* Pls. Ex. 18, Deposition of Cindy Timmerman at 93-94. All unblocking requests to date have been approved. *See* Def. Ex. 15, Decl. of Douglas Henderson ("Henderson Decl.") at ¶ 18.

Plaintiffs and intervenors both allege that the Policy, as written and as implemented, violates their First Amendment rights because it impermissibly discriminates against protected speech on the basis of content and constitutes an unconstitutional prior restraint. In response, defendant contends: (1) intervenors do not have standing; (2) the Policy does not implicate the First Amendment and is reasonable; (3) the Policy is the least restrictive means to achieve two compelling government interests; and (4) the library has statutory immunity from this action.

In the motions now before the Court, plaintiffs, intervenors, and defendant each ask the Court to grant summary judgement their favor. Intervenors also ask the Court to permit them to substitute for three of their parties.[3]

ANALYSIS

I. Standing

Defendant alleges that all of the intervenors lack standing. Intervenors include three websites (the Safer Sex Page, Banned Books Online, and the Books for Gay and Lesbian Teens/Youth page), two non-profit corporations with websites (the American Association of University Women and the Renaissance Transgender Association), one for-profit corporation with a website (The Ethical Spectacle), one newspaper columnist whose articles are published on a website (Rob Morse, writer for the *San Francisco Examiner*), and an artist whose work is published on a website (Sergio Arau). *See* February 6, 1998 Mot. Intervene as Pls.

A. Non-Jural Persons

Defendant argues that the three website intervenors lack standing because they are non-jural entities, being neither individual persons nor corporations. While intervenors assert that these three entities do have standing as alleged in their complaint, they have filed a motion to Substitute Parties to resolve this dispute. In each case, they wish to replace the web page with the individual who owns and operates it. Specifically, intervenors would substitute Christopher Filkins for The Safer Sex Page, John Ockerbloom for Banned Books Online, and Jeremy Meyers for Books for Gay and Lesbian Teens/Youth. These individuals are jural entities with a clear First Amendment interest in communicating the speech they have published via these sites.

Defendant contends that the Motion to Substitute Parties should be denied for two reasons. First, defendant alleges it would be prejudiced by adding these individuals as named intervenors at this late stage of the proceedings. All three individuals, however, were named in the original complaint and there has been no problem deposing them or obtaining discovery from and about them. Defendant cannot point to any specific actual or potential prejudice to its case and we find that there would be none. Second, defendant contends that the real party in interest in this litigation is the ACLU, which represents the Renaissance Transgender Association, and that the dismissal of the website intervenors would still leave the Renaissance Transgender Association as an adequate nominal party through which the ACLU could pursue this action. Defendant has not presented a single piece of evidence to substantiate this allegation or to demonstrate that these individuals have not asserted a real injury-in-fact that could be redressed by this Court. Therefore, intervenors' motion to substitute parties will be granted, which moots defendant's argument that these three intervenors do not have standing because they are non-jural entities.

B. Websites Never Blocked

Defendant next alleges that five of the intervenors, John Ockerbloom d/b/a Banned Books Online, the American Association of University Women, The Ethical Spectacle, Robert Morse, and Sergio Arau, have no standing because there is no evidence in the record that their websites were ever blocked. To the contrary, intervenors have submitted the Declaration of Alpna Cassidy Sehgal, a staff attorney for the ACLU. *See* Intervs. Decl. N ("Sehgal Decl."). In the Declaration, Sehgal alleges that she visited the Rust Branch of the Loudoun County Public Library on February 2, 1998 and, as a result of the Policy, was denied access, in whole or in part, to the websites of each of the intervenors. *See id.* at ¶¶ 2, 9-12, 14-16, 20.

Defendant first alleges that the Sehgal Declaration should be disregarded pursuant to the lawyer-witness rule. Intervenors respond that the lawyer-witness rule prohibits an attorney who may be called as a witness only from acting as an advocate at trial, and not from assisting with trial preparation. *See*, e.g., *Culebras Enterprises Corp. v. Riviera-Rios*, 846 F.2d 94 (1st Cir. 1988) (finding that lawyers who did substantial pretrial work did not violate lawyer-witness rule because they were not "advocates at trial"). Intervenors' statement of the law is correct. it is undisputed that Sehgal has not and will not act as an advocate in this action. We find no reason to disregard her declaration.

In the alternative, defendant contends that there is a material factual dispute as to whether these five sites were ever blocked. Defendant alleges that it attempted to access the sites of all eight intervenors on February 6, 1998, using a library computer employing the X-Stop software, and that only The Safer Sex Page, the Books for Gay and Lesbian Teens/Youth page, and the Renaissance Transgender Association page were blocked at that time. *See* Def. Ex. 18, Def. Answer to Intervs. Sec. Interrogs. Defendant asserts that this evidence contradicts Sehgal's declaration and, therefore, creates a dispute as to a material fact. Defendant's own witnesses, however, demonstrate the dynamic nature of the Internet, *see* Henderson Decl. at ¶ 14, and X-Stop, their filtering software. *See* Bradshaw Dep. at 49-51. It is entirely possible that these sites were blocked on February 2 but not blocked four days later.[4] Therefore, we find that the Sehgal declaration is unrebutted evidence that the sites, in whole or in part, were blocked by defendant on February 2, 1998, and therefore that these intervenors will not be denied standing on this basis.

C. Websites That Were Blocked

As noted above, defendant concedes that it blocked three of the intervenors' sites, The Safer Sex Page, the Books for Gay and Lesbian Teens/Youth page, and the Renaissance Transgender Association page, as of February 6, 1998, even though these sites admittedly did not violate the Policy. *See* Def. Ex. 18, Def. Answer Intervs. Sec. Interrogs. It is undisputed that by May 1998 defendant had unblocked these three sites, *see id.*, and there is no evidence that any of intervenors' sites have been blocked since then. Defendant asserts that none of the intervenors have standing to sue now because their sites are no longer blocked, they do not contain "any material that would even be considered a candidate for blocking," and "there is no reason to expect that any of these web sites will ever be candidates for blocking under the Internet Policy." Def. Mem. Support Motion Summ. J. at 6, 8. Therefore, defendant contends, intervenors cannot meet the burden of demonstrating that they have an "injury that could be redressed if the requested relief is granted." *Lujan v. Defenders of Wildlife*, 504 U.S. 555, 561 (1992). *See, Simon v. Eastern Ky. Welfare Rights Org*, 426 U.S. 26, 45-46 (1976) (stating that a plaintiff must demonstrate a "likelihood that the requested relief will redress the alleged injury").

In response, intervenors allege that they have standing to sue if there is a legitimate fear that the policy will be enforced against them, or if defendant, having blocked intervenors' speech on one occasion, is likely to do so again. *See ACLU v. Reno*, 929 F. Supp. 824, 851 (E.D. Pa. 1996) , *aff'd*, 117 S. Ct. 2329 (1997) (holding that plaintiffs had standing to bring pre-enforcement facial challenge against the Communications Decency Act). One way to demonstrate that a defendant is likely to block intervenors' speech is to show that it retains unfettered discretion in enforcing the Policy. *See 11126 Baltimore Boulevard, Inc. v. Prince George's County*, 58 F.3d 988, 993-94 (4th Cir. 1995) (finding a facial challenge to an ordinance restricting speech appropriate where a plaintiff alleges the ordinance does not contain "specific standards to guide the decisionmaker" or "appropriate procedural safeguards to ensure a prompt resolution").

Intervenors also argue that "'voluntary cessation of allegedly illegal conduct does not deprive the tribunal of the power to hear and determine the case.'" *Commonwealth of Virginia v. Califano*, 631 F.2d 324, 326 (4th Cir. 1980) (quoting *United States v. W.T. Grant Co.* 345 U.S. 629, 632 (1953)). In *W.T. Grant*, the Supreme Court warned that courts must "beware of efforts to defeat injunctive relief by protestations of repentance and reform, especially when abandonment seems timed to anticipate suit, and there is a probability of resumption." Id. at 632 n.5. The Court further explained that a voluntary cessation of wrongful activity would only moot an action if "the defendant can demonstrate that there is no reasonable expectation that the wrong will be repeated." Id. at 633. To do otherwise, the Court opined, would leave the defendant "free to return to his old ways." Id. at 632.

Defendant has failed to carry its burden of demonstrating that the wrong will not be repeated. Douglas Henderson, defendant's Director of Library Services, has acknowledged that the content and imagery on websites frequently changes. *See* Henderson Decl. at ¶ 14 (acknowledging "the changing nature of the WorldWideWeb"). In addition, the materials from one website also may be transferred to another website located at a different address. *See* Intervs. Decl. A, Decl. of Sergio Arau ("Arau Decl.") at ¶ 5. Such changes could lead X-Stop to block even previously unblocked material. Therefore, intervenors are justified in having a reasonable expectation that they may be blocked again in the future.

Furthermore, defendant's concession that none of the intervenors' websites contain or likely will ever contain material that violates the Policy does not prevent intervenors from having standing given defendant's admissions that X-Stop blocks websites that do not violate the Policy and that defendant does not even know what websites X-Stop blocks or how it selects them. *See* Henderson Decl. at ¶ 18 (stating that defendant is aware that X-Stop blocks websites that defendant would not block "if we knew about them"); Bradshaw Dep. at 12-13 (stating that Log-On Data Corp. has refused to provide defendant with the criteria it uses to censor websites); Pls. Ex. 2, Dep. of Douglas Henderson ("Henderson Dep."), at 494 (stating that defendant has never seen a list of the blocked sites). On this record, because defendant cannot "demonstrate that there is no reasonable expectation that the wrong will be repeated," and because a declaratory judgment would provide intervenors with relief, we find that the fact they are currently unblocked does not prevent intervenors from having standing to pursue this action.[5]

D. Banned Books Online

Defendant next claims that one of the intervenors, John Ockerbloom d/b/a Banned Books online, lacks standing because defendant has never blocked his website. Ockerbloom admits that there is no evidence that defendant has ever blocked his website, but asserts that he has standing because defendant blocked a link[6] from his website to a website providing the text of E for Ecstasy, a book about the history of the drug MDMA. *See* Sehgal Decl. at ¶ 15. Ockerbloom alleges that part of the mission of his website is to provide users with access to censored materials, such as E for Ecstasy. Therefore, blocking access to one of the links is a concrete injury to his free speech rights.

The extent to which free speech protection reaches links on the Internet has not been directly addressed by any court. In more traditional contexts, individuals are frequently found to have standing to challenge restrictions on speech in which they have a sufficient interest even where that speech is not originally theirs. For example, owners of adult bookstores can challenge censorship of books they intend to sell,[7] owners of adult movie theaters have standing to protest censorship of movies they intend to show,[8] and library patrons have standing to challenge library policies restricting their exercise of the First Amendment right to receive information.[9] In essence, intervenor Ockerbloom has sought to intervene in this action because he claims to have an interest in the E for Ecstasy page, material he explicitly and purposely has made available for use by others.

While this argument is initially appealing, its consequences would be unmanageable. Because of the ease of establishing links to any and every site on the Internet, if we find that

Ockerbloom has standing in this case it would be impossible to prevent anyone from asserting standing to protest alleged Internet-related First Amendment harms wherever, whenever, and to whomever they occur. For example, by virtue of the ACLU having placed links to each of the intervenors' web pages on its own Internet site, *see* Def. Ex. 18, thereby asserting an interest in the speech of the intervenors, it would be able to assert the rights of each intervenor in a lawsuit brought only in its own name. Such a result would make a mockery of traditional standing principles. Therefore, we find that John Ockerbloom d/b/a Banned Books On-Line, does not have standing and should be dismissed from this action.

E. Sergio Arau

Defendant also asserts that intervenor Sergio Arau does not have standing because he does not have any material published on the Internet to block. Arau responds that some of his work was blocked as of February 2, 1998, *see* Sehgal Decl. at ¶ 20, and that similar artwork and music of his are currently available on the Internet, although at a new website. *See* Arau Decl. at 5; Arau Decl. Ex. 7. Defendant has not rebutted this evidence. Therefore, we find that Arau's work is currently displayed on the Internet, that it is potentially at risk of being blocked again by defendant, and that he has standing to pursue this action.

F. Robert Morse

Lastly, defendant argues that intervenor Robert Morse, a columnist for the *San Francisco Examiner*, does not have standing because he gave up any First Amendment right in his columns by ceding the intellectual property rights in those columns to his newspaper. Morse counters that there is no legal support for the proposition that by relinquishing intellectual property rights in his work an individual also surrenders his First Amendment interest in that work. Indeed, authors and journalists who have given up the copyright to their work can still he sued for defamation resulting from that work and can still offer the First Amendment as a defense to such lawsuits. *See*, e.g., *Masson v. New Yorker*, 501 U.S. 496, 499 (1991) (noting that "[t]he First Amendment protects authors and journalists who write about public figures"). We find no legal or logical support for defendant's position and, therefore, find that Morse has standing to intervene in this action.

II. Immunity

Defendant has requested that we reconsider our previous finding that it is not immune from this litigation pursuant to a provision of the 1996 Communications Decency Act granting absolute immunity to good faith users of filtering software. *See* 47 U.S.C. § 230(c)(2)(A). In our previous opinion, we found that § 230 provides immunity from actions for damages; it does not, however, immunize defendant from an action for declaratory and injunctive relief. We see no reason to stray from our earlier decision, which is the law of this case. If Congress had intended the statute to insulate Internet providers from both liability and declaratory and injunctive relief, it would have said so.

IV. Strict Scrutiny Standard

Defendant has also requested that we reconsider our earlier findings (1) that the Policy implicates the First Amendment and (2) that the appropriate standard of review is strict scrutiny.

A. Implicating the First Amendment

Defendant first contends that the Policy should really be construed as a library acquisition decision, to which the First Amendment does not apply,[10] rather than a decision to remove library materials. Plaintiffs and intervenors contend that this issue has already been decided by this Court and is the law of the case. *See* Mainstream Loudoun v. Board of Trustees of the Loudoun county Library, et al., 2 F.Supp. 2d 783, 794-95 (E.D. Va. 1998) ("[T]he Library Board's action is more appropriately characterized as a removal decision"; "[W]e conclude that [*Pico*] stands for the proposition the First Amendment applies to, and limits, the discretion of a public library to place content-based restrictions on access to constitutionally protected materials within its collection.").

We addressed the acquisition/removal argument at length in our previous decision and defendant has not presented a single new argument or authority to support its position. Indeed, defendant's own expert, David Burt, undercuts its argument by acknowledging that "[f]iltering cannot be rightly compared to 'selection', since it involves an active, rather than passive exclusion of certain types of content." Def. Ex. 21, Rep. of David Burt ("Burt Rep.") at 15. Therefore, we decline to reconsider our earlier ruling on this issue.

B. Forum Analysis

Next, defendant contends that even if the First Amendment does apply, we should apply a less stringent standard than strict scrutiny. Specifically, defendant argues that because the library is a non-public forum, the Policy should be reviewed by an intermediate scrutiny standard, examining whether it is reasonably related to an important governmental interest. Citing *Kreimer v. Bureau of Police*, 958 F.2d 1242 (3d Cir. 1992), defendant argues that public libraries are non-public fora and, therefore, content-based speech regulations are not subject to the strict scrutiny standard. Rather, it asserts, such regulations need only be "reasonable and viewpoint neutral" to he upheld. Def. Brief in Opp. at 34-37 (citing *International Soc'y for Krishna Consciousness, Inc. v. Lee*, 505 U.S. 672, 694 (1992) (Kennedy, J. concurring)). Plaintiffs and intervenors respond that defendant has misread *Kreimer* and moreover that the library is a limited public forum in which content-based regulations are subject to strict scrutiny.

Defendant concedes that the Policy is a content-based regulation of speech and that content-based regulations of speech in a limited public forum are subject to strict scrutiny. Def. Brief in Opp. at 36-37. The only issue before us, then, is whether the library is a limited public forum or a non-public forum. In *Perry Education Ass'n v. Perry Local Ass'n*, 460 U.S. 37, 45-46 (1983), the Supreme Court identified three categories of fora for the purpose of analyzing the degree of protection afforded to speech. The first category is the traditional forum, such as a sidewalk or public park. These are "places which by long tradition or by government fiat have been devoted to assembly and debate". Id. at 4 5. Second is the limited or designated forum, such as a school board meeting or municipal theater. This category consists of public property which the State has opened for use by the public as a place for expressive activity". Id. The last category is the non-public forum, such as a government office building or a teacher's mailbox, which is not "by tradition or designation a forum for public communication." Id. at 46. It is undisputed that the Loudoun County libraries have not traditionally been open to the public for all forms of expressive activity and, therefore, are not traditional public fora.

A limited public forum is created when the government voluntarily opens a particular forum to the public for expressive activity. *See id.* at 45. The government can create a limited public forum for all, some, or only a single kind of expressive activity. *See, e.g., Kreimer,* 958 F.2d at 1259 (finding that the government had made the public library a limited public forum for the expressive activity of "communication of the written word"). Even though it is not required to operate such a forum, once the government does so it "is bound by the same standards as apply in a traditional public forum." *Perry,* 460 U.S. at 46. Therefore, content-neutral time, place, and manner regulations on the expressive activity or activities allowed are permissible if narrowly tailored to serve a significant government interest while leaving open ample alternative channels of communication, *see Kreimer,* 958 F.2d at 1262. Any content-based restriction, however, must he "narrowly drawn to effectuate a compelling state interest." *Perry,* 460 U.S. at 46.

The only court to have examined whether a public library constitutes a limited public forum is the Third Circuit in Kreimer.[11] In determining that the public library constituted a limited public forum,[12] the court considered three factors: government intent; extent of use; and nature of the forum. *See id.* at 1259. We agree that these are the crucial factors in determining whether a forum is a limited or a non-public forum.

1. Government Intent

The record establishes that the Loudoun County government, through defendant library board, intended to create a public forum when it authorized its public library system. In a resolution it adopted in 1995 and reaffirmed last year, defendant declared that its "primary objective . . . [is] that the people have access to all avenues of ideas." *See* Pls. Ex. 5, Loudoun County Library Board of Trustees Resolution, Freedom For Ideas — Freedom From Censorship, May 15, 1995 ("May 15 Resolution"). Furthermore, the same resolution states that the public interest requires "offering the widest possible diversity of views and expressions" in many different media, not diminishing the library collection simply because "minors might have access to materials with controversial content, not excluding any materials because of the nature of the information or views within, and not censoring ideas. Id. We find that defendant intended to designate the Loudoun County libraries as public fora for the limited purposes of the expressive activities they provide, including the receipt and communication of information through the Internet.[13]

2. Extent of Use

As to the extent of use the government has allowed, defendant has designated the library for the use of "the people" and has declared that "[l]ibrary access and use will not be restricted nor denied to anyone because of age, race, religion, origin, background or views." Id. Defendant has opened the library to the use of the Loudoun County public at large and has significantly limited its own discretion to restrict access, thus indicating that it has created a limited public forum. *See Kreimer*, 958 F.2d at 1260 (finding that the extent of use inquiry favored concluding that the library was a limited public forum because the library "does not retain unfettered discretion governing admission").

3. Nature of the Forum

The final consideration is whether the nature of the forum is compatible with the expressive activity at issue. While the nature of the public library would clearly not be compatible with many forms of expressive activity, such as giving speeches or holding rallies, we find that it is compatible with the expressive activity at issue here, the receipt and communication of information through the Internet. Indeed, this expressive activity is explicitly offered by the library.

All three of these factors indicate that the Loudoun County libraries are limited public fora and, therefore, that defendant must "permit the public to exercise rights that are consistent with the nature of the Library and consistent with the government's intent in designating the Library as a public forum." Id. at 1262. The receipt and communication of information through the Internet is consistent with both.

Because the Policy at issue limits the receipt and communication of information through the Internet based on the content of that information, it is subject to a strict scrutiny analysis and will only survive if it is "necessary to serve a compelling state interest and . . . is narrowly drawn to achieve that end." *Perry* 460 U.S. at 45 (citing *Carey v. Brown*, 447 U.S. 455, 461 (1980)).[14]

C. Renton/Time, Place, and Manner

Defendant also argues in the alternative that the strict scrutiny standard should not apply because the Policy is more appropriately viewed as a time, place, and manner restriction pursuant to *City of Renton v. Playtime Theatres, Inc.*, 475 U.S. 41 (1986), than as a traditional content-based restriction on speech. Plaintiffs respond that this analysis is inapplicable to the Policy, which is designed to address the primary effects of Internet speech and which defendant admits restricts speech based on content.

In *Renton*, the Supreme Court found that a zoning ordinance prohibiting adult movie theaters from locating within 1000 feet of residential neighborhoods, churches, and specific other structures was a content-neutral time, place, and manner restriction because it could be justified without reference to the content of the speech in the theaters. The city justified the ordinance as necessary to address the secondary effects of adult theaters in certain neighborhoods, namely preventing crime, protecting retail trade, maintaining property values, and preserving the quality of the neighborhoods, districts, and life. *See id.*, at 48. The Court found that none of these secondary effects were related to the content of the movies shown at the theaters. Therefore, the Court found the ordinance to be constitutional. *See id.* at 54.

In a subsequent decision clarifying what it meant by "secondary effects," the Supreme Court held that [r]egulations that focus on . . . [l]isteners' reactions to speech are not the type of 'secondary effects' we referred to in *Renton*." *Boos v. Barry*, 485 U.S. 312, 321 (1988). More recently, in construing the Communications Decency Act, the court stated that "content-based blanket restrictions on speech . . . cannot be 'properly analyzed as a form of time, place, and manner regulation'" *Reno v. ACLU*, 117 S. Ct. 2329, 2342 (1997).

Defendant contends that the Policy is designed to combat two secondary effects: creating a sexually hostile environment and violating obscenity, child pornography, and harm to juveniles laws. Neither of these are secondary effects and neither can be justified without reference to the content of the speech at issue. The defendant's concern that without installing filtering software, Internet viewing might lead to a sexually hostile environment is solely focused on the reaction of the audience to a certain category of speech. As the Supreme court noted in *Boos*, this is not a secondary effect. The defendant's second concern is the possible violation of various criminal statutes that address materials deemed to be obscene, involve child pornography, or are harmful to juveniles. These criminal statutes define prohibited speech only by and because of its content. Far from addressing secondary effects of speech, these statutes focus on the very speech itself.

Indeed, the Fourth Circuit has recently observed that content-neutrality is a prerequisite to the Constitutionality of time, place, and manner restrictions on expressive conduct on public grounds. *See United States v. Johnson*, No. 97-5023, 1998 WL 781215, *3 (4th Cir. Oct. 28, 1998). Therefore, defendant's admission that the Policy discriminates against speech based on content indicates that it would not be constitutional even if it were a time, place, and manner restriction.

III. Constitutionality of the Policy

Defendant contends that even if we conclude that strict scrutiny is the appropriate standard of review, the Policy is constitutional because it is the least restrictive means to achieve two compelling government interests: "1) minimizing access to illegal pornography; and 2) avoidance of creation of a sexually hostile environment. . . . Def. Brief in Opp. at 25. Plaintiffs and intervenors respond that there is no evidence that the Policy is necessary to further these interests nor that it is the least restrictive means available. Moreover, they argue that the Policy imposes an unconstitutional prior restraint on speech.

A content-based limitation on speech will be upheld only where the state demonstrates that the limitation "is necessary to serve a compelling state interest and that it is narrowly drawn to achieve that end." *Perry Educ. Ass'n. v. Perry Local Educators' Ass'n*, 460 U.S. 37, 45 (1983) (citing *Carey v. Brown*, 447 U.S. 455, 461 (1980)). This test involves three distinct inquiries: (1) whether the interests asserted by the state are compelling; (2) whether the limitation is necessary to further those interests; and (3) whether the limitation is narrowly drawn to achieve those interests.

A. Whether the Defendant's Interests Are Compelling

Defendant argues that both of its asserted interests are compelling. Although plaintiffs and intervenors argue that these interests were not really the motivating factors behind the Policy and that they are not furthered by the Policy, they do not argue that the interests themselves are not compelling. For the purposes of this analysis, therefore, we assume that minimizing access to illegal pornography[15] and avoidance of creation of a sexually hostile environment[16] are compelling government interests.

B. Whether the Policy is Necessary to Further Those Interests

To satisfy strict scrutiny, defendant must do more than demonstrate that it has a compelling interest; it must also demonstrate that the Policy is necessary to further that interest. In other words, defendant must demonstrate that in the absence of the Policy, a sexually hostile environment might exist and/or there would be a problem with individuals accessing child pornography or obscenity or minors accessing materials that are illegal as to them. Defendant "must demonstrate that the recited harms are real, not merely conjectural, and that the regulation will in fact alleviate these harms in a direct and material way." *Turner Sys., Inc. v. FCC*, 512 U.S. 622, 664; *see also*, *Johnson*, 865 F. Supp. at 1439 ("[S]imply alleging the need to avoid harassment is not enough[;] ... the defendant[] must show the threat of disruption is actual, material, and substantial."). The defendant bears this burden because "[t]he interest in encouraging freedom of expression in a democratic society outweighs any theoretical but unproven benefit of censorship." *Reno v. ACLU*, 117 S. Ct. 2329, 2351 (1997).

The only evidence to which defendant can point in support of its argument that the Policy is necessary consists of a record of a single complaint arising from Internet use in another Virginia library and reports of isolated incidents in three other libraries across the country. In the Bedford County Central Public Library in Bedford County, Virginia, a patron complained that she had observed a boy viewing what she believed were pornographic pictures on the Internet. Pls. Ex. 15 at 4-7. This incident was the only one defendant discovered within Virginia and the only one in the 16 months in which the Bedford County public library system had offered unfiltered public access to the Internet. After the incident, the library merely installed privacy screens on its Internet terminals which, according to the librarian, "work great". Id. at 4.

The only other evidence of problems arising from unfiltered Internet access is described by David Burt, defendant's expert, who was only able to find three libraries that allegedly had experienced such problems, one in Los Angeles County,[17] another in Orange County, Florida,[18] and one in Austin, Texas.[19] *See* Burt Rep. at 14. There is no evidence in the record establishing that any other libraries have encountered problems: rather, Burt's own statements indicate that such problems are practically nonexistent. *See* Burt Rep. at 253-55 (acknowledging that an e-mail requesting information about sexual harassment complaints relating to Internet use that he sent to "several thousand" librarians did not yield a single serious response). Significantly, defendant has not pointed to a single incident in which a library employee or patron has complained that material being accessed on the Internet was harassing or created a hostile environment. As a matter of law, we find this evidence insufficient to sustain defendant's burden of showing that the Policy is reasonably necessary. No reasonable trier of fact could conclude that three isolated incidents nationally, one very minor isolated incident in Virginia, no evidence whatsoever of problems in Loudoun County, and not a single employee complaint from anywhere in the country establish that the Policy is necessary to prevent sexual harassment or access to obscenity or child pornography.

C. Whether the Policy is Narrowly Tailored to Achieve the Compelling Government Interests

Even if defendant could demonstrate that the Policy was reasonably necessary to further compelling state interests, it would still have to show that the Policy is narrowly tailored to achieve those interests. The parties disagree about several issues relating to whether the Policy is narrowly tailored: (1) whether less restrictive means are available; (2) whether the Policy is overinclusive; and (3) whether X-Stop, the filtering software used by defendant, is the least restrictive filtering software available.[20]

1. Whether Less Restrictive Means Are Available

Defendant alleges that the Policy is constitutional because it is the least restrictive means available to achieve its interests. The only alternative to filtering, defendant contends, is to have librarians directly monitor what patrons view. Defendant asserts this system would be far more intrusive than using filtering software. Plaintiffs and intervenors respond that there are many less restrictive means available, including designing an acceptable use policy, using privacy screens, using filters that can be turned off for adult use, changing the location of Internet terminals, educating patrons on Internet use, placing time limits on use, and enforcing criminal laws when violations occur.

In *Sable Communications of Calif.. Inc, v. FCC*, 492 U.S. 115, 126 (1989), the Supreme Court noted that "[t]he Government may regulate the content of constitutionally protected speech in order to promote a compelling interest if it chooses the least restrictive means to further the articulated interest." In *Sable* the Court declared unconstitutional a statute banning all "indecent" commercial telephone communications. The Court found that the government could not justify a total ban on communication that is harmful to minors, but not obscene, by arguing that only a total ban could completely prevent children from accessing indecent messages. Id. at 128. The Court held chat without evidence that less restrictive means had "been tested over time," the government had not carried its burden of proving that they would not be sufficiently effective. Id. at 128-29.

We find that the Policy is not narrowly tailored because less restrictive means are available to further defendant's interests and, as in *Sable*, there is no evidence that defendant has tested any of these means over time. First, the installation of privacy screens is a much less restrictive alternative that would further defendant's interest in preventing the development of a sexually hostile environment. *See* Pls. Ex. 15 at 4, Letter from Tom Hehman to Douglas Henderson (stating that privacy screens "work great"). Second, there is undisputed evidence in the record that charging library staff with casual monitoring of Internet use is neither extremely intrusive nor a change from other library policies. *See, e.g., id.,* (noting no problems with the library staff being responsible for "'shooing' people away from sites we know are objectionable, just as we always have with prepubescent boys giggling over gynecological pictures in medical books"); *see generally* Pls. Ex. 15 (providing the Internet use policies of other Virginia libraries, many of which threaten loss of library privileges or prosecution for accessing illegal sites). Third, filtering software could be installed on only some Internet terminals and minors could be limited to using those terminals. Alternately, the library could install filtering software that could be turned off when an adult is using the terminal. While we find that all of these alternatives are less restrictive than the Policy, we do not find that any of them would necessarily be constitutional if implemented. That question is not before us.

2. Whether the Policy Is Overinclusive

Defendant contends that the Policy is neither overinclusive nor underinclusive because it is the least restrictive means available. Defendant also asserts that we should not focus on the specifics of what the Policy does and does not cover because that would detract from the broader issue of "whether a public library can or cannot filter obscene materials on its public Internet terminals and, if so, under what criteria and procedures." Def. Brief in Opp. at 4. In other words, the defendant asks this court to consider a hypothetical situation that is not before us. The federal courts, however, may not provide advisory opinions; we may rule only on the Policy before us. Defendant cannot save its Policy by asking the Court to decide hypothetical questions for which there is no case or controversy.

In examining the specific Policy before us, we find it overinclusive because, on its face, it limits the access of all patrons, adult and juvenile, to material deemed fit for juveniles. It is undisputed that the Policy requires that "[i]f the Library Director considers a particular website to violate . . . [the Virginia Harmful to Juveniles Statute], the website should be blocked under the policy for adult as well as juvenile patrons." Pls. Ex. 10, Def. Resp. to Pls. First Req. for Admiss. 35. It has long been a matter of settled law that restricting what adults may read to a level appropriate for minors is a violation of the free speech guaranteed by the First Amendment and the Due Process Clause of the Fourteenth Amendment. *See Reno v. ACLU*, 117 S. Ct. 2329, 2346 (1997) ("It is true that we have repeatedly recognized the governmental interest in protecting children from harmful materials but that interest does not justify an unnecessarily broad suppression of speech addressed to adults.") (citations omitted), *Butler v. Michigan*, 352 U.S. 380, 383 (1957) (restricting adults to what is appropriate for juveniles is "not reasonably restricted to the evil with which it is said to deal").

At issue in *Reno* was a federal statute, the Communications Decency Act ("CDA"), which established a criminal penalty for providing on the Internet material deemed harmful to minors although not obscene with the knowledge that such material could be accessed by minors. The Supreme Court found that because there was no way for an Internet provider to block minors from accessing such material, this statute effectively prohibited such material from being displayed at all. *Reno* at 2347. The Court held that

[i]n order to deny minors access to potentially harmful speech, the CDA effectively suppresses a large amount of speech that adults have a constitutional right to receive and to

address to one another. That burden on adult speech is unacceptable if less restrictive alternatives would be at least as effective in achieving the legitimate purpose that the statute was enacted to serve.

Id. at 2346. Because we have found that less restrictive alternatives are available to defendant and that defendant has not sufficiently tried to employ any of them, see III.C.1. the Policy's limitation of adult access to constitutionally protected materials cannot survive strict scrutiny.

3. Whether X-Stop Is the Least Restrictive Filtering Software

Defendant claims that X-Stop is the least restrictive filtering software currently available and, therefore, the Policy is narrowly tailored as applied. Our finding that the Policy is unconstitutional on its face makes this argument moot. A facially overbroad government policy may nevertheless be saved if a court is able to construe government actions under that policy narrowly along the lines of their implementation, if the policy's text or other sources of government intent demonstrate "a clear line" to draw. *See Reno*, 117 S. Ct. at 2350-51. we find no such clear line here. Defendant has asserted an unconditional right to filter the Internet access it provides to its patrons and there is no evidence in the record that it has applied the Policy in a less restrictive way than it is written. *See* Def. Resp. to Pl First Req. Admiss. 17 (denying that X-Stop does not block access to soft core pornography, which is protected). Therefore, our finding that the Policy is unconstitutional on its face makes any consideration of the operation of X-Stop moot.

V. Prior Restraint

Plaintiffs and intervenors allege that even if the Policy were to survive strict scrutiny analysis, the Court would have to find it unconstitutional under the doctrine of prior restraint because it provides neither sufficient standards to limit the discretion of the decisionmaker nor adequate procedural safeguards. Defendant responds that the Policy is not a prior restraint because it only prohibits viewing certain sites in Loudoun County public libraries, and not in the whole of Loudoun County.

Preventing prior restraints of speech is an essential component of the First Amendment's free speech guarantee. *See Freedman v. Maryland*, 380 U.S. 51, 58 (1965). "Permitting government officials unbridled discretion in determining whether to allow protected speech presents an unacceptable risk of both indefinitely suppressing and chilling protected speech." *11126 Baltimore Boulevard, Inc, v. Prince George's County*, 58 F.3d 988, 994 (4th Cir. 1995). In *11129*, the Fourth Circuit found that

[t]he guarantee of freedom of speech afforded by the First Amendment is abridged whenever the government makes the enjoyment of protected speech contingent upon obtaining permission from government officials to engage in its exercise under circumstances that permit government officials unfettered discretion to grant or deny the permission. . . . Such discretion exists when a regulation creating a prior restraint on speech fails to impose ad-

equate standards for officials to apply in rendering a decision to grant or deny permission or when a regulation fails to impose procedural safeguards to ensure a sufficiently prompt decision.

[The following procedural safeguards have been required by the Supreme Court:] "(1) any restraint prior to judicial review can be imposed only for a specific brief period during which the status quo must be maintained; (2) expeditious judicial review of that decision must be available; and (3) the censor must bear the burden of going to court to suppress the speech and must bear the burden of proof once in court."

Id. at 996 (quoting *Freedman*, 380 U.S. at 58-60 (1965)). In other words, even unprotected speech cannot be censored by administrative determination absent sufficient standards and adequate procedural safeguards. *See Southeastern Promotions, Ltd. v. Conrad*, 420 U.S. 546, 562 (1975) ("Whatever the reasons may have been for the board's exclusion of the musical, it could not escape the obligation to afford appropriate procedural safeguards. We need not decide whether the . . . production is in fact obscene.").

Defendant argues that prior restraint cases are limited to situations in which a government tries to restrict all speech within its jurisdiction. Because Loudoun County residents are still permitted to obtain unfiltered Internet access in their homes or offices, defendant asserts, this situation is distinguishable from those cases. We find no legal support for this argument. *See Reno*, 117 S. Ct. at 2349 ("'[O]ne is not to have the exercise of his liberty of expression in appropriate places abridged on the plea that it may be exercised in some other place,'") (quoting *Schneider v. New Jersey*, 308 U.S. 147, 163 (1939)); *Southeastern Promotions*, 420 U.S. 546. In *Southeastern Promotions*, a municipality had denied the use of a public facility for the production of the musical "Hair", which it deemed obscene. The Court found that "it does not matter . . . that the board's decision might not have had the effect of total suppression of the musical in the community. Denying use of the municipal facility under the circumstances present here constituted the prior restraint." 420 U.S. at 556.

It is undisputed that the Policy lacks any provision for prior judicial determinations before material is censored. *See* Pls. Ex. 10, Def. Res. to Pls. First Req. for Admiss. 31. We find that the Policy includes neither sufficient standards nor adequate procedural safeguards. As to the first issue, the defendant's discretion to censor is essentially unbounded. The Policy itself speaks only in the broadest terms about child pornography, obscenity, and material deemed harmful to juveniles and fails to include any guidelines whatsoever to help librarians determine what falls within these broad categories. *See* Pls. Ex. 12, Def. Answer to Pls. First Req. for Interrogs. 3 ("[T]here is no information beyond the Policy itself that constitutes the 'criteria' used for unblocking specific sites."). There are no standards by which a reviewing authority can determine if the decisions made were appropriate.

The degree to which the Policy is completely lacking in standards is demonstrated by the defendant's willingness to entrust all preliminary blocking decisions — and, by default, the overwhelming majority of final decisions[21] — to a private vendor, Log-On Data Corp. Although the defendant argues that X-Stop is the best available filter, a defendant cannot avoid its constitutional obligation by contracting out its decisionmaking to a private entity. Such abdication of its obligation is made even worse by the undisputed facts here. Specifically, defendant concedes that it does not know the criteria by which Log-On Data makes its blocking decisions. See Bradshaw Dep. at 12-13 (stating that LogOn Data has refused to provide defendant with the criteria it uses to block sites). It is also undisputed that Log-On Data does not base its blocking decisions on any legal definition of obscenity or even on the parameters of defendant's Policy. See Bradshaw Dep. at 36-37 (agreeing that "there is neither any attempt nor the ability by [Log-On Data] to apply a legal test") . Thus, on this record, we find that the defendant has not satisfied the first prong of prior restraint analysis, establishing adequate standards.

In addition, the Policy also fails to include adequate procedural safeguards. The three minimum procedural safeguards required are (1) a specific brief time period of imposition before judicial review; (2) expeditious judicial review; and (3) the censor bearing the burden of proof. The Policy, even including the alleged protections of the unofficial unblocking policy, is inadequate in each of these respects.[22] First, the Policy itself contains no provision for administrative review, no time period in which any review must be completed, and no provision for judicial review. See Pls. Ex. 1, Policy. Under the unofficial unblocking policy,, a library patron who finds herself blocked from an Internet site she believes contains protected speech is required to request in writing that the librarians unblock the specified site. See Pls. Ex. 4, Internet Procedures at ¶ 13. If the librarian determines that the site does not fall within the Policy's prohibitions, he will unblock it, although there is no systematic way in which this is done. See Henderson Dep. at 368-71. There is no time period during which this review must occur and there is no provision for notifying the requesting patron if and when a site has been unblocked. See Timmerman Dep. at 93-94 (stating that neither patrons nor staff are informed when the defendant unblocks a site).

The second required procedural safeguard is expeditious judicial review after the administrative decision is made. There is no provision whatsoever in the Policy for judicial review of any blocks. See Pls. Ex. 1, Policy. This makes the question of who carries the burden of proof in any judicial review proceeding, the third required procedural safeguard, moot. Because the Policy has neither adequate standards nor adequate procedural safeguards, we find it to be an unconstitutional prior restraint.

VI. Severability

While neither party addresses the issue, the Policy includes a provision that if a part of it is overruled, "remaining portions remain in effect." Pls. Ex. I at 2. In Reno, the Supreme Court severed provisions of the CDA, declaring its prohibition of "indecent material" unconstitutional but allowing the prohibition on obscene material to remain in effect "because [obscene materials] enjoy[] no First Amendment protection." 117 S. Ct. at 2350. The CDA, however, unlike the Policy, did not operate as an unconstitutional prior restraint; rather, it provided for criminal penalties only after a judicial determination that obscene material had been furnished. Because we have concluded that section 2 under the heading "Internet Services Provided" constitutes an unconstitutional prior restraint on speech, and that section 2 permeates the rest of the Policy, we hold that defendant's Policy on Internet Sexual Harassment is unconstitutional.

VII. Conclusion

Although defendant is under no obligation to provide Internet access to its patrons, it has chosen to do so and is therefore restricted by the First Amendment in the limitations it is allowed to place on patron access. Defendant has asserted a broad right to censor the expressive activity of the receipt and communication of information through the Internet with a Policy that (1) is not necessary to further any compelling government interest; (2) is not narrowly tailored; (3) restricts the access of adult patrons to protected material just because the material is unfit for minors; (4) provides inadequate standards for restricting access; and (5) provides inadequate procedural safeguards to ensure prompt judicial review. Such a Policy offends the guarantee of free speech in the First Amendment and is, therefore, unconstitutional.

For these reasons, the intervenors' Motion to Substitute Parties will be GRANTED; the plaintiffs' and intervenors' motions for summary judgment will be GRANTED; and the defendant's Motion for Summary Judgment will be GRANTED as to the standing of John Ockerbloom d/b/a Banned Books on-Line and DENIED in all other respects. Defendant will be permanently enjoined from enforcing its Policy on Internet Sexual Harassment. An appropriate order will issue.

The clerk is directed to forward a copy of this Memorandum Opinion to counsel of record. Entered this 23rd day of November, 1998.

_____

Leonie M. Brinkema
United States States District Judge

Alexandria, Virginia

NOTES

1. Although plaintiffs and intervenors have refused to admit that the Internet contains child pornography and obscene materials, defendant has provided unrebutted evidence strongly suggesting that such materials can be found there. For purposes of this opinion we will assume that such materials are accessible through the Internet. *See* Def. Exs. 4-14; *see also Reno v. ACLU*, 117 S. Ct. 2329, 2336 ("Sexually explicit material on the Internet includes text, pictures, and chat and 'extends from the modestly titillating to the hardest-core.'") (citing *ACLU v. Reno*, 929 F. Supp. 824, 844 (E.D. Pa. 1996)).
2. Defendant admits to having blocked The Safer Sex Page, the Books for Gay and Lesbian Teens/Youth page, and the Renaissance Transgender Association page, even though it recognizes that none of them contain prohibited material. *See* Def. Ex. 18, Def. Answer to Intervs. Sec. Interrogs.
3. We have also considered the Amici briefs filed by the Commonwealth of Virginia and the National Organization for Women-Dulles, et al., on behalf of defendant. Because we find that the issues raised in these briefs were adequately covered in the briefs submitted by the parties, we do not address them specifically in this opinion.

4. Indeed, one of the websites defendant did find to be blocked on February 6, 1998, the Books for Gay and Lesbian Teens/Youth page, had not been blocked four days earlier when Sehgal had tried to access it, although links from it to other websites were blocked. *See* Sehgal Decl., ¶ 11.

5. Even absent the above analysis, intervenors would likely have standing to pursue this action as a challenge to a government action that is "capable of repetition, yet evading review." *See*, e.g., *Morse v. Republican Party of Virginia*, 116 S. Ct. 1186, 1213 n. 48 (1996). If defendant could evade court challenges to its Policy by unblocking the protected speech only of entities that filed lawsuits against it, it would be able to continue indefinitely its unconstitutional censorship against most of the now 80,000 websites it currently blocks. *See* Pls. Ex. 13, Dep. of Def. Expert David Burt ("Burt Dep."), at 222.

6. "Links" are text, icons, or images located on a web page that allow the user, by the click of a mouse, to switch to another specific document "located anywhere on the Internet." *See Reno v. ACLU*, 117 S. Ct. 2329, 2335 (1997); *see* also *ACLU v, Reno*, 929 F. Supp. 824, 836-37 (E.D. Pa. 1996) (finding that links "are short sections of text or image which refer to another document. Typically the linked text is blue or underlined when displayed, and when selected by the user, the referenced document is automatically displayed, wherever in the world it actually is stored. Links for example are used to lead from overview documents to more detailed documents, from tables of contents to particular pages, but also as cross-references, footnotes, and new forms of information structure. . . . These links . . . are what unify the Web into a single body of knowledge, and what makes the Web unique.").

7. *See 11126 Baltimore Boulevard v. Prince George's County*, 58 F.3d 994 (4th Cir. 1995).

8. *See Drive In Theatres, Inc. v. Huskey*, 435 F.2d 228 (4th Cir. 1970).

9. *See Kreimer v. Bureau of Police*, 958 F.2d 1242 (3d Cir. 1992).

10. Defendant has consistently relied on *Board of Education v. Pico*, 457 U.S. 853, 889 (1982) (Burger, J. dissenting) ("[T]here is not a hint in the First Amendment, or in any holding of this Court, of a right, to have the government provide continuing access to certain books."). *Pico*, however, was limited to the context of school libraries. It is notable that even justice Rehnquist's dissent in that case explicitly recognized the difference between school libraries, which serve unique education purposes, and public libraries, which are "designed for freewheeling inquiry." *Pico*, 457 U.S. at 915 (Rehnquist, J. dissenting).

11. At issue in *Kreimer* was a First Amendment challenge to content-neutral library rules that addressed only conduct, not access to specific materials. The rules: (1) required persons who were not engaged in "reading, studying, or using library materials" to leave the library; (2) prohibited patrons from engaging in various forms of behavior that would harass or annoy other patrons; and (3) required patrons "whose bodily hygiene is offensive so as to constitute a nuisance to other persons" to leave the library. 958 F.2d at 1262-64.

12. Defendant's assertion that the *Kreimer* court found the public library to be a non-public forum is simply wrong. *See Kreimer*, 958 F.2d at 1262 ("Hence, as a limited public forum, the Library is obligated only to permit the public to exercise rights that are consistent with the nature of the Library and consistent with the government's intent in designating the Library as a public forum.").

13. This includes both the right to provide information and the right to receive information. *See Kreider*, 958 F.2d at 1250-55 (citing, *inter alia*, *Martin v. City of Struthers*, 319 U.S. 141 (1943); *Lamont v. Postmaster General*, 381 U.S. 301 (1965); *Griswold v. Connecticut*, 381 U.S. 479, 482 (1965) ("The right of freedom of speech and press includes not only the right to utter or to print, but the right to distribute, the right to receive, the right to read. . . .")).

14. In *Kreimer*, the Third Circuit determined that none of the regulations at issue were subject to strict scrutiny review because none of them were content-based limitations on the kind of expressive activity permitted in the library. *Kreimer*, 956 F.2d at 1262 ("Significantly, the parties do not contend that any of the challenged regulations purport to restrict First Amendment activities on the basis of content or viewpoint.").

15. *See* Protection of Children Against Sexual Exploitation Act, 18 U.S.C. §§ 2251-2260 (1984 &

Supp. 1998) (criminalizing activities related to child pornography); 18 U.S.C. § 1465 (1984 F. Supp. 1998) (criminalizing transportation of obscene materials in interstate commerce). However, to the extent defendant's concern is with its own criminal liability, the Fourth Circuit has clearly stated that service providers are not liable "for information originating with a third-party user of the service." *See* Zeran v. America Online Inc., 129 F.3d 327, 330 (4th Cir. 1997).

16. We note, however, that the legal concept of a sexually hostile work environment has traditionally been limited to the employment context, see, *e.g.*, Title VII of the Civil Rights Act of 1964, 42 U.S.C. §§ 2000e *et seq.* (1994); *Johnson v. Los Angeles Fire Dept.*, 865 F. Supp. 1430, 1439 (C.D. Cal. 1994) ("There is no doubt that the prevention of sexual harassment is a compelling government interest."), and, more recently, the education context, *see Gebser v. Lago Vista Independent School District*, 118 S.Ct. 1989, 2000 (1998).

17. Quoting a newspaper article, Burt reported that library computers "are regularly steered to online photos of naked women, digitized videos of sex acts and ribald chat-room discussions," causing legitimate researchers to have to wait in line while others read "personal ads or X-rated chat rooms." Burt Rep. at 14 (quoting *Public Libraries Debating How to Handle Net Porn*, August Chron., July 3, 1997).

18. Burt alleges that filters had to be installed in Orange County libraries after patrons were accessing hard-core porn sites "for hours on end." Id. (quoting Pamela Mendels, *A Library That Would Rather Block Than Offend*, N.Y. Times, Jan. 18, 1997).

19. The Austin library installed filters after two incidents. In the first, a librarian caught a patron printing child pornography on the library printer. In the second incident, at a different branch, an adult patron was caught teaching children how to access pornography on the Internet. *See id.* at 14-15 (citing Mark Smith, Meeting the Pressure to Filter, Tex. Library J., Feb. 1997).

20. Although they dispute the legal conclusion to be drawn from the facts in the record, the parties do not dispute the facts themselves. Therefore, summary judgment remains the appropriate vehicle for resolving this dispute.

21. Defendant claims that the library staff has reviewed "more than 172" websites, see Henderson Decl. at ¶¶ 9-10, out of the approximately 80,000 that X-Stop currently blocks. *See* Burt Dep. at 222.

22. The defendant relies on the undisputed evidence that it has not denied any of the eleven unblocking requests it has received thus far to save the Policy. *See* Henderson Decl. at 16. This is insufficient because, as we noted in our previous opinion, "forcing citizens to publicly petition the Government for access to" disfavored speech has a "severe chilling effect." *Mainstream Loudoun*, 2 F. Supp. 2d at 797 (citing *Lamont v. General*, 381 U.S. 301, 307 (1965)); see also *Elrod v. Burns*, 427 U.S. 347, 373-74 (1976) ("[T]he loss of First Amendment freedoms, for even minimal periods of time, unquestionably constitutes irreparable injury."). At least one patron has stated that he failed to request access to a blocked site he believed was improperly blocked because he was "intimidated to have to go through that procedure." Pls. Ex. 19, Kropat First Decl. at ¶ 7.

Index

A

Academic libraries, 16–17, 25, 29–31, 115–116
Acknowledgment forms, 35–36, 66
Alpine School District (American Fork, UT), 159–161
American Civil Liberties Union, 77–78
American Family Association, 83
American Libraries, 82
American Library Association, 12, 16, 35, 76–77, 80, 81, 88, 90, 94, 104, 167, 168–184
    Association for Library Service to Children, 88
    Office of Intellectual Freedom, 35, 167, 184
Anne Arundel County (MD) Public Library, 54
Anti-obscenity statutes, 62–63, 78

B

Baltimore County Public Library, 104
Bellingham (WA) Public Library, 11, 26, 28
Berkeley (CA) Public Library, 2, 92, 103
Bloomingdale (IN) Public Library, 36
Boston Public Library, 93, 94
Brown University, 51, 55–57, 122
Burt, David, 7, 78

C

Canyon (TX) Public Library, 40
Carnegie-Stout Public Library (Dubuque, IA), 133–134
Cedar Falls (IA) Public Library, 49
Chat Rooms, 42–43, 51
Chicago Manual of Style, 121
Child Safety on the Information Superhighway, 88, 104
Collection development policy, 14–15, 79
College of the Holy Cross, 152–158
Communications Decency Act, 41, 77–78
Community High School (Ann Arbor, MI), 69, 162–165
Confidentiality, 122
Copyright, 60–61, 119–122

Cortland College, 30
Crane, Nancy B., 121
Cyber Patrol (software), 82

D

Dallas Public Library, 111
Danbury (CT) Public Library, 11
Dartmouth College, 25, 30
Denver Public Library, 51, 52
Dylan, Bob, 48

E

EDUCAUSE, 7, 116
Ela Area (IL) Public Library, 12
"Electronic Style: A Guide to Citing Electronic Information," 121
E-mail, 44–45
Evanston (IL) Public Library, 33

F

Farmers Branch (TX) Manske Public Library, 26
Filtering, vi, 75–99
Filtering and materials selection, 79
Filtering Facts, 78
Filtering software packages, 82–86
Florida Atlantic University, 113, 120
Fort Smith (AR) Public Library, 11
Fortres (software), 21
FTP (file transfer protocol), 46
Freedom to Read Statement, 90, 167, 168–172

G

Ginsberg, Allen, 63
Grande Prairie (IL) Public Library, 31
Guided use, 88, 101–113
Guidelines and Considerations for Developing a Public Library Internet Use Policy, 180–184

H

Handicapped accessibility (to Web pages), 118
Houston Public Library, 94, 95, 138–140
Hypertext Markup Language (HTML), 117, 118, 123

I

Interactive games, 44
Internet Filter Assessment Project (TIFAP), 86
Internet Kids Yellow Pages, 104
Internet policy
  Acceptable use, 40–57
  Access to workstations, 24–37
  Archives of policies, 7
  Checklist, 194–195
  Commercial uses, 46–47, 64–65
  Content-based restrictions, 41–42, 61–64, 121–123
  Consequences of unacceptable use, 66–67
  Downloading files, 48, 50
  Employee use, 63–64
  Filtering, vi, 75–99
  Guided use, 103–104
  Illegal activities, 62, 123
  Institutional values, 12
  Misrepresentation, 61
  Network and file directory access, 47
  Non-library software, 49
  Physical location in library, 19–24, 86–88
  Prohibited use, 59–73
  Resource guides, 104–105
  Scheduled use, 27–29
  System security, 65
  Updating, 131–132
  Use by children, 31–37, 76, 104–109
Internet Service Provider, 65, 103

J

Jervis Public Library (Rome, NY), 148–150
Joyce, James, 63
Juneau (AK) Public Library, 113

K

Kimmel, Stacey, 7
Kuntz, Jerry, 82

L

Lake Oswego (OR) Public Library, 7
Las Vegas-Clark County (NV) Library District, 89
Lawrence (KS) Public Library, 27, 49
Lehigh University, 7
Li, Xia, 121
The Librarian's Guide to Cyberspace for Parents and Kids, 104
Library Bill of Rights, 12, 16, 77, 80, 81, 90, 168

Library Bill of Rights, Interpretation, 173–174
Library policy
  Fees, 13–14
  Mission, 3, 9–17
  Model for adoption, 6
  Parties responsible for developing, 4–5
  Posting, 6–7
  Procedures, 5–6
  Process of writing, 1–7
  Scope, 2–4
  Type of library, 2–3
Loudon County (VA), 78, 90, 197ff

M

Mainstreet Loudon vs. Library Board of Trustees, Loudon County, Virginia (U.S. District Court Decision), 197ff
Medina County (OH) Library District, 112–113
Minnesota Library Association, 186
Mission, 3, 9–17
MLA Handbook, 121
Modern Language Association, 121
Monitors, recessed, 23
Montana Library Association, 187

N

Nassau Community College, 51, 53
National Center for Missing and Exploited Children, 88
Net Nanny (software), 82
New Jersey Library Association, 189–190
New Hampshire Library Association, 188
New York Public Library, 88, 105, 106–108
Norwood Independent School District, 53
Nueva Net, 17

O

Ohio State Library, 7

P

Parental consent forms, 31–35, 90, 161
Peachtree (GA) City Library, 50
Peterson, Christine, 84
Planning and Role-setting for Public Libraries, 9–10
Planning for Results: A Public Library Transformation Process, 10
Platform for Internet Content Selection (PICS), 83
"Plug-in" software, 48
Polly, Jean Armor, 104
Port Isabel (TX) Public Library, 31–32
A Practical Guide to Internet Filters (Schneider), vi, 76, 86
Printers, 21
Privacy screens, 22–23, 87–88

Procedures, 5–6
Protocol blocking software, 46
PUBLIB listserv, 82
Public libraries, 25
Public Library of Charlotte and Mecklenberg County (NC), 33
Public Library of Cincinnati and Hamilton County (OH), 67, 68

Q
Queensboro (NY) Public Library, 10, 11

R
Ramapo Catskill Library System (NY), 82
Real Audio (software), 48
Reno v. American Civil Liberties Union (U.S. Supreme Court decision), 78
Resolution on the Use of Filtering Software in Libraries, 176
Rice University, 7
Rio Grande Valley Library System (Albuquerque, NM), 112

S
A Safety Net for the Internet, 104, 106–108
San Antonio Public Library, 115
San Diego (CA) Public Library, 105, 109
School libraries, 16–17, 25, 33–35, 42, 92–94
School Library Journal, 92
Schneider, Karen, vi, 76, 82, 86
Seneca College, 128–129
"700+ Great Sites for Kids," 105
Sexual harassment, 64
Sexually explicit materials, 41, 62–64, 67, 75–99
Spokane (WA) Public Library, 10, 135–137

Statement on Library Use of Internet Filtering Software, 177–179
Stoner, Michael, 116

T
Telnet, 45–46
Texas, State of, 63
Time limits, 20–21
Training, 16, 110–113

U
Unger Memorial Library (Plainview, TX), 105
University of Texas at Austin, 29
University of Pennsylvania, 16, 70–73
U. S. Constitution, First Amemdment, 41, 62, 80, 81, 121–122
U. S. Supreme Court, 41, 78
Urofsky v. Allen (U.S. District Court decision), 64

V
Virginia Library Association, 191
Virginia, State of, 64

W
Web policies, 115–130
"Web Policies that Work," 116
West Warwick (RI) Public Library, 41
Wicomico County (MD) Free Library, 91
Winona (MN) School District, 124–127

X
X-Stop (software), 83

Y
"Youth Wired," 115

About the Author

Mark Smith is the director of communications for the Texas Library Association, where he monitors government relations activities including policy development in and concerning Texas libraries. Previously he worked as a public library director in two communities in New Jersey and as the library systems administrator at the Texas State Library and Archives Commission.